Training Within Industry:
The Foundation of Lean

Donald A. Dinero

Productivity Press
NEW YORK, NEW YORK

Most Productivity Press books are available at quantity discounts when purchased in bulk. For more information, contact our Customer Service Department (888-319-5852). Address all other inquires to:

Productivity Press
444 Park Avenue South, Suite 604
New York, NY 10016
United States of America
Telephone 212-686-5900
Fax: 212-686-5411
E-mail: info@productivitypress.com

Text Design by William H. Brunson Typography Services
Page composition by William H. Brunson Typography Services

Library of Congress Cataloging-in-Publication Data

Dinero, Donald A.
    Training within industry : the foundation of lean / Donald A. Dinero.
      p. cm.
    Includes bibliographical references and index.
    ISBN 1-56327-307-1
    1. Employees—Training of.   2. Industrial efficiency   3. Organizational effectiveness.   4. Industrial management. I. Title.
    HF5549.5.T7D526   2005
    658.3′124—dc22

2005005986

10 09 08   10 09 08 07 06 05 04 03 02

To my loving wife Maureen,
who has always been there for me and
has always believed in me.

CONTENTS

Bulletins included on CD:

1: Training Workers to Meet Defense Needs
2: Tying-In Pre-Employment Training with On-the-Job Training
3: The Training Within Industry Program
4: Developing All-Round Skilled Craftsmen Through Apprenticeship
5: Expanding the Managerial Organization
6: Strengthening the Managerial Organization
7: How to Prepare Instructors to Give Intensive Job Instruction
8: Training Aids
9: Training Production Workers
10: Upgrading
11: Increasing War Production Through Employment of Women
12: Safety on the Job for the New Employee
13: Supplementary Instruction for Upgrading
14: How to Improve Job Methods
15: How to Improve Job Relations
16: How to Meet Specific Needs
17: How to Select Supervisors—A 6-Step Program
18: Introducing the New Employee to the Job
19: How To Instruct a Man on the Job
20: Management and Skilled Supervision
21: How to Get a Plant Training Plan into Action
22: How to Get Continuing Results from Plant Training Programs
23: Improving Supervisors' Knowledge of the Work
24: Keeping Supervisors Informed About Their Responsibilities
25: How Training Can Be Done—Methods, Aids

FOREWORD

You are about to read an important book because it tells the story of the most underrated achievement of 20th century American industry—Training Within Industry (TWI). Anyone familiar with the Toyota Production System (TPS) is well aware of its roots in Henry Ford's system. But few people are aware of the role of the TWI program developed by the United States during World War II.

My own "discovery" of the TWI programs occurred in Toyota City, Japan in 1984. My job at that time was assisting the training and education department of Toyota Motor Corporation in developing training programs to transfer the company's production system to its new joint venture with General Motors in Fremont, California, later to become famous as New United Motor Manufacturing Inc. (NUMMI). Our challenge was to "adapt" various Toyota training materials to make them appropriate for NUMMI. I was faced with what appeared to be two conflicting objectives: The training had to remain true to TPS, yet at the same time be compatible with American "culture" and palatable to American workers.

As it turned out, General Motors' workers at NUMMI took to TPS far more smoothly and effectively than anyone had anticipated. Still, there were many struggles along the way. One of my own struggles involved a standardized training process intended to assist plant floor frontline supervisors in teaching new operations to workers quickly and effectively. In my view, the program Toyota used was too standardized, rigid, and rote in nature; in short, simply too "Japanese." So, I protested to my Japanese colleague, declaring that the program as configured just wouldn't do and required radical revision before being unleashed on the NUMMI workforce.

My Japanese colleague, Isao Kato (Toyota's Master Trainer of the TWI programs) had been quite patient with me up to this point, knowing that his job was to mentor me as well as get the job done. Finally, however, exasperated with my protestations and frustrated with my stubbornness, he stormed out and fetched from a back room file a yellowed, dog-eared, coffee-stained copy of the English-language original training manual, just as they had received it (minus the coffee stains, I trust) some 30 years before. To my absolute amazement, the program that Toyota was going to great expense (including retranslating from Japanese to English) to "transfer" to NUMMI was exactly what the Americans had taught the Japanese decades earlier. Of course, it was JI, the Job Instruction module of TWI. Toyota still used it in 1984 and continues to use it today, yet rarely do I find a U.S. manufacturer who has even heard of it, much less uses it here in its the country of origin. Through NUMMI, Toyota began the repatriation of this expatriated technology.

The re-importation of this technology has long struck me as so significant that when I established my consulting group in 1997, I chose the name "The TWI Network, Inc." (although the focus of the group's consulting work is TPS and Lean Enterprise transformation rather than strictly TWI training).

Toyota still uses Job Instruction in its original form as the key to its training efforts. While that is not exactly true for the other "J" courses, the training programs with which Toyota has replaced them still follow the same principles, and to some extent, even the same format. Toyota drastically altered the Job Methods course in the 1950s to reflect the results of the radical production system experiments that Ohno was initiating, and the company substantially modified the Job Relations course shortly before I arrived in Toyota City in the early 1980s. Despite these changes, the essence of the "J" courses is still found in Toyota's current training.

Your guide into the world of TWI, Don Dinero, approaches the topic from a variety of perspectives. In addition to an in-depth description of the programs, he also provides rich detail about the development of the TWI programs as different companies and organizations have applied it. The astute reader will find layered meaning in these pages—the *development* of TWI actually *embodies its fundamental character*. TWI wasn't developed on paper, in a laboratory, and then rolled out to the masses. Rather, it was developed over time through actual practice and implementation—each iteration adapting the continuous improvements of the program. Were the programs standardized? Yes, certainly. Were they static? Absolutely not.

In addition, this dynamic captures one of the most important and often overlooked aspects of the Toyota Production System: the central role of Standardized Work. TPS and TWI take us away from the command and control of the typical application of "Scientific Management" to true *Management by Science*. A common misperception of standardization is assuming it is simply regimentation, or command and control, when in fact its true value is to serve as the basis of experimentation. Standards are set—as bases of comparison—and are used as baselines for improvement. Far from reducing individual work into regimented chores, Standardized Work can enable individual innovation at every level of the organization. We have come to call this process "continuous improvement." Deming called it PDCA. You can learn about it through learning about, and practicing, TWI.

John Shook
Senior Advisor, Lean Enterprise Institute
President, TWI Network, Inc.
Ann Arbor, Michigan

ACKNOWLEDGMENTS

Many people, sometimes unknowingly, can influence the creation of a book. I am most grateful to Tony Carlisi of the CMS Consulting Group because it was he who first introduced me to TWI, and who subsequently encouraged my pursuit of it. That is where my TWI journey began and therefore this book would not have existed had it not been for Tony. I also want to acknowledge Bob Wrona of the Central New York Technology Development Organization who saw the TWI footnote in *Kaizen* (by Masaali Imai) and had the foresight and persistence to resurrect TWI for companies in the United States.

Many people become passionate about TWI because they recognize that it fills in a gap between mass production and Lean production. My passion led me to speak about TWI to anyone who would listen and give presentations as often as I could. That led to an IIE conference in Atlanta and a fortuitous meeting with Mike Sinocchi, senior acquisitions editor of Productivity Press. In addition to being easy to work with, I must thank Mike for his ability to sort through all the information on Lean he received that week and focus on TWI as a subject that should be broadcast to more people.

Editing is critical to the writing process, and I am extremely grateful to Gary Peurasaari, the development editor of this book, for his efforts. Gary skillfully read my manuscript and understood not only what I had written but also what I was thinking. At times he made it more Lean, and at other times he asked me to elaborate. In the end, Gary helped me write a much better book. I'd also like to acknowledge Bob Cooper, the production manager, and Megan Foley, assistant editor, for all of their work in bringing this manuscript to its final form.

TWI is more than just theory; its value lies in its use. Therefore, I am indebted to the many people at Gray-Syracuse, Inc. and Schneider Packaging, Inc. who added to my TWI experience. I would especially like to thank Paul Smith, Vice President of Human Resources at Gray-Syracuse for his help and contributions.

When I learned that John Shook was willing to write a foreword for this book, I was truly pleased because I respect the work he has done and continues to do in the area of Lean thinking. It is no surprise to me that someone who understands both Lean and TWI is not only enthusiastic about both, but sees the connection between the two. I expect to meet Mr. Shook someday and thank him in person, but for now this entry must suffice.

I cannot conclude without thanking the members of my family for their contributions. My brother Tom provided insight and helpful suggestions in the initial stages of the manuscript. My sons Dan and Doug listened patiently as I bounced ideas off of them and occasionally rambled on about TWI. Finally, my wife Maureen offered support, encouragement, strength, and inspiration. For that I am deeply grateful.

INTRODUCTION

I remember, as a boy, watching my mother iron clothes in the kitchen. When she stopped ironing, either she would lay the iron down on the heating surface or she would stand it up on its heel. After a while I concluded that there was a reason for what she did. Standing the iron up on its heel took longer and thus she would do this only if she knew she would need extra time to rearrange the article of clothing. If she knew that moving the clothing would require only a fraction of a second, she would slide the iron out of her way (heating surface down), arrange the clothing, and quickly pick up the iron again. If she left the iron in that position too long, it would burn the ironing board cover. I was in grade school at the time when I made this observation, which would have made me about eight or nine years old. At the time and for many years after, I thought everyone took this type of logical approach to doing things. Of course, I was wrong.

I always thought about why things are the way they are and why people do the things they do, and when I became an engineer, naturally, this thinking was reinforced by associating with other engineers. It was here that I began to develop a fascination with why people work in certain ways—especially why they didn't automatically take a scientific approach to solving problems. I also learned that you need to step back and consider other perspectives to understand fully what it is you are 'seeing'—that peoples' approaches and processes for doing things are predicated on many criteria and circumstances, not the least of which is being *trained to see*. But I am jumping ahead.

I did my first "Lean" project in the mid-eighties when a vice president charged the materials manager and me, then an engineering manager, with reducing the lead time of a product line from 6 to 8 weeks to less than two weeks. Naturally, our first reaction was that this objective was considerably unrealistic and the VP was just slightly crazy. However, since our competition was delivering their product in about 2 weeks, we knew not only that it was possible, but also that we had to do better.

The first thing we asked was, "Why does an order take 8 weeks to ship?" I can clearly remember saying to Mike (the materials manager), "It takes us 2 weeks to get the paper work from order entry to the shop. We're going to have to make a lot of changes to shorten the entire cycle to 2 weeks." We stated our objective, listed all the details, analyzed all the details, and then eliminated or changed what did not help us accomplish the objective. The result was a standard delivery in less than 1 week, and if an order came in by 9 AM, we could ship it by 4 PM. Additionally, costs, WIP (work in process) and inventory were all drastically reduced. The point of this story is that we never really recognized the impact that this project had on our organization at that time, although we had actually already implemented some process adjustments that were considered "cutting edge." We felt we were just doing our jobs and responding to a management request.

As I was involved with or led other projects, I noticed how some results were more successful than others and wondered why. I could never identify any one reason, though I surmised that the heart of the issue had to do with "how people did work" and that not everyone analyzes everything he or she sees. Some people may automatically use an analytical thinking process in problem solving within their own field of expertise, but they may not know how to apply that process to areas outside of their field. For example, an engineer may be able to debug a complicated software program or layout an assembly area, but not know how to make it easier on himself to apply for a day of vacation. Given an existing procedure, he will probably follow it even if he sees it as inefficient and frustrating.

I knew I should focus more on the "people element" when implementing projects, but there was no commonly accepted method to use in doing this. About the same time, I read the book by Womack, Jones, and Roos, *The Machine That Changed the World*. The subtitle says that it is "The Story of Lean Production." The book describes the success of the Toyota Production System (TPS), and why it was a "Lean" approach with respect to say, the General Motors Production System of the 1980s. As I read the book, I was looking for some key as to why U.S. auto manufacturers consistently underperformed Toyota and other Japanese manufacturers. Yes, there was the argument about mass production's waste, but why? One sentence in the middle of page 99 jumped out at me. "So in the end, it is the dynamic work team that emerges as the heart of the Lean factory." Although I felt this was a key to implementing Lean, I knew there was still something missing. The "people" aspect was again touched on, but the subject was not expanded beyond that.

Even then, the term "teamwork" was overused. There are many books on "teamwork" and one could spend a fortune going to teamwork seminars. But, I did know from my experience that people who truly believed in and practiced teamwork were more successful implementing Lean than those who strictly used mass production's "command and control" or top-down management approach that didn't empower employees. It was not until I learned about Training Within Industry (TWI) that I understood the significance of this and why Toyota was so successful with TPS. (In the 1940s, the U.S. War Department created the TWI Service, which developed four training programs to help organizations train millions of people at their worksite to quickly increase production. TWI was later exported overseas.) TWI teaches the basic skills that enable employees to make the transition from hierarchical "command and control" organization to a flatter, team-oriented organization. Immediately I thought, "TWI is the missing link that makes Lean successful." As I learned more about TWI and began training others in it, I realized that it was much more than a missing link. TWI is a foundation on which you can build and sustain a Lean enterprise. Simply put, TWI provides the necessary skills that make everyone in the organization think Lean—if your employees know and practice TWI skills, your organization will be practicing Lean Thinking everyday.

There are many management techniques that have worked wonders in improving organizations, and were published nationally or internationally, generating terms that have become the current buzzwords for success. MBO (management by objectives), QC (quality circles), reengineering and TQM (total quality management) are four such techniques that come to mind. But how many of these techniques have met the test of time industry-wide? One reason for these failures is that the successful results evolved in a specific environment, and what works in one environment may not in another. Lean Manufacturing evolved out of a Japanese culture and society devastated by war, and though there are cultural differences with the United States, Lean techniques are time-tested and seemingly applicable to any environment. But when U.S. organizations apply Lean, they often fail, and ask, "How can this idea be so successful, seem so simple, and yet be so difficult to implement?" Is Lean just another buzzword or is something missing?

We now know that 'Lean' is not just another buzzword, but organizations are still struggling to implement it. Why? Because they do not understand the importance of TWI. Yes, Womack's and Jones's later book, *Lean Thinking*, stresses that managers need to specify *value* clearly, and that organizations need to focus on identifying value-creating activities along specific product *value streams* to make value *flow* smoothly according to the *pull* of customer demand. All the while the organization pursues *perfection* (continuous improvement). (We will discuss this in Chapter 3). But how does an organization get people to understand, implement, and sustain this behavior? It comes back to how people work. TWI is a tool that teaches people to think and approach their work analytically. It is not about providing a solution to a problem, but rather it is about teaching people how to look at a problem so that they can develop effective solutions (countermeasures). As one of TWI's program's state, "Make best use of each person's ability." Training and empowering its employees to use Lean techniques proactively and analytically is one of the secrets to Toyota's success. And where did they learn how to do this? From TWI.

Although TWI training is not a silver bullet that will eliminate all problems, it does form the basis for solving them and, as this book shows, it can be the basis for modifying an organization's culture and a foundation of Lean Thinking. Most readers have heard or read how Japanese assembly line workers have the authority to stop an entire assembly line. How do you create a culture that empowers the hourly worker? Training. TWI teaches people to think on their own, act on their decisions, and work as a team to increase the bottom line. This is not done in great leaps as is done, for example, in a *Kaizen Blitz*; it occurs in small increments that are within the scope of the individual. Over time, small steps equate to a giant leap. More importantly, however, as many people make many small improvements they create an organization where employees believe that they can have a positive affect on their jobs and the corporation as a whole. As such, TWI is a foundation for Lean Thinking and it has the power to act as a catalyst to change a culture from mass production to Lean production. My belief is that in understanding TWI concepts, Lean practitioners will have a new appreciation for Lean and a new tool for implementing it.

Before concluding, I'd like to address a few things about the book's structure. One of my goals in writing *TWI: The Foundation of Lean* was to chronicle how the TWI founders developed all four training programs (Job Instruction, Job Relations, Job Methods, and Program Development) for a 1940s wartime economy; and how the founders developed a very basic and condensed training program that, to this day, doesn't require modifications. This is basic training material that should not be hidden in a library, but rather should be disseminated as widely as possible. As a result, I spend a lot of time in Parts 1 and 2 of this book highlighting the history, structure, and characteristics of the four programs. Part 3 covers the methodology for delivering the programs to participants. Throughout the book, I stress TWI's successes and relationship to Lean Thinking. To cover all of this, I divided the book into three parts. (The included CD contains the TWI bulletins and gives additional information, some of which is currently applicable, while some is of interest from only a historical perspective.)

- **Part 1: Chapters 1–4.** Chapters 1 and 2 deal with the history of TWI. Chapter 3 defines TWI's relationship to Lean, and Chapter 4 defines the characteristics which make TWI's four programs successful. Chapter 4 defines the common characteristics of the programs, especially the four-step method which lays the way for understanding Part 2. This chapter is important for people who want to use TWI, but believe they can improve it before they have delivered it properly several times.

- **Part 2: Chapters 5–8.** Each program has its own chapter. These chapters discuss the versions that the TWI developers went through to design each program. I also highlight the time-tested and successful characteristics that are common to all four programs.
- **Part 3: Chapters 9–12.** Each program has its own chapter. These chapters cover some of the same ground as Chapters 5–8 but this time I discuss each program's methodology (four-step method) as well as how the trainer uses Sessions to deliver each program. (Chapter 13 is the conclusion.)

The historical material and discussion on how TWI developed the characteristics of the four programs in Parts 1 and 2 lay the groundwork for the reader to understand Part 3. If the reader is familiar with the history of TWI and convinced of its merits, he or she can jump ahead to the Lean discussion in Chapter 3. If the reader wants to get to the core of delivering TWI, he or she can jump ahead to Part 3 after reading Part 1, and then return to Part 2 to understand how each program evolved. If you choose the latter approach, I would recommend you read the first part of Chapter 5.

I base much of *TWI: The Foundation of Lean*, on the *TWI Report* and TWI training manuals. Quoting from these resulted in some anomalies. For instance, the 1940s terminology used in the *TWI Report* and what I use will differ at times—the *TWI Report* uses gender-biased terms such as *foremen, manpower,* or *girls*. It also uses the term "plant" which I replace with "organization" or "company." However, I do use the same term for "supervisor" because, by TWI's definition, supervisor applies more broadly *to what a person does, rather than as a title.* Also, I created Tables 5-1 and 5-2 to clearly identify the roles and responsibilities of the trainers and participants in the four TWI training programs, or who should be taking each program.

TWI: The Foundation of Lean is for organizations needing to train trainers, employees, managers, and supervisors. For those who are unfamiliar with TWI, it will be a true eye-opener. For those in the Lean world who have struggled with Lean implementations, it may provide the missing link that explains what may have gone wrong with an implementation. For those planning a Lean initiative, I advise you to read this book; it may save you some grief. For those just learning about Lean Thinking, my advice is to add this book to your arsenal of learning—it should become part of your Lean nomenclature. As you will see in the coming pages, TWI is the 'real thing' for all levels of training and for all organizations. It has been time-tested, is still being taught today, and is still being used by some of the "world's greatest manufacturers." TWI is the "missing link" and foundation that will help an organization make the necessary cultural changes to solve problems and sustain a Lean transformation.

A Note about the CD

I included the text of the bulletins because I believe the information is too valuable not to. Note, however, that they have been reproduced exactly as they were written 60 years ago and thus, as with all reading, the reader must take the useful "gems" and leave the rest. For example, the bulletin on "Upgrading" states:

> From the company's standpoint the development of each employee to his highest level of usefulness is requisite to company success. Building competent manpower is considered one of management's primary functions in many companies ... Nothing is so destructive to employee efficiency, loyalty, and morale as to have a man hired from the outside and given a higher rated job for which someone already employed feels he could qualify.

The theme of eliminating waste reappears and a reason is offered on how to increase productivity and morale, which are two characteristics on which some companies seem to be constantly working. On the other hand, between these sentences is inserted the following:

> From the employee's standpoint, growth and advancement through his work should represent the central core of his life.

One must put this sentence within the context it was written. U.S. society had been mainly agrarian 40 years before, had gone through the Great Depression and now was in a fight for its survival. The majority of the population was not yet to the point where they could afford for their jobs, or professions or careers not to be the "central core" of their lives. We know today that a balanced life is usually happier and more successful than one that focuses on only one aspect; but even today, many people are not to that point.

Readers especially need to read the bulletin *Increasing War Production Through Employment of Women* in its context. The authors were addressing those people who may have believed that just as women don't belong on ships, they don't belong in the workplace. Looking back at this today, it is easy to see this prejudiced thinking. However, it may be easier for some to see that if you have a job to get done, you should choose the best person to do it regardless of gender, race, etc. Women generally are smaller than men are, but not all women are smaller than all men and sometimes we overemphasize the importance of size or strength. The key point is that everyone who is unfamiliar with a job will need training, so we must find out what they know about it and build on that. This article is probably best summed up by one of the sentences in the forward letter by the director, C.R. Dooley:

> The employer who has never had any women employees on his force may need to be reminded, in some cases, that a new woman worker is just a new worker.

The main point to glean from this bulletin is that one must not make assumptions about people. Base your decisions on facts already known. Collecting more facts allows one to make better decisions. Thus, one should not only read the bulletins in the context in which they were written, but they should also look for the main message that is conveyed.

Some bulletins seem to be so out of date that they may appear to be worthless; but if one looks for the main message, they will find value. There are two bulletins on training aids: *How Training Can Be Done—Methods, Aids,* and *Training Aids.* Again, you must understand the context here, but the main message is to be aware of available audio visual aids and make the best use of them. A corollary would be to use the simplest medium that is effective. The first bulletin mentioned gives a table of various aids and describes their characteristics so that one can *Select the Most Effective Aid.* Naturally, videos, computers, and LCD projectors were not on the list, but they could easily be added. Recently, I attended a presentation at a local professional society to which I belong. The presentation was on how to make the best use of PowerPoint® software when making a presentation. The point not made by the presenter was how to determine when PowerPoint® software should be used. Many people use it because they can and not because the application is particularly effective. One should understand what the medium does and then select the simplest form to accomplish one's objective.

Some people may still see certain organizations' activities as necessary evils to be done for social or legal purposes. Safety programs or counseling services are two that come to mind. A main concept favored by the TWI Service that stands against that idea comes out in the bulletins, which is that all the activities they encourage people to do have one objective: *to increase production.* A basic reason for enforcing safety rules is that accidents (with or without personal injuries) impede the flow of production. That is not to say that people were callous and didn't care if people were injured. The point is that a successful organization is one where the flow of production is continuous and uninterrupted. Anything that interferes with that flow should be eliminated.

Thus, read the bulletins because they do possess valuable ideas, but keep them in context and look for the main message.

PART 1

History, Benefits, and Characteristics of TWI

CHAPTER 1

Benefits of the TWI Programs

"The TWI programs are distinctive, not because of the accepted principles of good management they cover, but because they are successful in getting these used."[1]

In early 1940, if a company had all the available equipment necessary to make lenses and wanted to increase its lens-grinding capacity by training another lens grinder, it would have to wait 5 years because that is how long it would take the average person to master the art and science of lens grinding. By the end of 1940, that time period was reduced to 4–6 months. In 1945, it was again reduced to less than 6 weeks.[2] The equipment, the companies, the employees, the supervisors, and the management all remained essentially the same. The major change was in how the company trained its employees. Training a lens grinder in 6 weeks instead of 5 years is impressive given the fact that producing optical lenses is a complicated process. I cite this lens-grinding example because during World War II (WWII), there was an urgent need to increase productivity in lens grinding, and the fledging government agency, Training Within Industry Service (TWI), used this urgency to help launch four training programs. Between 1940 and 1945, these programs were monumental in changing how organizations in the United States trained people to improve production. The four programs were:

1. *Job Instruction Training (JI)*. Trained workers in how to instruct a person to perform a job correctly and safely; and to be productive as quickly as possible, while creating less scrap, rework, and damage to tools and equipment. (Chapters 6 and 9)
2. *Job Relations Training (JR)*. Trained employees in how to solve personnel problems using an analytical, nonemotional method combined with some basic foundations of human relations. JR emphasizes that you must treat all people as individuals and by understanding people on all levels, supervisors can achieve results working through people. (Chapters 7 and 10)

3. *Job Methods Training (JM)*. Trained employees in how to improve the *way* jobs are performed in order to consistently produce greater quantities of quality products in less time using the available manpower, machines, and materials. (Chapters 8 and 11)
4. *Program Development (PD)*. Trained employees to solve production problems that were unique to their organizations. PD solves problems related to personnel through training while problems related to other resources are solved through technical means. (Chapters 9 and 12)

The first three programs were generally referred to as the "J" programs. Table 1-1 illustrates some testimonials and statistical data to illustrate some of the benefits of the TWI program during WW II.

The examples in Table 1-1 may be more interesting to the reader in what they *don't* show. Here are a few:

- Except for the union example, these are all *manufacturing examples*. What about service industries like the medical field or financial sector?
- These examples are over 60 years old! Organizations have introduced many new approaches and techniques to the world of manufacturing and services over the last 60 years and companies today are more advanced, at least technologically, than companies back then. So how relevant can these TWI results be to contemporary business practices?
- The United States (and the World) was at war then and people were in an environment where they often had no choice but to take jobs they did not want or for which they were not properly trained. Our culture is different now.
- If TWI training was so beneficial at improving productivity, why aren't companies applying these practices today?
- Just because TWI worked for those companies during those times, it doesn't mean it'll work for my company or my situation today. After all, a lot of business buzz-word-promoting programs have come and gone and often have very little substance, are too difficult to apply, and aren't the panacea they make themselves out to be. How do I know that TWI isn't just another fad?
- These statistics are not all that convincing since all of them cite "one-time" cases with no mention of follow-through or continuation. What I need is *a program that sustains improvements*.

In the remainder of this chapter, and in Chapter 2, we'll touch on some of these concerns, as well as how these four programs dramatically increased productivity during wartime and the 1940s. In Chapter 3 I cover some of the

Table 1-1. TWI Success Stories

Companies	TWI Results	Statistics Increased/ Reduced/Saved
Machinery Plant	In 1945, the Vice President of the Food Machinery Corporation at Lakeland Florida, Mr. H. L. Austin, wrote: "Because of poor morale, our labor turnover was terrific; complaints and grievances were multitudinous; production schedules lagged. We sent our top production superintendent and our director of training to a Job Relations Institute. They came back and presented the program to all our supervisors. Within a fortnight, complaints and grievances ceased, labor turnover stopped, and production went ahead of schedule."[1]	
A Cable Producer	Eight hundred people were employed in the Long Island City plant of the General Cable Corporation. Although they were working three shifts a day and 6 days a week, their production of 7-strand field wire was many thousands of miles of wire below requirements. The plant had been in operation for only about 5 months and had 52 stranding machines. It was considered to be operating at about 50 percent of normal production for these types and numbers of machines. The next column shows the improvements that resulted within 4 months after 67 supervisors were given Job Instruction Training.	• Production: more than doubled • Scrap: went from 15% to 1% • Turnover: reduced by more than 70% • Absenteeism: cut in half[2]
The Easy Washing Machine Corporation	After using all three "J" programs at the Easy Washing Machine Corporation, the director of training reported: "In the overall analysis, the following figures indicate types of improvements as a result of training" (see next column).	• Production: increased 10% to 50% • Absentees: reduced from 15% before [training] to 2% after • Rejects: reduced to less than 1% from 5%–10% • Scrap: reduced from 5% to less than 1% • Learning time: on certain jobs reduced as much as 50%[3]

Table 1-1. *Continued*

Companies	TWI Results	Statistics Increased/ Reduced/Saved
The Moore Dry Dock Company, Oakland, CA	"Job Methods improvement proposals actually in effect are saving, according to craft superintendents' own estimates, 8,332 man-hours per month. This amounts to 99,984 man-hours per year, and at a commonly accepted value of $1.50 per man-hour, represents a savings of almost $150,000 each year. *This figure is constantly being raised by a flow of new Job Methods improvements coming in from the several hundred foremen, quartermen, and leadermen, trained in JM in the past 6 months.*"[4]	
Consolidated Steel Corp.	This company had a small fabrication yard located in Orange, Texas. In 1940, the Navy contracted with them to build destroyers. At the height of employment, the facility had 20,000 workers.[5] The data in column three reflects the efforts of 18,749 employed at the time and the 15,000 who had received some form of TWI training. "These results were arrived at by comparison of production department records, based on the construction of the first 50 destroyer escorts as compared with the last 50. The credit for these beneficial results is largely attributed to the successful continuous use of TWI programs."[6]	• Production: increased 45% • Training: reduced 78% • Scrap: reduced 69% Tool breakage: reduced 75% • Manpower: saved 45% • Accidents: decreased 70%
Oregon Shipbuilding Corporation	"...[T]he superintendent reported that, before Job Instruction, department output was 800 rivets per man, per day, per shift. After Job Instruction, the superintendent reported enthusiastically that the output had increased to 3,200 rivets per man, per day, per shift; that the workers were doing the work easier and were happier."[7]	• Production: increased 400%

Table 1-1. *Continued*

Companies	TWI Results	Statistics Increased/ Reduced/Saved
Northrop Aircraft Inc. Hawthorne, CA	Although little known before World War II, Northrop produced the P-61 "Black Widow" Night Fighter and the "Flying Wing" Army bomber and thus became a valuable defense contractor. "Job Instruction Training, beginning in the fall of 1942, was given to 1,241 supervisors of all levels. By February 1944, as a result of consistent coaching, Northrop was experiencing such plantwide results as listed in column three: The reduction in injuries enabled this company to receive the Department of Labor Safety Award. The Safety Engineer gives Job Instruction the major credit for this accomplishment."[8]	• Production: increased 17% • Break-in time to train a person on a new job: reduced 22% • Rejections: reduced 12% • Scrap: reduced 27% • Injuries: reduced 45%
Texas Oil Companies	"The tangible results from one department of the Port Arthur Works are indicative of results already obtained in other departments and plants ... Since Job Instruction was put on a continuing use basis early in 1944, the following results have been obtained."[9]	• Manufacturing costs: reduced 20% • Accidents resulting in lost time: reduced 75% • Minor accidents: reduced 20% • Break-in time: reduced 40% • Scrap/rework: reduced 20%
Applying Job Methods in Coal Mines	See next column for typical results.	• Saved 60% labor in construction of a road. • Freed 2 men out of 4 in rock-dust unloading • Saved 63% of time required for handling war bonds • Increased 20% handling coal per day through new method of spotting cars[10]

Table 1-1. *Continued*

Companies	TWI Results	Statistics Increased/ Reduced/Saved
Hawaiian Air Depot	After using the Job Instruction Program: "In one unit, the average time for a complete maintenance job was thirty-five to forty hours. After training for one-third of the personnel, maintenance was cut to an average time of twelve to fourteen hours."[11]	• Maintenance time cut by 60% or more
Job Relations Training With Unions	You can measure benefits from process improvements and training, but human relations are more difficult to measure unless there is a union involved. "The business agent for five New York locals of the International Brotherhood of Electrical Workers (A.F.L.) reported that since Union Job Relations [a modified JR program] was given to the stewards in one local, not a single grievance had come to him to handle (three months). In the past at least two cases a week were referred for attention and handling. "One local on the Industrial Union of Marine and Shipbuilding Workers (C.I.O.) at Sun Shipping & Drydock Company, before using the Union Job Relations Program, had ten to twenty cases a week that went to the third step of the grievance procedure. This was cut to a weekly average of two."[12] "The U.A.W. – C.I.O. at Chance Voight, brassworks in Waterbury, and the Machinists (A.F. of L.) in Stamford have stated that they were able to reduce by over 50% the number of grievances which had to be sent to the second level of the grievance procedure. In other words, the steward became capable enough to handle them on the first level. This eventually reduced, of course, the number of grievances going into arbitration and saved the union considerable money in that respect."[13]	• Grievances reduced from an average of 8/month to zero for a 3-month period • 3rd step grievances reduced by over 80% • 2nd step grievances reduced by over 50%

1. TWI Report, p. 91.
2. TWI Report, p. 96.
3. TWI Report, p. 96.
4. TWI Report, p. 97.
5. www.domeisland.com/destroyers/ consolidated.html
6. TWI Report, p. 94.
7. TWI Report, p. 98.
8. TWI Report, p. 137.
9. TWI Report, p. 147.
10. TWI Report, p. 149.
11. TWI Report, p. 156.
12. TWI Report, p. 98.
13. TWI Report, p. 87.

reasons why TWI is not only relevant in today's industry, but is a foundation for sustaining any successful Lean initiative. In Chapter 4, I identify the unique and timeless characteristics that make all four of these programs critical to today's industry.

TWI Is Not Just for Manufacturing

The examples cited in Table 1-1 are from the TWI Services' *The Training Within Industry Report* (TWI Report). I will be referring extensively to the TWI Report, as well as the TWI training manuals, throughout this book. As you will learn in more detail in Chapter 2, the government created the TWI Service solely to help defense contractors, which is why most of the examples are limited to manufacturing firms. However, in reviewing Table 1-2, it is obvious that the TWI Service programs were widely used in a variety of organizations, including service organizations listed in the last group in the table. The report doesn't specify exactly what is included in "Transportation, Communications, and Utilities," but since "Aircraft, Ships, and Autos," and "Other Transportation Equipment" are listed separately, we can surmise that the former category was limited to service organizations. The "Service Industries," as stated in the report, are mainly hospitals and laundries. As an example of its broad application and flexibility, the TWI Service realized early on that instead of modifying its programs at the request of a particular office or hospital it was just as effective to change some terminology. For example, they changed the word "bench" (used in a shop environment) to "desk" (for use in an office environment) or "table" (for use in a hospital environment).[3] This flexibility to adapt terminology enabled TWI to be used by diverse entities, from libraries in New Jersey to the Department of Agriculture. The Department of Agriculture used TWI to introduce the TWI Job Methods Training Program to Westinghouse's Better Farm and Home contest—a program designed to get boys and girls living on farms to look at better methods for performing "chores."[4]

Also, the "Government Establishments" group mainly represented the Army Service Forces (ASF), which was the supply and administrative arm of the army that fed, clothed, housed, and equipped the Army. At that time, it was the largest supply organization in the world.[5] Most of the positions in the ASF were supervisory and clerical and the number of personnel trained in service organizations noted here amounted to about 16 percent of the total.[6] TWI consulted with the Civil Service Commission to make a version of the Job Methods Training Program for offices, which was subsequently used by the ASF. Table 1-3[7] clearly shows that TWI training went beyond the ASF for service organizations resulting in over a half million certificates issued by other groups.[8]

Table 1-2. Companies Using TWI from 1941–1945

Groups Served	Units Served								Certifications			
	Under 100 Emp.	100–499 Emp.	500–999 Emp.	1,000 Emp. & Over	Total No. Plants	Total Employees in plants	Job Instruction	Job Methods	Job Relations	Program Development	Union Job Relations	Total
Industrial Groups												
Agriculture	2	19	21	12	54	49,191	3,252	760	2,904	8		6,924
Mining	26	103	112	61	302	238,915	9,034	1,748	5,286	10		16,078
Contract Construction	8	17	15	9	49	88,401	5,182	424	1,123	3		6,732
Ordnance and Accessories	54	291	171	240	756	1,063,225	83,079	16,933	36,641	169		136,822
Food	293	562	333	160	1,348	689,141	33,931	10,183	15,269	71		59,454
Textiles Mill Products	16	262	247	143	668	540,021	29,921	8,556	13,442	83		52,002
Apparel, Fabric Products	56	250	131	49	486	240,736	12,628	2,915	3,657	33		19,233
Lumber, Lumber Products	66	240	81	20	407	139,899	6,667	1,698	2,162	17		10,544
Paper and Printing	51	240	127	66	484	250,646	16,517	4,654	6,425	67		27,663
Chemicals, Allied Products	62	217	150	82	511	344,787	23,898	7,108	15,945	72		47,023
Petroleum, Coal Products	37	103	113	65	318	310,046	16,639	2,580	9,452	36		28,707
Rubber, Leather, Glass	94	318	182	106	700	503,097	31,198	9,192	15,906	60		56,356
Iron, Steel, Metal Products	404	1,015	509	355	2,283	1,712,980	94,118	26,346	49,701	225		170,390
Aircraft and Parts	54	228	140	206	628	1,640,348	156,739	50,615	78,668	149		286,171
Ships, Ship Repair	30	133	72	125	360	1,222,101	84,306	17,865	43,686	41		145,898
Autos, Auto Equipment	58	43	62	41	204	213,724	12,111	3,947	5,504	25		21,587
Other Transp. Equipment	24	57	33	31	145	109,898	4,796	2,030	2,001	11		8,838
Elec., Mech. Machinery	252	682	305	238	1,477	1,088,176	70,617	22,702	28,860	167		122,346
Transp., Comm., Util.	227	377	492	234	1,330	1,505,266	53,037	16,230	38,344	118		107,729
Service Industries	205	348	275	23	851	271,507	16,791	1,775	4,671	16		23,253
Miscellaneous	957	497	339	75	1,868	465,425	152,581	17,741	57,703	312		228,337
Trade and Finance	47	40	100	32	219	189,728	9,418	1,461	4,102	18		14,999
Government Establishments	106	186	448	137	877	808,549	78,653	17,290	48,214	76		144,233
Unions	4	13	141	28	186	263,040	57	20	356	42	8,856	9,331
All Groups	3,133	6,241	4,599	2,538	16,511	13,948,847	1,005,170	244,773	490,022	1,829	8,856	1,750,650

*Punch-card tabulation made for TWI by National Roster of Scientific and Specialized Personnel

Table 1-3. Certificates Issued to Nonmanufacturing Groups

	JI	JM	JR	Total
Army Service Forces	150,000	75,000	100,000	325,000
Civil Service Commission	67,000	26,000	20,000	113,000
U.S. Dept. of Agriculture	11,000	10,000	4,000	25,000
Social Security Board	1,800	7,200	800	9,800
Dept. of Labour, Canada	55,000	14,000	12,000	81,000
Ministry of Labour, England	15,600	240	2,000	17,840
TOTAL	300,400	132,440	138,800	571,640

Sixty Years Old, but Some Things Remain the Same

TWI developed its training programs by gathering the accumulated knowledge of experienced professional trainers at the time and combining this know-how with new ideas that were tested through numerous trial sessions. Because of the constraints of WWII, referred to many times in the TWI Report as an "emergency," the founders of TWI came up with four essential requirements to turn these three facets (existing knowledge, new ideas, and thorough testing) into workable programs. They were:

1. The programs must be simple.
2. The programs must be prepared using a minimum amount of presentation time.
3. The programs must be built on the principle of demonstration or "learning by doing."
4. The program should provide a "multiplier effect" so that a group of employees who have been trained can, in turn, train other employees.[9]

Because of these requirements, the TWI founders developed a very basic and condensed training program—there was no extraneous text or training. In a sense, it was "pure" training because everything was geared toward quickly making workers effective and efficient so the requirements only included basic information for vital functions. Consequently, there has been no need to make major changes or improvements in these programs in over 60 years of use. That is not to say that changes have not been made and will not be needed in the future. However, most changes, to date, have been made to accommodate cultural issues such as eliminating gender-bias from the terminology. (These changes are discussed in Chapter 9.[10]) The results achieved from the TWI programs in training millions of people in jobs they knew little or nothing about—getting employees productive as quickly as possible, finding and implementing improved ways to do things, and successfully dealing with personnel situations—are results any business in any age desires. Remember, these successes were during a difficult time in the United States, having just come out of a depression when unemployment was hovering around 25 percent.

There are some U.S. companies currently resurrecting TWI, and the successes so far are similar to those of 60 years ago. Interestingly, the current companies that are reaping the benefits of TWI without having current TWI examples are those that were already engaged in significant and successful training programs. Usually these companies have implemented Lean Manufacturing initiatives and routinely offer their employees a wide variety of training such as Total Quality Management (TQM), Covey, and various leadership training programs. Though these companies used training to solve production problems, it wasn't until they used TWI that they tapped into the real potential of using training as a foundation to sustain improvement programs. Here are two current examples.

Schneider Packaging Equipment Company

This company makes automatic machinery in upstate New York. During January 2003, they trained ten of their manufacturing floor personnel in the Job Methods Program. During this particular training, each participant is required to select a method and improve it, the purpose being to practice and to learn. The participants' improvements from learning these methods during the training resulted in $34,300 in savings, realized within the first 30 days after the training. The projected annualized savings for those improvements was $124,690, and the estimated investment of the company was approximately $11,000 for the training and the employees' time. That resulted in a 312 percent ROI in the short term and an 1134 percent ROI for the year.[11]

These figures prompted the engineering department to undergo the same training the following month, but because the engineers and project managers do not do physical assembly work, their improvement projects were procedural in nature. They considered procedures such as writing and editing service manuals, allocating time for specific jobs, creating final documentation for a project, and clearing approval for a vacation day. Although they could estimate time saved, they could not obtain precise costs until they experienced the number of iterations of the procedure in question. Comments on the Participant Response Sheets included the following:

> "... [Job Methods will give us the] discipline to capture the details and carefully think about why we do what we do ... makes company-

wide implementation smoother ... This process can make simple improvements to our process that can, in turn, save money, time, and most importantly, grief. ..."

Gray-Syracuse

Gray-Syracuse (GS) is a world-class producer of precision casting parts for highly engineered products used in aircraft engines, power generation equipment, and missiles. After creating a new strategy, GS realized that it had a great opportunity to improve productivity by addressing the front end of the production process. Most of their previous efforts in flexible manufacturing were done at the back end of the process where higher skills are required.[12] GS's attitude was one of opportunity:

"Even though we manage everyone's competencies, we had been biased toward the high-skill jobs. The identification of strategic job families brought something to the forefront that we wouldn't have seen otherwise ... It showed us an entry-level job that was just as important. The benefits of focusing on this job will be huge."[13]

The strategy of applying flexible manufacturing to the front-end mold assembly was a challenge since it required a broad new set of competencies for the process of eight distinct configurations of activities (known as cells) to produce different types of products. The simplest cell required 11 different activities, while the most complex cell required 27. Since the assembler position is an entry-level position, employees were trained by assigning the best employees to train new employees using the buddy technique. According to Paul Smith, the Human Resources Director at Gray-Syracuse, GS realized it needed a way to train employees that was repeatable and verifiable and they found what they were looking for in TWI Job Instruction Training.

Using ... Training Within Industry (TWI), experienced GS experts developed activity and competency profiles for each cell, summarized in a TWI template. All thirty current assemblypersons would have to master the activities required by each cell. The supervisor, the quality inspector, and/or the trainer used the TWI template to evaluate each of the thirty assemblypersons monthly and quarterly. They had a target to bring all assemblypersons to level 3 ("in training") as soon as possible, and then quickly to level 4 ("certified: within cell") ... According to the human capital readiness report, "The readiness level was 400, an average level of 1.6 per person per cell, when the program was introduced in 2001. This level was only 40 percent of phase 2 objective. One year later, the readiness level had risen to 810, an average level of 3.3 and 84 percent of the phase 2 objective."

Paul Smith attributed the speed with which the competency levels rose to the TWI Job Instruction Program, which requires breaking a job into important parts, and then designing training for each of these parts. This includes having the trainee demonstrate performance to confirm that she or he has in fact learned the job. Since the Job Instruction training was implemented, GS achieved these results:

- Raised the Human Capital Readiness Report from 40 percent to 84 percent in the twelve-month period JI was being implemented. This effort focused on the mold assembly job family cutting the time in half to achieve strategic readiness.
- Reduced by 73 percent the 2002 versus 2003 Initial Wax Department Assembly Defects. As of the first three quarters of 2004, these defects have been reduced 96 percent compared with defects reported in 2002. Continuing reduction in defects continues to enable the Wax Department to improve mold release (delivery) time to the Casting Department:
  - 2002—Average on-time delivery to Casting Dept. 73.2 percent
  - 2003—Average on-time delivery to Casting Dept. 89.6 percent
  - 2004 (first 3 quarters)—Average on-time delivery to Casting Dept. 98.6 percent[14]

These improved Mold Release times contributed to increasing productivity in other areas:
  - Cycle Time Reduction: 64 percent
  - Inventory Reduction: 50 percent
  - Improved On-time Delivery: 80 percent

One final point. Because Gray-Syracuse at the time did know how to best apply TWI to their operation, they trained their personnel in all three of the "J" programs. Once they got started, however, they found the best strategy was to emphasize Job Instruction to standardize processes. In administering TWI programs, once you obtain consistency in operations, you can more effectively employ Job Methods to make improvements and, finally, Job Relations to help maintain good employee relations.

Why TWI Fell Out of Use in the United States

As discussed in more detail in Chapter 2, the U.S. government created the TWI Service for the war effort, and though it was extremely successful, the government disbanded it when WWII ended. Some TWI professionals continued to offer the programs in the United States, but were not very successful, though TWI continued to have successes overseas. There are several possible explanations for this.

After WWII, the United States had the strongest and largest production facilities in the world. The purpose of TWI is to increase productivity. If your productivity is the best in the world, there would seem little motivation to improve it. Although this may seem very shortsighted now, consider what the United States was like immediately after the war. Companies were shifting production from war material to civilian goods. With no competition to speak of from war-devastated countries, companies operated at full production to meet both U.S. and worldwide demand. Demand was such that companies could not make goods fast enough, and because there was little or no competition, there was no need to improve or increase worker productivity. These companies may have also believed that there was no time for training.

Secondly, the TWI Service designed the programs to be very simple and basic for quick and effective results and insured its operational integrity through a strict quality control procedure. But once the government disbanded TWI, there was no organization to control the program's content. Therefore, when U.S. companies did adopt TWI, they changed the programs, and consequently, the programs lost their effectiveness. Why did TWI fail them? According to the scientific view, the simplest solution is usually the best solution. That is, taking a solution that was derived from the scientific method and making it more complex will most likely not improve the solution. The TWI founders and practitioners understood this and *made sure they maintained strict quality control on their procedures.* (I will have more to say on the scientific method later.) Yet it is human nature that when confronted with something very simple, people tend to want to improve or modify it. Today, we can see the remnants of these modifications in bits and pieces of the TWI programs in current use. For example, the term *Key Point* as originally used in Job Instruction may be in a company's training manual today, but it has little to do with the original meaning. Instead of using five 2-hour sessions over a week to teach someone a training technique, today, organizations commonly use one 10-hour training session. We will discuss later how changes like these can nullify the intended effects of TWI Training. In a direct answer to the question, "Why aren't companies using TWI today?" the answer is, "They are." You know their names: Sanyo, Yamaha, Kawasaki, Nissan, and especially, Toyota. We'll have more to say about Toyota in Chapter 3.

TWI—A Precursor to the Learning Organization

Although the TWI founders' initial intention was to address problems and improve efficiencies in the production of manufactured goods, they soon realized they had created training programs that were universally applicable to any type of organization. Table 1-2 shows the wide spectrum of companies signed up for the TWI programs.

The U.S. Army Basic Training or "boot camp" provides a good parallel for the skills a person gains in the TWI programs. The U.S. Army's basic 8-week training prepares a person to function in the army. Once "privates" complete this training, they move on to the advanced training for whatever specialty they may engage in. The U.S. Army does not consider the 8 weeks of basic training to be sufficient to prepare a person to be productive in the army, but it is important groundwork to prepare the person for what to expect while they serve. In the private sector, however, companies usually expect prospective employees to be already fully trained in the basic skills. They assume the employees' work history, or previous job skills, are sufficient. As a result, companies seldom offer any basic or preparatory training. If required, companies may test for reading, writing, and math skills, but they usually don't test for or teach specialty areas such as problem-solving skills.

However, there are skills people learn through TWI training that will help a person perform optimally, no matter what his or her job function. Job Instruction teaches employees to instruct others on how to perform a task, follow a procedure, or understand a process. Though people already instruct other people every day, TWI uses formal and well-tested programs that ensure employees will learn the job quickly yet capably; make as few errors as possible while performing their tasks' and do so without injuring themselves, creating excessive scrap, or damaging equipment. This quality of performance builds employees' confidence which in turn improves morale.

Because of the competitive nature of people and business, an organization will not survive if it is satisfied with the status quo. If an organization cannot find ways to produce products in less time or with less expense, its competitors will. Therefore, changing methods and processes to produce products in less time is something to which every organization should pay attention. There is a big difference, however, between "doing a job in less time" and "doing a job faster." Merely working faster without improving processes can introduce more errors or waste and you approach a "fast" limit quickly. The true focus, and one that TWI uses, is to look at "doing a job correctly in less time" and to achieve this by continuously training employees who immediately apply what they've learned and continually improve their jobs. This further fits in with the Lean manufacturing approach of removing waste in your processes.

Furthermore, having an idea or developing a plan achieves only half of the objective for making improvements. Knowing how to put your plans into action no matter what level you are in an organization requires a methodical and proven approach. Finally, at every level in an organization, management must deal with people and culture, which can mean obstacles, especially when faced with changing the way you do work. You can read a service manual when a *machine* has problems, but there is no such manual when *people* have problems. TWI teaches some simple methods to deal with personnel issues. The skills people learn through the three TWI "J" programs will spread throughout the organization. TWI is not just an idea; it is a practical series of short training courses that teach employees "how" to practice their skills. In a fundamental sense, TWI is a precursor to a learning organization. In *The Fifth Discipline*, Peter Senge says, "A learning organization is a place . . .

> . . . where people continually expand their capacity to create the results they truly desire, where new and expansive patterns of thinking are nurtured, where collective aspiration is set free, and *where people are continually learning how to learn together.*"[15]

Senge also discusses the importance of *learning to learn*, as well as, *how* to learn new skills, knowledge, and capabilities. In other words, an organization has to do more than develop new business or technical skills. And it is not enough to be innovative. Organizations need to be continuously developing its "learning capacity" and to have a standardized method for transferring skills and knowledge to its employees. We learn by asking questions and getting feedback. We improve when we change our actions according to that feedback. We improve on a continuing basis when we keep repeating that process. This is the process taught by Job Methods, which has as a main principle: Question everything. When people are comfortable questioning what they do and are empowered to make improvements, the culture begins to reflect that of a learning organization.

TWI is Self-Sustaining

Anything an employee does can become a habit if he or she does it often enough. Some job training is so specific to a situation, however, that repeated practice sessions might be rare. Thus, it is unlikely for that process to become a habit. TWI, on the other hand, addresses broader skills that most people usually need every day. Basic issues of how to teach a person a job, how people can make small but continuous improvements in whatever tasks they perform, standardize these tasks, and how to improve communications and people skills to better deal with coworkers and management, are important skills that should also become "habits" in an organization's culture.

TWI skills are as necessary and almost as basic as the "3 *Rs*": reading, writing and arithmetic. No one questions the value of these basic subjects and their importance is reflected in the fact that we teach them to our children at the earliest possible age. Furthermore, we consider these subjects *skills*. That is, once the teacher instructs the student, he or she practices these skills until reaching a "passing" level of performance. To become competent in these skills, students must do many arithmetic problems, write many essays, and read many books, all the while advancing to the next level. However, organizations often do not actually train people in the TWI skills. They may give a "presentation" of the material, but they do not require drills (work projects) or activities that engage the person to demonstrate *how* it works. Only by "doing" can employees learn how to perform the skill competently.

The power of TWI is that whether you are learning how to calculate sales tax, or figuring out a bus schedule, the training is basic, yet the effect is far reaching, like introducing a common language into the Tower of Babel and turning it into a single community focused on being successful and productive. Once an organization embeds TWI skills into its culture, it will soon see its employees learning on a continuous, self-sustaining level. This is attributed to the fact that TWI emphasizes keeping an open mind to accept new changes, and making further improvements. This is why many people view the TWI Job Methods as the origin of the concept behind continual improvement, or *kaizen* in Japanese.[16] I take this one step further by saying TWI is a foundation of Lean. But before discussing this, let's look at the birth of the TWI Service and some of the many challenges it faced.

---

1. Robinson, Alan G., and Schroeder, Dean M., *Training, Continuous Improvement, and Human Relations: The U.S. TWI Programs and the Japanese Management Style*, California Management Review, The Regents of the University of California, CMR, Volume 335, Number 2, Winter 1993, p. 36.
2. Training Within Industry Service, *The Training Within Industry Report: 1940–1945* (Washington, D.C.: War Manpower Commission Bureau of Training, 1945), pp. 18–20.
3. *TWI Report*, p. 159.
4. *TWI Report*, p. 159.
5. TWI Report p. 153; "It is necessary to picture the world's largest manufacturer, merchant, supplier, transportation service, contractor, and storage company all unified under one control in order to get a picture of the ASF during wartime."

6. Transp., Comm., Util.; Service Industries; Trade and Finance; Government Establishments.
7. *TWI Report*, p. 151
8. *TWI Report*, p. 151; Table 1-3 lists approximately twice as many certificates for the ASF as does Table 1-2 (144,233 versus 325,000) because those in Table 1-2 "represent the work done by TWI for the Army Service Forces (*TWI Report* p. 129). TWI Training was deemed so successful that the ASF decided to run the program themselves and then TWI conducted (train the trainer) Institutes for ASF.
9. *TWI Report*, p. 32.
10. The TWI Service was created to help the defense industry and initially, the founders had no preconceived idea of how to do that. As programs were developed, their content was set in response to the requests from the defense industry to solve specific problems. This is in contrast to creating a training program and then attempting to sell it to someone.
11. www.trainingwithinindustry.com; Slide show; slide #33.
12. *Strategy Maps: Converting Intangible Assets into Tangible Assets,* Robert S. Kaplan and David P. Norton, Harvard Business School Publishing Corporation, 2004 p. 237. Other quotes can be found on pp. 237–239 in the book.
13. Ibid, p. 4.
14. Per telephone conversation with Paul Smith, September 7, 2004.
15. *The Fifth Discipline: The Art and Practice of the Learning Organization*, New York: Doubleday, 1990, p. 1.
16. *The Roots of Lean Training Within Industry: The Origin of Kaizen*, Jim Huntzinger; The Tribune, published by The Society of Manufacturing Excellence, Second Quarter 2002.

CHAPTER 2

A Brief History Outlining the Principles of TWI

"The mistake made and not recognized for a long time was that the programs were described in terms of their techniques and not their accomplishments."[1]

For all the evils that war brings, it often forces nations to be creative and innovative. When the United States entered World War I (WWI), there was a great need for ships, especially since ships were the only mode of transportation for traveling anywhere around the world. The United States had 37 steel shipyards and 24 wood shipyards employing 50,000 people, but the defense department needed ten times that.[2] Although manpower was available, they were untrained in the art and science of building ships. The obvious solution for the U.S. government was to devise a way to train these people quickly, so they turned to industry trainers and teachers and asked them to develop a program for accomplishing what seemed to be an impossible task: Train 500,000 people in a matter of months to build ships to win a war. They did, and when this mission was accomplished, the people responsible for the program realized that they had gained a great deal of knowledge in the field of instruction, and summarized all of the principles they developed (see Exhibit 2-1).[3]

Unfortunately, most organizations only gave these principles "lip service" during WWI and ignored these training principles between the two world wars. This was unfortunate, because these principles are as true today as they were at the beginning of the twentieth century. You can do preparation or training in universities, colleges, and vocational schools, but the most effective training occurs when a person performs the actual work while on the job. Here you can make the instruction more specific, the learner becomes more engaged, and the parent organization has a 'stake' in the outcome. In addition, the instructors typically come from the pool of employees because they already know the work and processes, although they will need some help in learning how to instruct. Some of the items in Exhibit 2-1 may seem quaint today such as number 6 referring to creating "worker loyalty," though corporate

Exhibit 2-1. Training Principles Developed in World War I

World War I Training Principles

The Emergency Fleet Corporation experience and that of the Army can be summarized as establishing these principles:

1. Training must be done *within* industry.
2. Instructors should be plant men, preferably supervisors.
3. These supervisors would need help in the method of instruction.
4. Break-in time is cut by training on the job.
5. The most effective size of group for training by one instructor is from 9 to 11.
6. Spelling out the importance of work and giving of personal attention develops worker loyalty.
7. Training is an investment—its costs are paid by eventual increased production.
8. Ability to instruct is an important supervisory qualification.
9. The four steps in good instruction are:
   a. Preparation
   b. Presentation
   c. Application
   d. Inspection (or test)
10. Job analysis or the making of job breakdowns is an important preliminary step before instruction.

Many industrial people "accepted" those principles verbally, but there were few indications of their use.

---

assets such as loyal employees can be priceless when an organization is changing and when seemingly insurmountable obstacles arise. The point is that these training themes are good ideas that work throughout time, becoming more like universal principles that any company can use.

World War I ended in November 1918, but there was a farm depression in the early '20s, and with the stock market crash on October 2, 1929, the United States and the world began its slide into the Great Depression. By 1932, unemployment in the United States was estimated to be 25 percent[4] and the total value of goods and services fell to about half of what it had been before the crash. Franklin Roosevelt's New Deal began to take effect in 1933 and helped to lift the country out of the Depression, but the onset of World War II (WWII) was the biggest factor in turning the economy around.

September 1, 1939, Germany invaded Poland: the beginning of World War II. On June 22, 1940, France fell to Germany, leaving Great Britain as the only western European country that could oppose Hitler's forces.[5] In June, Italy joined forces with Germany and the fighting soon spread to Greece and North Africa.[6] Even so, many Americans didn't want the United States to enter the war. One of the reasons for this isolationism may have been the Depression—unemployment was still high and production capability was extremely low. Though the United States wasn't sending troops overseas, Franklin Roosevelt still believed that the Allied Powers could win the war if the United States became the "arsenal of democracy," supplying them with the necessary materials. This required the U.S. government to prepare the nation for an increase in production capacity. One of the requirements, of course, was an ample supply of trained workers to churn out the new "arsenal." Although there was no lack of manpower because of high unemployment, there were too few people trained with the appropriate skills to carry out the government's plans. To further complicate matters, supervisors and leadmen (team leaders) were in short supply because many of these skilled people were enlisting or being drafted[7] into the military. It was the sudden increase in factory orders though, which necessitated hiring additional workers.

"In 1942, approximately 6,000 new workers were reporting for work every day as night shifts and extra day shifts became necessary. Four hundred workers who had had no experience in directing the work of other people were being appointed as supervisors every day. Some were experienced operators, but some of those who were going to direct the work of these new workers had neither the knowledge of the job nor of how to break-in new people."[8]

Congress had specified that an Advisor on Industrial Production and an Advisor on Employment be part of the Advisory Commission to the Council of National Defense. Owen D. Young, Chairman of the Board of the General Electric Company and an assistant to the Commissioner of Employment, suggested that industry be given some help with manpower requirements. "The plan was simple—there would be a volunteer staff of industrial men, on loan for full or part time, to provide consulting, advisory, and clearing-house service."[9] Hence, the government created the Training Within Industry Service (TWI) in August 1940.

Looking back from the final product of the three "J" Programs and Program Development, the accomplishments of TWI look obvious and straightforward. Looking forward from 1940, however, the future was very uncertain. The TWI Service knew what it had to do, but not how to do it. Furthermore, no one could imagine the vastness of the project undertaking. "If anyone had pictured an armed force of 14,000,000 and the national war production force needed to supply it, the job would have seemed impossible."[10]

Initial Start-up Challenges

The government first turned to the participants who had gained so much training experience during WWI. Channing Rice (C.R.) Dooley was loaned from the Socony Vacuum Company, where he was the industrial relations manager, to be the Director of the Service, and Walter Dietz was loaned from the Western Electric Company, where he was personnel relations manager of the Manufacturing Department, to be the Associate Director and Head of Development.[11] "They came to Washington in August 1940 for 6 weeks, and stayed until Training Within Industry closed its operation in the fall of 1945."[12] At the time, both men each had 38 years of industrial experience. Both were in charge of personnel relations when they came to Washington. Dooley also had extensive experience in the planning and development of training. They brought with them Michael J. Kane from American Telephone & Telegraph where he was staff engineer on training.[13] The government had previously "borrowed" these three men for the WWI shipbuilding project, so they were immediately able to lend that expertise to the TWI challenge. The *TWI Report* provides detailed information on how the developers set up TWI along with an organizational chart (see Figure 2-1). It is important to note:

> From the beginning, TWI has operated as a decentralized service. In September 1940, TWI divided the country into 22 geographical districts according to the main industrial areas. In each, an informal group was to be headed by a prominent local production executive or industrial personnel man who would continue on his company's payroll while he gave TWI part-time service as a "dollar-a-year" man.[14]

> Although Dooley, Dietz, and Kane set out to immediately plan this organizational structure to deal with production and personnel shortages, an urgent request came to them during their first week in the summer of 1940 that derailed these planning efforts. This was the severe shortage of experienced lens-grinders and polishers mentioned in Chapter 1. This challenge led directly to the creation of the Job Instruction Training, the first of three "J" programs. Before this, however, Dooley and Dietz were not focused on creating training programs because their general charge was to "provide consulting, advisory and clearing-house service." To meet this immediate challenge, they decided to issue informative bulletins to the industry-at-large. The first bulletin issued on September 24, 1940, stated the purpose of the TWI Service:[15]

Figure 2-1. Basic Organizational Chart for TWI

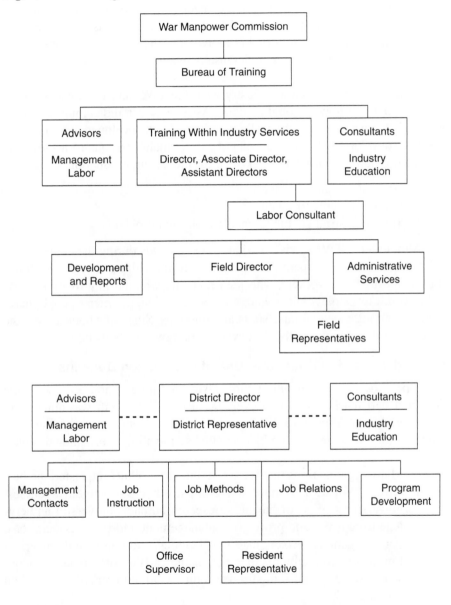

"The Office of Production Management has established this service for defense contractors and sub-contractors to assist them in meeting the increasing needs for skilled workers and supervisors.

"The underlying *PURPOSE* of this activity is:

To assist defense industries to meet their manpower needs by training within industry each worker to make the fullest use of his best skill up to the maximum of his individual ability, thereby enabling production to keep pace with defense demands."

Though the bulletins told industry what the TWI Service intended to do, it didn't spell out how it would be done. As we'll see in the coming chapters, initially TWI was very much "feeling their way" and developed over time, but the TWI developers did quickly identify three main methods to achieve the goal of providing a sufficient workforce for increasing production.

1. Give advice and information.
2. Solve problems for plants.
3. Train industrial people to handle their own problems.[16]

Although the TWI service used all three methods during the course of its existence, in the end it spent the bulk of its efforts with number three—training people to train workers. The idea that this was the key to its success didn't come to Dooley, Dietz, and Kane as an epiphany; many people hammered it out after several false starts and missteps. Since this book covers the third method in detail, we'll only cover the first two methods here.

Give Advice and Information—Use of Information Bulletins

TWI spent the first year mainly giving advice and information because, while "the paid staff reached a peak of over 400 in 1944,"[17] the staff was quite small in the early years. Although TWI continued writing bulletins throughout its existence, there were three main problems with disseminating information this way.

1. Many organizations that were not industrial plants requested the bulletins. "Vocational education groups, other government agencies, university schools of business, research bureaus, university and college executives and professors, management and trade associations, youth organizations, engineering societies, and public and university libraries were recipients of much of the early printed material. Consequently, much of it misfired as a direct aid with regard to war plant training . . ."[18]
2. Defense plant trainers always had questions regarding the quantity and the quality of the results. The bulletins were intended to increase productivity, but there was no way of knowing if companies accomplished that purpose to any degree.

3. As the war continued, paper was in short supply, which made issuing bulletins a questionable use of an important commodity. TWI issued the last bulletin in March 1942, while the last one was *written* in April 1945.

The "TWI Materials, Preface to Bulletins" states the initial purpose of the TWI Service as:

> Training Within Industry was organized in August 1940. Its immediate purpose, as far as could be seen then, was to provide a clearinghouse service in industrial training techniques, and to make training consultation available to contractors that requested this service. This objective, of course, expanded as conditions of war production changed.
>
> During the first year of existence, a number of bulletins on the need for training in expanding plants and on generally accepted training techniques were written for defense contractors. Later, a few bulletins were added to the series in order to provide materials needed in the TWI programs.

This section includes, in their latest editions, a list of all of the Training Within Industry bulletins. Many of them, since they were prepared for use on problems of conversion and expansion, were allowed to go out of print when war production struck its full stride and have not been distributed during the past two to three years. They are included in this complete list in order to give a picture of industrial conditions and problems at the time they were written.[19]

Table 2-1 shows a complete list of the bulletins and dates published. (*Note:* I organized the bulletins by first release dates and numbered them accordingly in the last column, which is the bulletin number I will refer to in this book.)

Although the *Training Within Industry Report* does not explicitly state why the bulletins were not as effective as intended, the reason might lie in the difference between presenting information (learned through reading or listening) and the need for skills (developed through practice).[20] The bulletins told the plant personnel *what to do*, but they did not tell them *how to do it*. Perhaps this was the reason that the bulletins were so popular among vocational schools, universities, and libraries where the focus is on learning concepts, but lost favor in the hands-on world of production facilities where plant personnel need instruction in how to do a job.

The existing bulletins are in their entirety and are on the CD accompanying this book. When you read them, you might be struck by how contemporary some

Table 2-1. Complete List of Issued TWI Bulletins

TWI Bulletin #	Title of Bulletin	Date Released/ Revision Date	CD Bulletin #
TWI Bulletins Organized by First Date of Release			
YEAR 1940			
N/A	Training Workers to Meet Defense Needs	N/A (intro)	1
N/A	Tying-in Pre-employment Training With On-The-Job Training	1940 rev. 6/44	2
1	The Training Within Industry Program	9/24/40 rev. 8/5/41	3
N/A	Developing All-Around Skilled Craftsmen through Apprenticeship	10/40 rev. 6/43	4
4A	Expanding the Managerial Organization	11/1/40	6
4	Strengthening the Managerial Organization	11/1/40	5
2B	How to Prepare Instructors to Give Intensive Job Instruction	12/1/40	7
YEAR 1941			
5	Training Aids	8/1/41	8
2A	Training Production Workers	8/15/41	9
N/A	Upgrading	8/15/41 rev. 6/44	10
YEAR 1942			
7	Increasing War Production Through Employment of Women	3/1/42	11
8A	Safety on the Job for the New Employee	5/1/42	12
N/A	Supplementary Instruction for Upgrading	5/42 rev. 6/44	13
4C	How to Improve Job Methods	12/1/42	14
YEAR 1943			
N/A	How to Improve Job Relations	1/43 rev. 6/44	15
N/A	How to Meet Specific Needs (What Training is Needed in Your Plant)	4/43 rev. 6/44	16
N/A	How to Select Supervisors—A 6-Step Program	6/43 rev. 11/43	17
8	Introducing the New Employee to the Job	6/1/43	18
N/A	How to Instruct a Man on the Job	12/1/43	19
YEAR 1944			
N/A	Management and Skilled Supervision (How the TWI Programs Operate)	6/1/44	20
N/A	How to Get a Plant Training Plan into Action	12/1/44	21
N/A	How to Get Continuing Results from Plant Training Programs	12/1/44	22
N/A	Improving Supervisors' Knowledge of the Work	12/1/44	23
N/A	Keeping Supervisors Informed About Their Responsibilities	12/1/44	24
YEAR 1945			
N/A	How Training Can Be Done—Methods, Aids (How to Conduct a Plant Meeting)	4/1/45	25

Note: Bulletins 14–25 were all included in the original PD training. (16 is a summary of the training.) Numbers 14 (JM), 15 (JR), & 19 (JI) were dropped because other material forced them out and the people in PD should have received that training already. The remaining bulletins (17, 18, 20–25) were all included in the PD program.

of them are. For example, in the bulletin, "Expanding the Managerial Organization" (Bulletin 5), the authors wrote that, when selecting a supervisor:

"Experience proves conclusively that intelligence, personality, vitality and other leadership abilities should outweigh technical or trade ability when such selections are made. Of course, there are some functions where technical knowledge is essential, and in such cases it should be recognized."

The bulletin "How to Get Continuing Results from Plant Training Programs" (Bulletin 22), describes a four-step process:

1. Assign responsibility.
2. Get adequate coverage.
3. Provide for coaching.
4. Report results and give credit.

The bulletin continues to describe how one should coach a supervisor and recognizes that coaching is important after training has been completed.

"Keeping Supervisors Informed About Their Responsibilities" (Bulletin 24), begins with an introduction by C.R. Dooley, the TWI Director. He states:

"It is important that every supervisor know not only the technical phases of his job but also just what his responsibilities are. Since these responsibilities change, it is necessary that the plan for keeping supervisors informed of their responsibilities shall operate continuously.

"No plant management can hold a supervisor responsible for things about which [he] has not been informed . . ."

Finally, "Increasing War Production Through Employment of Women" (Bulletin 11), relates that organizations should select and train women the same as they do men. In fact, after TWI issued this bulletin in March of 1942, C.R. Dooley was quoted in *Fortune* magazine (February 1943) as saying:

"We have had so many requests from nervous employers for special material on the training of women that I've asked my secretary to go out and buy a rubber stamp to use on every printed piece we send out, reading "This includes women, Negroes, handicapped, Chinamen, and Spaniards." The only difference between . . . men and women in industry is in the toilet facilities."[21]

It appears that TWI was already promoting diversity training in the 40s. In an attempt to help employees recognize and meet the needs of other employees and not blindly enforce rules, the same bulletin included this note:

Safety and the Woman Worker

"The safety records of women are better than those of men, but there are special hazards to be recognized. It may be necessary to require the wearing of protective clothing. The safety engineer who selects caps and jumpers will do well to consult with the women who will wear the clothing—his interest may be in finding a cap which will insure that the hair will not catch in a machine, while the employee may also be concerned about a cap which will protect hair from dust and not ruin a new hair-do. *It is poor practice to select clothing which requires disciplinary action to enforce wearing or which causes resentment.*" (My emphasis)

This bulletin also addresses a prejudice of the times: "A common opinion is, 'Women have no mechanical ability.' It is more accurate to say that they have little 'mechanical familiarity.' A main thought that one obtains from reading the TWI Report and the TWI training manuals is that the basic concepts proposed are universal and span both time and culture—one would only need to add contemporary phrasing. Treating people as individuals as well as recognizing and utilizing a diverse workforce are as important today as they were then. A company that makes the best use of the skills of all its employees will surpass a company that restricts problem solving to a select few. As discussed in Chapter 1, TWI helped lay the bases for "learning organizations," where successful companies train their employees to question, think, and solve problems. This is especially true where TWI promoted its training as a production tool—properly training and empowering employees to use that training to create a successful organization. We'll have more to say on this later.

Solve Problems for Plants—Consulting

Another way TWI assisted production facilities was by using consultants to help them solve their problems. TWI recognized that the first step in any problem-solving program would be to do an inventory of existing skills in the plant. This "inventory of present skills" is called a "needs analysis" today and TWI addressed that task by sending consultants into plants to do surveys. They conducted several hundreds of these during the first 6 months of 1941, and several hundred more plants received consultations without formal surveys. Although TWI was providing the "consulting, advisory and clearinghouse service" as it was charged to do, the personnel in TWI realized in mid-1941 that these actions had no effect on increasing productivity in plants. Even though ". . . in all some assistance was given to 892 plants, employing over a million and a half people,"[22] nothing of note had been accomplished.

The consultants taking the surveys felt they had wasted their time since almost no action had been taken within any of the plants visited. They did discover, however, that nearly all the supervisors in these plants were engaged in training employees and that many of them were not very well qualified to do so. It was TWI's view that an outside facility could provide only about 5 percent of what was required to prepare a worker for a specific job, meaning, the worker would have to do the remaining 95 percent of the training on the job. This started them focusing on what would be the core of the Service: training trainers.

Training Industrial People to Solve Problems

During this same period, the New Jersey District of TWI had been successfully standardizing the job instruction training program TWI had developed for the lens grinders because of the crisis in 1940. Organizations had provided job instruction training before, but no one had ever standardized it. TWI realized that through standardization it could quickly spread any program across the country successfully. As a result, in November 1941, TWI nationally released a Job Instruction Program based on the New Jersey District Program. TWI also recommended developing a similar instruction program "in the field of conserving manpower, machine capacity, equipment and material."[23] This suggestion led to the Job Methods Program, reducing the use of surveys, and emphasizing training programs with individual counseling only provided for specific programs or occasionally done for specific problems. TWI's main thrust from 1942 to 1945 was the development and application of the three "J" Programs: Job Instruction, Job Methods, and Job Relations. These three programs specifically addressed instruction, methods, and human relations. Program Development, on the other hand, addressed a much larger issue and, although it was issued nationally in the fall of 1944,[24] its development continued until 1945.

The Role of TWI in the War Manpower Commission

The United States started becoming an "arsenal for democracy" in 1940 and then officially entered the war after Japan attacked Pearl Harbor on December 7, 1941. As production increased through the end of the war in 1945, various supplies also became scarce resulting in rationing of sugar, meat, butter, shoes, and tires. Communities conducted salvage drives (recycling) of wastepaper, fat, tin cans, rags, and iron and steel scrap. It was during this time that the TWI Service was absorbed into the War Manpower Commission in 1943.[25] "The War Manpower Commission (WMC) held virtually dictatorial powers over all essential workers and was empowered, if the emergency warranted, to mobilize every adult in the country.[26] In fact, on April 17, 1943, the WMC essentially "froze" the positions of 27,000,000 workers in the United States, effectively preventing them from leaving their jobs.[27] One reason such an extreme measure was necessary was that many workers were leaving entry-level jobs within the first week or two because they became disgruntled. An underlying cause of why they quit was that their "breaking in" training was inadequate, making it more likely they would be unsuccessful performing their jobs, thereby causing the supervisors to place even more pressure on them. The Job Instruction Program greatly improved this "break-in" period, making people feel productive in their jobs quickly, which helped them stay. Even after the WMC issued their mandate in 1943 and people no longer had the option of leaving, the JI training continued to improve morale,

Because the WMC had such great authority, initially there was some confusion over how to share responsibilities. On February 4, 1944, the WMC issued a policy statement to clarify its role, but it seemed to have little effect since nothing changed. In August of that year, WMC issued another statement to clarify its national policy. The second policy letter was hand delivered to each WMC and TWI field staff and discussed with all districts in the late summer and early fall of 1944.[28] The policy basically stated that the WMC personnel would determine *when and where* training was to be done, while the TWI personnel would determine *how* it would be done.[29] The Report states that these memos did not solve all of the problems, but they did help the TWI Service focus on their objective.[30] TWI defined a concept of "production urgency" that mandated 'what to work on when.' It outlined a hierarchy of activities to be done in the following order:

1. Critical Plants and Services *behind* schedule,
2. Critical Plants and Services *on* schedule,
3. Essential Production and Services (inclusion on the permanent eligibility list), and
4. Other Civilian Activities—of local importance.[31]

This list became very important as the war went on especially when resources became scarcer and supervisors had to be very discriminating on where to allocate manpower. In addition, the government placed program restrictions on each TWI program when it had to reduce funding. As of August 18, 1945, this included:

- *Job Instructions:* supervisors and experienced employees.
- *Job Method:* any designated employee.
- *Job Relations:* supervisors, union stewards, and union officers.
- *Program Development:* individual with assigned functional responsibility for identifying production problems and for planning training to meet those needs.

The program restrictions are significant because they show that TWI didn't just develop the programs for training supervisors. Even when funds were scarce, TWI recognized that it should offer Job Instruction to experienced employees because, like supervisors, one of their duties could be training. Likewise, Job Methods training is useful to all employees on a daily basis. As for Job Relations, it was limited specifically to supervisors, union stewards, and union officers, only because "management staff" positions were normally responsible for routinely handling personnel problems.

Promotional Efforts

Because TWI was created about 18 months before the United States entered the war, many of its potential clients had no perceived need for what TWI offered because they were either under no pressure and felt no need for training or they had just received a defense contract and were too busy for training.[32] Initially TWI had no clear program that companies could buy into. As mentioned, TWI conducted many surveys but they served only to make the community aware of the TWI Service and did little to "sell" programs.[33] To be successful, the TWI staff knew they needed to use a variety of ways to get the word out. One method TWI used throughout its lifespan was speeches. Chambers of Commerce, trade associations, technical societies, hospital councils, and even service groups and the American Legion, were used to publicize the programs.[34] Since each of the 22 TWI districts had some staff, a representative from the district would choose one of these venues to speak about TWI. If possible, managers who had already used the program would accompany the speaker. Initially it was difficult to do this because the JI program could not be referenced, nor were the first JI trainers certified until October 1941. As a result, TWI was more dependent on consulting. Even after October 1941, it took some time for TWI to create a list of companies that had used TWI. Despite the slow start, Job Instruction was "eagerly accepted by plants—it was a usable remedy for a generally acknowledged problem—getting inexperienced people to do skilled operations quickly."[35] As time went on, and more companies used TWI, the promotional efforts had a greater impact because they used testimonials such as:

- "Here is a government agency whose men will come into your plant only when invited, help you, get out, and when they are gone, you still own your plant."
- "This is a government war agency that helps instead of hinders."
- "If anyone had told me that I would be hiring theater ushers, musicians, and manicurists to operate lathes and milling machines in my plant, and that I would not only like it but get standard production from them, I would have called him a liar; today, I do it gladly, get results, and only TWI has made this possible."[36]

Bulletins were the third main vehicle used to promote TWI, but again, as mentioned, they proved to be ineffective. By the early 1940's, TWI spread its message through radio because most U.S. households had radio. In March 1941, the first TWI national broadcast announced the beginning of a cross-country trip promoting TWI. These radio broadcasts were then followed by newspaper accounts of the radio programs.[37]

What the Service Learned—Results Are Vital

C.R. Dooley wrote, "We have learned so much about the techniques of training that what we knew before is as nothing." I believe his use of the word "techniques" is much broader than one might initially think and was meant to include *results*: the outcome and by-products of training, and the requirements and methods for selling and promoting the training. The TWI Service discovered early on that results were vital from two perspectives: 1) Selling the Programs and, 2) Sustaining the Programs. Even before TWI developed the "J" programs, its objective was to convince management that companies could use training as a production tool to solve production problems.

Because the TWI Service was not allowed to go into a plant without a request from management, their first step was to secure this request before they could deliver their programs. This was often a roadblock because many managers did not see the value in training, even though the main problem in industry at the time was a lack of trained workers. Another impediment for TWI was that its sales effort initially only focused on describing the programs and their techniques. Although people from divergent industries presented the TWI programs to management in many different ways, they "all tended to make their approach on the basis of what a program was, not what it would accomplish."[38] Therefore, they failed to get management buy-in, even though TWI was designed to address industry's need for workers across the board. The following describes how one TWI person broke through this impasse:

. . . Rome Collin . . . was in charge of TWI's field activities in upstate New York in 1942. Mr. Collin in one town had the unenviable duty of approaching a corporation president noted for his directness. When he entered the executive's office, the greeting he received was a sharp "Well, what do you want?" "I don't want anything," Mr. Collin answered. "But if I had a dozen tool makers I'd bet you'd give me a warmer reception. I don't have the tool makers, but I have something that will help you get along without them.[39]

It became apparent to TWI that selling results worked best. What TWI obviously needed was an ample supply of successful results for its sales promotions, but at first, these were not available because they had not delivered programs, and even when they delivered programs, no one was rushing to gather results. This was a catch-22 for this reason. The first program developed was Job Instruction and was well received by executives and supervisors because of the need it filled—quickly training inexperienced people to do skilled jobs that in turn solved management's manpower and production needs. However, the resulting success of this program stifled management's incentives to quantify results.

Early in its history, TWI knew that results were vital to sustaining the programs. Again, quantifying it was problematic since the District Representatives from the 22 geographical districts were volunteers on loan from existing companies. They were familiar with the companies and the managements in their geographical areas, and during the initial months of TWI, management often accepted their offers to come into their plants based on friendship without asking to see evidence of production results. Because these companies did not require results, results were not collected or recorded. Without such documentation of improvement, the enthusiasm of the program quickly cooled after the trainers left.[40]

TWI didn't resolve this catch-22 until Job Methods could provide readily quantifiable results in terms of savings in manpower and money. At the same time (1943), the House Appropriations Committee began to ask for data to back up the cost of the Job Instruction program. This prompted TWI to gather results of the programs for Congress and its potential clients.[41] TWI subsequently devised a reporting form that would help companies more easily report results from the training activities (see Exhibits 2-2 and 2-3). Part of TWI's success was that it learned to utilize these reports to cite results when selling the program. These reports also became a vital tool in sustaining programs already in use.

Exhibit 2-2. Typical Result Form (Denver)

TWI OUTSTANDING "RESULT OF THE WEEK"
IN DENVER DISTRICT

Result was noted and reported to us on (Date)   __April 16, 1945__

Result of: J.I.   J.M.   J.R.   P.D.

Kind of establishment (name of product or service)   __Rubber products__

1. Name and location of plant   __Gates Rubber Company, Denver, Colorado__

2. May we use company name?   ☐ Yes   ☐ No

3. Number of employees in plant   __5,000__

4. Number of employees affected   __40__

5. Just what happened in "before and after" terms:
   (State evidence in facts, figures, man hours, etc.)

Before "J" Programs:
   In one clerical department, where 46 were employed, 375,000 units were
   produced in one year.

After "J" Programs:
   By applying the three "J" methods conscientiously and continuously,
   450,000 units were produced by 40 workers.

This is an increase of 20% or 75,000 units, in output by a work force reduced
by 13%, or 6 workers.

The quality of the work was also greatly improved.

*Note: Most credit is given to J.I. and J.R., as the work force has always been
method-improvement minded.*

Obtaining Management Support: The Management Contact Approach

As will be discussed later, any manager who has the authority to use training dollars can profit from any of the TWI training programs. However, the
greatest returns come when the entire organization makes use of the training. This requires having all of management informed on the use and benefits of TWI. It took TWI nearly 3 years to understand this, but once it did, it
adopted the policy that no program could be started in a plant unless *all*
management was informed and willing to take on the responsibility for making it work.[42]

Exhibit 2-3. Typical Result Form (Dallas)

TWI OUTSTANDING "RESULT OF THE WEEK" IN DALLAS DISTRICT

Result was noted and reported to us on (Date)   <u>May 3, 1945</u>

Result of: J.I.   J.M.   J.R.   P.D.

Kind of establishment (name of product or service)   <u>Shipbuilding</u>

1. Name and location of plant   <u>Consolidated Steel Corp., Orange, Tex.</u>

2. May we use company name? ☐ Yes ☐ No

3. Number of employees in plant   <u>18,749</u>

4. Number of employees affected   <u>15,000</u>

5. Just what happened in "before and after" terms:

   (State evidence in facts, figures, man hours, etc.)

During the past 4 years four different types of vessels have been built. When the yard opened, only 2% of the workers had previous shipbuilding experience. About 50% had no previous experience in any related industry.

The average employment during this 4 years has been 18,000. The number of certificates issued in the three TWI "J" programs are:

     J.I. - 2850   J.M. - 800   J.R. - 540

Mr. Newell Hogan, Training Director, and Mr. James D. McClellan, Production Manager, reported the following beneficial results from TWI programs:

Increase in production	−45%
Reduction in training time	−78%
Reduction in scrap	−69%
Reduction in tool breakage	−75%
Saving of manpower	− 45%
Reduction of accidents	−70%

These results were arrived at by comparison of production department records, based on the construction of the first 50 destroyer escorts as compared with the last 50. The credit for these beneficial results is largely attributed to the successful continuous use of TWI programs.

All levels of supervision in both the yard and the office have been processed in one or more of the "J" programs. This accounts for the large number of employees affected.

"In general, the plants where Job Instruction was started on a "Sure, go right ahead and do anything you want" basis, failed to get the values they should have received. It was a long time before TWI learned that it was important to start programs only when management demanded them, not merely accepted them, and operated them, themselves."[43]

As we now know, TWI is more than just a series of training programs. TWI contains basic training that has the potential for driving a culture change in an organization. Only when the entire organization is aware of that potential will you meet it. If the president of a company understands and accepts the program but the plant superintendent is unaware of it, there is a danger of jeopardizing the success of the program. To ensure success, TWI created a standard procedure in the training program to emphasize that every intermediate supervisor had to understand that making the program work was part of his job. Management support is a concept repeated often throughout the TWI Report, "Only when top management understands, sponsors, participates and demands production results, can full usefulness of the program be obtained."[44]

The message TWI continuously repeated was that TWI training was a tool like any other production tool. That is, a training class was not effective unless the participants specifically used the skills they learned. Although this may sound like an obvious statement today, requiring management to have their employees use and apply TWI skills after a class required a concerted effort. The trainers needed this commitment to achieve their objective of getting trainees to believe their training would be useful by the end of the session. Solving a problem with a particular method that will make an employee's job easier is a good way to convince someone to use that method. Job Instruction required that all participants handle a project from their own workplace and consequently trainees were more enthusiastic about using their training. However, workers and management both have work habits that must change if they are to use the new training. It is essential that *everyone* agree to the new training.

As part of their concerted effort, TWI held more management orientation meetings. These meetings evolved into what was called the *Management Contact Approach*. The first step entailed meeting with top management from one to six times so that managers could understand the program and their responsibility for getting increased results through the programs.[45] That is, they were responsible for its implementation and ultimate success. For the same reasons, TWI held meetings with all levels of management staff and developed the set of important ideas below that they shared at these meetings:

1. Results would vary from plant to plant because results depend upon personnel. However, a result smaller than seen in published results might still be worthwhile.
2. Overall results are not accomplished by individuals, but getting the results "was a team job involving the whole organization."[46]
3. TWI programs were developed to be useful to supervisors at all levels.
4. "The program was described as having two parts—ten hours of *basic training*, then *continuing use* so that management would get maximum returns . . . like any production tool, a supervisory skill is used over and over, day in and day out . . . while the basic training did develop a skill, this skill would be lost unless used."[47]

TWI gave management some guidance with "continuing use," not least of which was to have a plan of action to sustain the initial training so there wasn't anything left up to chance. As good as the TWI programs are they still have to overcome the influence of existing habits. All employees have habits in how they operate. If these habits are contradictory to TWI, they must be "unlearned" before TWI can become habitual. Furthermore, the programs differed in their ease of "sustainability." Whereas the Job Relations and Job Instructions programs might require only one employee to perform functions without any interaction with others (though not preferable), Job Methods usually requires cooperation with others in the organization. If the methods change is small, a supervisor can make it within his or her realm of authority. Sooner or later the supervisor will desire a change that will require a higher level of management to implement. If management is not aware of the forms and procedures involved with Job Methods, they will be unaware of these needs and the program is very likely to fail. To facilitate sustainability in all scenarios, TWI adopted an "Operating Plan" which required that no program would start without a definite plan to sustain it. This plan contained the following parts:

1. Assign responsibility.
2. Give the basic training to all supervisors.
3. Coach supervisors.
4. Report results.
5. Give credit for results.

These are not responsibilities that, once filled, are ended. They continue if results are to continue.[48]

"Assign responsibility" means assigning a specific person to follow up on getting continuing results. This brings to mind the adage, "If everyone is responsible, no one is responsible." You must hold someone accountable for making sure everyone is trained, that supervisors receive the coaching they need, that results are recorded and reported, and especially that credit is given for those results. At a textile plant in eastern Pennsylvania with an employment of about 5,000, an individual was assigned to being in charge of the TWI activities.

> In getting Job Methods started, the company realized that this was a production tool, and getting the desired results would require the full-time services of a man to look after these activities. With some advice from TWI, he was not given the title of "Training man" but "Assistant to the General Manager." Most of the man's efforts are devoted to making the three "J" programs work. He has been able to get the majority of all levels of supervision through the 10 hours of each program, and definitely intends to continue with this policy until everyone in the organization, who is in a supervisory capacity, has gone through the 10 hours. This includes people from not only the manufacturing division, but also such staff divisions such as the laboratory, engineering, and office.[49]

The five steps listed above are contained in a TWI Bulletin "How to Get Continuing Results from Plant Training Programs" (Bulletin 22). The bulletin includes steps in coaching workers and supervisors with different levels of skills, needs, and abilities.

TWI's Workable Solution: The "J" Programs

After some missteps, the Service settled on four programs. In February 1943, with the national launching of the Job Relations Program, all of the "J" programs were now functioning on a national level and selling the programs had become more sophisticated. TWI used the Management Contact approach and when talking with management, plant surveys. Now, however, instead of focusing on the plant's training program, TWI analyzed and reviewed the most urgent problems facing management. Now there was compelling evidence that the "J" programs not only worked in training programs for improving methods and solving personnel problems, but for production problem-solving tools as well.

> "Because of [the wide applicability of the "J" programs], it became virtually impossible for any manager to name a problem involving people on which TWI could not give assistance."[50]

One reason the developers of TWI were successful is that they were not afraid to extensively experiment with the programs. Within two years they had been through several thousand plants and tested, applied, and revised many different approaches. Although TWI was clearly in an emergency, the sheer volume of what they had to do afforded them a great opportunity to fully test many ideas in a short period. The result is that they streamlined the "J" programs, making them basic, succinct, and pure. They are so simple that when one looks at them the first impression is that something is missing. TWI designed the three "J" programs, Job Instruction, Job Methods, and Job Relations, and the fourth one, Program Development, with the objective of increasing productivity through training with these important and effective constraints:

- Industry must be convinced to do it (TWI had no authority).
- Industry must do it alone (The government would not fund it).
- The Service was small compared to the size of the assignment.
- As time went on, demand for their service increased dramatically.

By providing such clear boundaries and goals, the three "J" programs plus Union Job Relations and Program Development issued 1,750,650 certificates of completion, which meant that almost two million people were spreading the word of TWI. See Exhibit 2-4 for a breakdown of the four TWI programs.

Exhibit 2-4. Total Number of TWI-Issued Certificates Between 1941–1945

Number of TWI Certificates Issued	
Job Instructions:	1,005,170
Job Relations:	490,022
Job Methods:	244,773
Union Job Relations:	8,856
Program Development:	1,829
Total Certificates Issues :	**1,750,650**

The End of One Story Is the Beginning of Another

The government created the TWI Service for the war effort, and when the war was over, so too was the agency, which disbanded on September 28, 1945.[51] (See Appendix A for the complete TWI timeline.) Many members of the staff at TWI, including the four original men, Dooley, Dietz, Kane, and Conover, who had been "borrowed" from companies though were still on the payroll, naturally returned to the private sector to their former jobs.[52] The thinking was that the government appropriately ran such a training agency during a war, but, in a time of peace, organizations could run these programs.

"During a period of national emergency it was right to set up and operate a federal group such as TWI at public expense. In peacetime the development of techniques for in-plant training and their use to get production results is so profitable that it is properly something which private enterprise should operate and pay for."[53]

The TWI staff, however, didn't just want to let all they had accomplished and learned go by the wayside, and because the TWI Service was a "reoccurring assignment" for many of them, just as it was for Dooley, Deitz, Kane, and Conover in WWI, they decided to document their accumulated experiences in the *TWI Report*. This report, the bulletins, and training manuals were disseminated in libraries in the 48 contiguous states.[54] In a final letter dated September 1945, C.R. Dooley, the director of the Service, wrote:

"We have learned so much about the techniques of training that what we knew before is as nothing. This learning has been at the expense of the taxpayers and therefore should be preserved and used in peacetime. These techniques are as applicable to peace as to war production."[55]

Dooley's point about the techniques being applicable to peacetime was correct, but it would be a long while before organizations in the United States would resurrect these proven techniques. Unlike the war-ravaged countries of Europe, Japan, China, Korea, the Philippines, etc., U.S. factories and the accompanying infrastructures were intact. All that companies had to do was to switch from military production to consumer production and because there was no appreciable competition, there was little incentive to increase productivity using TWI methods.

Worldwide Use of TWI After World War II

The people who had gained from their experience with TWI saw an opportunity to share this knowledge with the rest of the world. The following excerpt from a 1993 white paper attests to their success for the worldwide use of the TWI programs.

- "TWI had actually been started in Great Britain at the peak of the war in 1944. Its lasting impact there was testified to in a 1969 speech by Mr. Roy Hattersley, then a senior official in the British Department of Employment and Productivity:

  TWI is Britain's most widely used supervisor training scheme and has been sponsored and developed by my Department for almost a quarter of a century. During that time more than one million supervisors have attended courses and many of the largest firms in the country have based their own comprehensive training schemes on TWI's foundations . . . the demand continues to grow. The number of supervisors trained has almost quadrupled over the last five years. The demands on the D.E.P. training services have increased six-fold over the same period.

These are improvements that must be maintained if the country is to achieve lasting prosperity, for our industrial training [programs] are an essential part of our more general plans for building a strong and productive economy. They are irrevocably linked with our proposals for improved productivity.

- "As part of the reconstruction of Europe, TWI training programs were set up in France, Italy, Belgium, Holland, Luxembourg, Denmark, Sweden, Norway, and Finland.
- "In 1947, New Zealand set up its own government-run TWI Service. Department of Labor reports indicate that TWI was very widely used at least up until 1969. The "J" programs were taught to supervisors in the railways, the post office, the meat industry, the wool industry, utilities, auto dealerships, banking, grocery stores, and even in the Treasury when it had to convert New Zealand's currency over to the decimal system. New Zealand's TWI Service, together with private industry, introduced TWI programs into many other countries, including Australia, New Guinea, Hong Kong, Fiji, Taiwan, Singapore, Western Samoa, Iraq, Uganda, and South Vietnam.
- "TWI programs were prepared for Korea, although they were never run owing to the Korean War. TWI did eventually percolate into Korea through Japanese companies, and it is used there today.
- "Over 3 million supervisors in Indonesia were TWI-certified in the period 1951–1953.
- "1,000 Mexican supervisors from 50 plants received TWI certification under the aegis of the Centro Industrial de Productividad in Mexico City in 1956 and 1957.
- "5,000 Turkish supervisors from 100 companies, collectively employing over 200,000 people, had received TWI training by 1956.
- "1,226 supervisors were trained in Nepal in 1958.

"While TWI had an impact on many countries around the world, it had its greatest effect on Japan, which embraced the "J" programs more whole-heartedly than any other nation."[56]

We will discuss this in more detail in the next chapter. What is clear is that since 1945 the Japanese have incorporated TWI in its companies, while the use or even awareness of TWI and its contributions have nearly disappeared in the United States. It is important to point out, however, that the U.S. government does carry on aspects of TWI's tradition to assist companies. The U.S. Department of Commerce together with the National Institute of Standards and Technology operate a network of centers, known as Manufacturing Extension Partnerships (MEP), that work with small- to medium-size manufacturers. There are 400 centers located throughout the United States. The MEP centers offer products and services related to training people in, among other things, Lean Production. What many people don't realize, and what we will discuss in the next chapter, is that true Lean training incorporates the programs of TWI.

---

1. Training Within Industry Service, *The Training Within Industry Report: 1940–1945* (Washington, D.C.: War Manpower Commission Bureau of Training, 1945), p. 52.
2. *TWI Report*, p. 186.
3. Taken from *The Training Within Industry Report: 1940–1945*; p 188.
4. The 1940 Census was 131,699,275. If ¼ were eligible workers, the potential workforce would be about 33 million. Of those, 8 million were out of work (p. 3, *TWI Report*).
5. Although the fall of Poland is generally considered the start of WWII, some historians believe that it actually started in 1931 when Japan seized Manchuria. Also, by 9/1/39, Austria and Czechoslovakia had been acquired by Germany.
6. World Book Ency, vol 21, p. 470.
7. The Selective Service Act was passed by Congress on Sept. 16, 1940 initially conscripting up to 900,000 individuals per year.
8. *TWI Report*, p. 36.
9. *TWI Report*, p. 4.
10. *TWI Report*, p. 5.
11. *TWI Report*, p. ix.
12. *TWI Report*, p. 5. Before closing the service, a Final Report was written, which gives a history of the Service.
13. *TWI Report*, p. ix.
14. *TWI Report*, p. 7.
15. TWI Service Bulletin #1.
16. *TWI Report*, p. 16.
17. *TWI Report*, p. 14.
18. *TWI Report*, p. 51.
19. TWI Materials, Preface to Bulletins.

20. The concept of differentiating between presenting information and mastering skills lies at the core of TWI's success and will be discussed further in Chapter 4. We can read many books on losing weight, playing tennis or getting rich, but until we practice and master the required skills, we will never achieve our goal.
21. *TWI Report*, p. 52.
22. *TWI Report*, p. 30.
23. *TWI Report*, p. 223.
24. *TWI Report*, p. 249.
25. *TWI Report*, p. 114.
26. Gordon Carruth, *What Happened When: A Chronology of Life and Events in America* (New York: Signet Books, 1991), p. 777.
27. *What Happened When*, p. 785.
28. *TWI Report*, p. 117.
29. *TWI Report*, p. 116.
30. This is important to understand because it lies at the heart of the Quality Control of the programs, which is greatly responsible for their success. The TWI Service believed that it had to have control over content and delivery in order to maintain effectiveness. As we will see, TWI was correct in this determination. In the ensuing 60 years, the programs have been universally successful only when there has been a group overseeing content and delivery.
31. *TWI Report*, p. 118.
32. *TWI Report*, p. 50.
33. In February 1943, TWI asked its district representatives to again review whether or not surveys could be of any use. Since the only value the surveys could offer was to point out training needs, it was finally decided to officially discontinue their use at this time. Final Report, pg. 51.
34. *TWI Report*, p. 53.
35. *TWI Report*, p. 53.
36. *TWI Report*, p. 54.
37. *TWI Report*, p. 55.
38. *TWI Report*, p. 52.
39. *TWI Report*, p. 75.
40. *TWI Report*, p. 52.
41. *TWI Report*, p. 89.
42. *TWI Report*, p. 61.
43. *TWI Report*, p. 35.
44. *TWI Report*, p. 185.
45. *TWI Report*, p. 64.
46. *TWI Report*, p. 62.
47. *TWI Report*, p. 63.
48. *TWI Report*, p. 63.
49. *TWI Report*, p. 71.
50. *TWI Report*, p. 60.

51. The following dates in 1945 may be of interest: May 5—Office of Education announces all war training programs will be concluded on May 31 (p. 72); May 7—Germany Surrenders; July 28—TWI notified that its last day of operation will be September 30 (p. 124); August 6—Hiroshima bombed. Refer to Appendix A, TWI Timeline for additional dates.

52. "All four of these men [Dooley, Deitz, Kane, Conover] were originally borrowed from their companies for short periods of a few weeks, 6 months at the most. Socony-Vacuum, Western Electric, American Telephone & Telegraph, and U.S. Steel often asked how much longer their men were going to be needed in Washington, but it was always possible to arrange for just a little more time. A great debt is owed these companies for their cooperation and generosity." Final Report, p. X.

53. *TWI Report*, p. XI.

54. *TWI Report*, p. 182.

55. *TWI Report*, Letter of transmittal to Philip S. Van Wyck

56. Robinson & Schroeder, *Training, Continuous Improvement, and Human Relations: The U.S. TWI Programs and the Japanese Management Style*, pps. 45–46.

CHAPTER 3

Why TWI Is a Foundation
of Lean Thinking

"This is the foundation for the Toyota Way of learning—
standardization punctuated by innovation, which
gets translated into new standards."[1]

From 1945 to 1951, General Douglas MacArthur headed the Allied occupation of Japan with the basic mandate to demilitarize Japan and re-establish it as a democratic nation. Several members of MacArthur's staff were familiar with TWI and recognized two main benefits it could offer.[2] First, since the war had decimated the Japanese economy, rebuilding it would include a significant amount of training. TWI had proven that the use of its programs resulted in exceptional productivity gains through training. Secondly, the United States recognized that democratic principles were inherent in the TWI "J" programs. The Job Relations program teaches one to "Treat people as individuals," "Let each worker know how he/she is doing," and "Tell people in advance about changes which will affect them," as examples. The Job Methods program teaches one to check with all concerned when making changes. These concepts emphasizing that everyone is valuable and has something to offer were important in helping Japan transform into a democratic society.

The Japanese did embrace TWI completely and are still using the programs today. In fact, the Japanese Labor Ministry still controls the use of TWI by administering programs and licensing other organizations to conduct the "J" courses.[3] The dissemination of TWI throughout Japan is so widespread that it appears to have assimilated into the culture. *Kaizen* (kai = change, revise, and zen = goodness, virtue) (continuous improvement) is a term that is used in the Toyota Production System (TPS), which many companies are trying to emulate today as Lean Manufacturing.[4]

TWI was one of the early seminal forces in developing TPS and one could debate whether TPS could have fully evolved and been sustained without the practice of TWI. This is evident when one studies TPS or Lean and sees the many similarities it has with the TWI approach of using teams, continuous training and improvement, learning by doing, standardization, and developing a learning organization. Research by Alan G. Robinson and Dean M. Schroeder gives further evidence that TWI was a basis to the success of TPS, specifically the use of the concept *kaizen*.

"Each of the "J" programs has influenced Japanese management in its own way. According to Mr. Nobuo Noda, a prominent Japanese business scholar, both JI and the TWI programs as a whole offered a new pattern of "how to teach." Because Japan had lost much of its skilled labour force during the war, it was just what was needed and soon spread throughout the country until TWI-instructed trainers could be seen in almost every factory."

People often credit Job Methods for its role in developing *kaizen* ("continuous improvement") in Japan, which is now a distinctive part of the Japanese management. For example, *The Idea Book*, a translated Japanese book about *kaizen*, states that:

"The forerunner of the modern Japanese-style suggestion system undoubtedly originated in the West ... TWI (Training Within Industry), introduced to Japanese industry in 1949 by the U.S. occupation forces, had a major effect in expanding the suggestion system to involve all workers rather than just a handful of the elite. Job modification constituted a part of TWI and as foremen and supervisors taught workers how to perform job modifications, they learned how to make changes and suggestions ... Many Japanese companies introduced suggestion systems to follow up on the job modification movement begun by TWI."[5]

Toyota has been training its employees in TWI continually since it started the programs in 1951 and it has been receiving benefits ever since. For example, Toyota had a total of 2,003,646 employee suggestions in 1990, which equated to 35 ideas per person.[6] Although currently, employment figures are more difficult to find, the Toyota Motor Manufacturing, Kentucky website states that, "More than 90,000 employee suggestions are adopted each year" [at the Georgetown facility].[7] The value of Toyota's version of TWI, Toyota TWI (TTWI)[8] is further confirmed by the following quote:

"The Toyota Way of going to the source, observing in detail, and learning by doing were all very much influenced by TWI (Dietz and Bevens, 1970) and became the backbone of Toyota's standardization philosophy."[9]

When Alan G. Robinson and Dean M. Schroeder researched the white paper from which the above quotation was taken, they also interviewed Japanese who had first-hand knowledge of TWI. By using all three "J" programs, TWI becomes more than just a training package.

"A good number of our Japanese interviewees stressed that TWI has done much more for Japan than just bequeathing it a collection of techniques to it embodying basic good management. First, it has taught managers and supervisors to appreciate the scientific and rational approach to management. Although each "J" course is about a different aspect of the manager's job, each teaches the same approach to a situation: get the facts, analyze them, and then act on the resulting information. The second important thing that TWI has done, it was felt, has been to get the message across that good human relations are *good business practice*, a message that is given credit for helping to break up the tradition of autocratic management prevalent in Japan before and during the war."[10]

TWI to TPS to Lean Thinking

To understand the evolutions of TPS, the reader must be somewhat familiar with the concept of Lean Thinking, which is the generalization of the term "Lean Manufacturing" or "Lean Production," which was coined in the book *The Machine That Changed the World* by James P. Womack, Daniel T. Jones, and Daniel Roos. Lean Thinking is a philosophy that entails more than just applying the techniques and objectives of the Lean production system. It is a thought process and way of thinking that ties all of the world-class manufacturing techniques into a complete system. Ultimately, it is a new way to look at how you do business and its role in the community. The Lean production paradigm, which evolved from the Toyota Production System (TPS), is still in the process of replacing the mass production paradigm developed by Ford. If you have not already done so, I would recommend reading *The Machine That Changed the World* and the subsequent book titled *Lean Thinking* by James P. Womack and Daniel T. Jones. For the purposes of this book, my simplified definition of Lean Thinking is *a process whereby you understand exactly what it is you do, and eliminate any wasteful activities doing it while enhancing all value-added activities*. A wasteful activity is the opposite of a value-added activity, a term that defines any work and process that directly adds customer value to a product. A wasteful activity is not required in reaching your objective, while a value-added activity is.

Lean Thinking evolved from the manufacturing sector and though there are sources promoting Lean Thinking for office administration, software production, and product development, it is easier to discuss Lean concepts when applied to producing a tangible product. In manufacturing, you can readily see how assembly, machining, and welding are all value-added processes because these activities change the shape of the work piece and thus get you closer to your goal of the final product. As such, the ultimate objective is to eliminate non-value added work or waste. Once you eliminate waste, the overall process will take much less time. Material handling, motion and inspection, and office administration services, are seldom value-added activities simply because they do not directly change (add value to) a final tangible product.

In their first book, Womack, Jones, and Roos give an excellent history of automobile production. Henry Ford was a Lean thinker who reportedly said, "The longer an article is in the process of manufacture and the more it is moved about, the greater is its ultimate cost." As a result, in the early 1900s, Ford earned unprecedented profits by eliminating waste to reduce the cycle time from iron ore to finished product to 81 hours.[11] Ford gave us mass production, as we know it, and because it was so successful, companies around the world copied it. The system included an assembly line staffed by workers who do one specific job, supported by engineers who design and support the system. This amounted to a division of labor. The engineers determined the best way to do something and the assemblers did it that way. When TPS and Lean Thinking came around, it completely turned this idea upside down.

Toyota, TWI, and Teams

When Taiichi Ohno of Toyota wanted to increase automobile production at Toyota, he and other Toyota managers often collectively visited Detroit and were generally impressed with what they saw. However, Ohno's budget did not match that of Ford's and he soon concluded that Detroit's methods wouldn't work for Toyota because Detroit was producing millions of parts, and Toyota only thousands. Furthermore, Ford's mass production techniques used lots of equipment, making large quantities of products, inventory, and process steps based on large volumes, with interruptions between these steps. This caused large amounts of material to sit in inventory and wait.[12] In Lean Thinking, inventory is nearly the worse kind of waste. Ohno recognized that his production methods must be more flexible so that he could get the most out of limited resources. He also recognized that he needed to eliminate waste, which required continuous flow, or one-piece flow. To accomplish this he could not use nor afford a division of labor. That is:

> "Ohno needed both an extremely skilled and a highly motivated workforce. If workers failed to anticipate problems before they occurred

and didn't take initiative to devise solutions, the work of the whole factory could easily come to a halt. Holding back knowledge and effort—repeatedly noted by industrial sociologists as a salient feature of all mass-production systems—would swiftly lead to disaster in Ohno's factory."[13]

For many years, people believed that the development of "Lean" production was only possible because of the nature of the Japanese culture. Therefore, the United States imported only aspects of it, such as Just-in-Time (JIT). Actually, Lean's creation depended on many contributing factors that are not unique to Japan's culture and occurred over an extended period. Besides using aspects of Ford's mass-production techniques, Toyota borrowed many of its ideas from the United States, one of which was the concept of the *pull system* that was inspired by the stocking/inventory system in American supermarkets and became the key to JIT. Toyota also borrowed ideas from W. Edwards Deming such as "meeting or exceeding the customer's requirements are the task of everyone within an organization." Toyota also broadened the definition of "customer" to include both internal and external customers which means, "the next process is the customer" and borrowed the Deming Cycle of Plan-Do-Check-Act (PDCA) Cycle, a cornerstone of continuous improvement.[14]

One very important foundation for helping TPS ultimately come together is noted in Womack, Jones, and Roos—the Japanese relied on teams to implement and accomplish much of this change to Lean Thinking. Womack and company do not detail how the Japanese formed those teams, but the authors do say:

> "... In the end, it is the dynamic work team that emerges as the heart of the Lean factory. Building these efficient teams is not simple. First, workers need to be taught a wide variety of skills—in fact, all the jobs in their work group so that tasks can be rotated and workers can fill-in for each other. Workers then need to acquire many additional skills; simple machine repair, quality checking, housekeeping, and materials-ordering. Then they need encouragement to think actively, indeed *pro*actively, so they can devise solutions before problems become serious."[15]

To teach workers a *wide variety of skills*, Toyota needed a reliable method of training workers so they could learn a job thoroughly and quickly while minimizing scrap and damage to equipment and tools. Toyota also believed you should do this with a high degree of safety so they did not view job instruction as a "necessary evil," but a main component of a supervisor's skill set. Perhaps Toyota's greatest accomplishment was creating a workforce to "... think ... *pro*actively, so the employees themselves, the workers who were actually "doing" the work, could "devise solutions before problems become serious." You can attribute this approach directly to TWI. John Shook, who started at Toyota in 1983 and co-authored *Learning to See* writes:

> "I discovered them (TWI materials) in a round about way in the process of "adapting" some Toyota training materials to make them appropriate for NUMMI. When I found myself struggling with some of the concepts of a certain training program, my Japanese colleague fetched from a back-room file a yellowed, dog-eared, coffee-stained copy of the English language original training manual, just as they received it (minus the coffee stains I trust) some 30 years before. To my amazement, the program Toyota was going to great expense to "transfer" to NUMMI was exactly that which the Americans had taught the Japanese decades before."[16]

What Toyota needed was a simple method to enable employees to analyze what they did and quickly implement changes. Toyota determined that by making the employees' jobs easier, the employees would have the intrinsic motivation to use the method rather than wait to be prodded to make improvements. And if the training method required that employees use only existing resources, then the changes would be economical and management would not need to request more funds or personnel.

TWI: The Missing Link

What kept Toyota on the right track goes back to the basics of successfully getting many employees quickly trained in a variety of jobs, thinking proactively and analytically about their jobs, and having supervisors deal positively with personnel situations. You can attribute these factors directly to the concepts of TWI and subsequently to Toyota's version, TTWI. For example, Lean Manufacturing depends on proper training and standardization, which comes from Job Instruction Training (JI), and continual improvement and innovation, which Job Methods Training (JM) encourages. More importantly, however, the concepts of the Job Relations Training (JR) contributed to the humanization or respect for the individual, which enabled a democratic culture to evolve in Japan.

In an August 1951 interview conducted as part of a survey of the effects of TWI on Japanese management by International Economic Services Ltd., a Tokyo consulting firm, Mr. Takei of the Mitsui Mining Co., the largest coal mining company in Japan at the time, said that he felt the "concept of humanism in industry" was one of the most appreciated ideas transmitted into Japan by TWI.[17]

It is clear that the TWI training (and Toyota's subsequent program TWII) *is a foundation of TPS and what is now Lean Thinking*. I believe the biggest mistake many organizations make in attempting to implement Lean, and the reason why so many fail, is that they only adopt Lean tools and techniques and ignore this foundation. One need only look at the experience of Toyota to see how TWI is the "missing link" that will help an organization make the necessary cultural changes to solve problems and sustain a Lean transformation.

Becoming Lean Requires a Culture Change

One of the reasons Lean Thinking is an entirely new production paradigm rather than just a new methodological approach to improvement, is that you can apply Lean concepts to all types of industries and throughout their entire supply chain (suppliers). The five main principles of Lean as distilled by Womack & Jones in *Lean Thinking*:

1. Specify the *value*.
2. Identify the *value stream*.
3. Make the value *flow* without interruption.
4. Let the customer *pull* value from the producer.
5. Pursue *perfection*.[18]

The purpose of Womack and Jones' book is to explain the above principles (Part I) and then prescribe a practical plan of action to change an organization from one of mass production to one of Lean production (Part II).[19] Concepts are discussed at or above the level of plant manager. At the time the authors wrote *Lean Thinking* there were already many books on the subjects of TPS, JIT, and other Lean techniques and tools. What the authors wanted to do was address questions regarding the key principles in switching to Lean.[20] The "Lean" books they refer to describe fairly simple approaches to implementing such basic tools and techniques as 5S, a series of activities to eliminate wastes that contribute to errors, defects and injuries, mistake proofing, devices to prevent a defect or equipment malfunction, and ways to reduce set-up time or provide quick changeover. Unfortunately, the simplicity of these techniques is probably the main reason why many companies became so frustrated when their Lean implementations failed. For example, statistics have been cited that say that 98 percent of 5S implementations are dormant after 18 months. Although I cannot verify that statistic, it is in agreement with my experience. In many companies, the only evidence of a 5S implementation months afterward is an empty tool shadowboard or striping on the floor. If Lean is so simple, if there are seminars, conferences, and books extolling the virtues that everyone agrees with, why do companies constantly fail at implementing it?

Some Lean practitioners say that switching to Lean requires a cultural change, which means changing the way people think and what they think about. An organization's culture is, among other things, determined by the way it gets work done and what it does. How does management go about changing an organization's culture? There are books on that too, but basically these practitioners are correct, *one must change the way people think*; only then will companies change what they do and how they do it. One of the benefits of TWI's three "J" programs (JI, JR, JM) is that it changes the way people think about performing their work. Once you change employees' thinking to include instructing, learning, and improving, they will become more open to the application of the Lean techniques. Furthermore, you will have created an environment to sustain these changes because your employees will want to make changes on their own.

The three "J" training programs clearly contribute to changing an organization's culture. Furthermore, they change the culture in a specific way. Jeffrey K. Liker has studied the TPS extensively and has described the Toyota Way in 14 principles in his book. He makes the point that to be successful in today's marketplace, one must create a learning organization. In Liker's opinion, Toyota is the best learning organization he knows of. He then goes on to say "This is the foundation for the Toyota Way of learning—standardization punctuated by innovation, which gets translated into new standards."[21]

JI Training leads to standardization of processes and JM Training leads to innovation of processes. When JM results in an innovation, companies must repeat JI training so they can correctly incorporate the innovation into the work scheme. This cycle keeps repeating. Job Relations, then, is a stabilizing activity that keeps employees properly focused. We will discuss the three "J" programs at length in the coming chapters, but here is a brief description of how they lead to a cultural change in an organization.

Job Instruction Training (JI) and Cultural Change

JI training is a simple way for someone to quickly teach a person a job and improve productivity. Conventional training usually pairs a trainee with an experienced person who becomes the "trainer," which creates stress because the "trainer" has to train and continue performing his or her job simultaneously. To these trainers, training becomes a chore. The JI training process reduces stress on both individuals involved, making training less of a chore. JI Training results in standardized instruction and standardized instruction results in standardized methods. JI training requires a trainer to list the steps involved in completing a job. Unless an improvement is made, this same list can be used for the next trainee, no matter who the trainer is. If two trainers make two different lists, they are taught to compare notes and choose one list over the other. As a result, TWI trains all employees in a given method in the same way. Also, the JI training is such that a person learns the job correctly and safely in the shortest amount of time possible. This reduces waste in time, material, and damage to tools and equipment. Proper training with the resulting standardization will help an organization change its culture.

Job Methods (JM) Training and Cultural Change

JM training is a simple method to improve whatever it is you do. Many Lean implementations result from *kaizen* events where workers do hands-on training in Lean techniques. The event leader could be an outside Lean consultant, industrial engineer, Lean manager, or even a group's team leader. When an event leader is present, assisting in specific activities in a specific time period, everything goes well. After the necessary employees participate in these activities, the company hopes that the employees "get it," but somehow they often don't, and after the event leader leaves, employees tend to revert to their old habits. As a result, the company is unable to sustain the Lean techniques.

Job Methods training, on the other hand, is a method that an employee uses to make his or her own job easier, which means the motivation to do the job is intrinsic and the employee has neither to be told to do it, nor shown the best way to do it. The improvement is something the employee will have thought of on his or her own and is therefore more likely to have the initiative to implement because of its direct benefits. As Lean Thinking has shown, many small, continuous improvements help to significantly increase productivity. While making improvements, employees are exchanging ideas while watching employees implement the changes around them. As this behavior spreads, employees will soon get together to discuss more significant changes that will help them individually, but ones they can't implement on their own, and which might require management's cooperation. Thus, the JM method includes how to create a change that management will accept, if management's acceptance is required, thus facilitating continuous improvement. In many respects, this behavior is the same as forming a Quality Circle, which is a very potent tool for changing an organization's culture.

Job Relations (JR) Training and Cultural Change

Addressing employee relations, or how you work with other people, may seem intuitive, but when it comes to addressing personnel issues most managers need training. JR Training is an analytical method for addressing personnel issues. The best plan can result in utter failure because of a small personnel problem. Job Relations teaches people how to solve those problems success-fully as they occur. With further practice in the method, supervisors learn how to anticipate problems so they can deal with them before they balloon out of hand. This type of proactive management will assist any organization in help-ing its employees through cultural changes.

The Power of the "J" Programs

When I picture TWI graphically, I envision a three-legged stool: the "J" pro-grams are the legs and Lean is the seat. Teaching employees to think analyti-cally and for themselves, embracing change, as well as training others goes to the very core of what you need to do to change an organization's culture. Organizations tend to assume employees naturally have problem-solving skills. The fact is, most people have never been instructed in the scientific method or any other common problem-solving technique. Though TWI offers a simple method that instructors can easily teach and participants easily learn, its power to transform organizations lies in the approach of *never giving the answer to a problem*. The instructors rely on the participants to think and dis-cover the answers on their own, which is a skill everyone needs to be truly suc-cessful.

Sustaining a Lean transformation and embracing Lean Thinking will be successful to the point where employees understand and *practice* the skills of the three TWI programs and management promotes this behavior throughout the organization. Although it is not necessary that employees learn these skills through the specific TWI programs, it is necessary that they learn and practice them. Finally, none of this will happen if management does not accept and promote it. This is not difficult to do, but management must do it. Without complete management support, the TWI programs will never reach their potential. Successful supervisors and employees will use the skills learned in TWI whether or not management endorses them. But without such endorse-ment the skills will not become widespread across the organization, nor will a culture change likely take place. In the end, organizations follow their leaders.

The "J" Programs Connect Hard and Soft Management Skills

Finally, I believe another power of the three "J" programs is that you can use them to connect the two main schools of management thought, sometimes referred to as "hard skills" and "soft skills." Successful people often use a combination of these skills even though they may not realize it. The hard skills include such things as Value Stream Mapping and other types of flow diagrams; and Statistical Process Control, and other statistical methods, simulations, and so forth. The 'soft skills' include goal setting, conflict management, team building, and coaching, among others. Professional societies have a tendency to concentrate their programs on either the hard or the soft skills because one or the other offers what their members want. Occasionally a society will sponsor a conference where some of the other skills are discussed, but I know of no society that embraces both hard and soft skills. The TWI programs apply equally well to both areas of study and actually would serve as a link to help people on one side cross over to the other. The hard skill people could learn from the Job Relations program to "treat everyone as an individual" and to "make the best use of each person's ability." The soft skill people could learn to "define your objective, get the facts, weigh and decide, take action and check results." There is too much information for anyone to become an expert in everything, but when it comes to management approaches and skills, it is prudent to have a functional understanding of the premises and principles of the other side.

Now that you have a better understanding of how TWI is a foundation to Lean, we will step back and focus on defining the characteristics that made TWI so successful, why these characteristics continue to sustain TWI today, and why organizations should not arbitrarily make changes to TWI's format or content.

---

1. *The Toyota Way: 14 Management Principles from the World's Greatest Manufacturer*, Jeffrey Liker. The McGraw Hill Companies, 2004, p. 251.
2. Robinson & Schroeder, p. 46. (Original source: The Japan Human Relations Association, Summary of Japanese Suggestion Activities Survey, 1991.)
3. Robinson & Schroeder, p. 48. (Original source: The Japan Human Relations Association, Summary of Japanese Suggestion Activities Survey, 1991.)
4. Robinson & Schroeder, p. 52. (Original source: The Japan Human Relations Association, Summary of Japanese Suggestion Activities Survey, 1991.)
5. Robinson & Schroeder, p. 51. (Original source: The Japan Human Relations Association, Summary of Japanese Suggestion Activities Survey, 1991.)
6. Robinson & Schroeder, p. 52 (Original source: The Japan Human Relations Association, Summary of Japanese Suggestion Activities Survey, 1991.)
7 http://www.toyotageorgetown.com/qualdex.asp, p. 3.
8. Robinson & Schroeder, p. 48. (Original source: The Japan Human Relations Association, Summary of Japanese Suggestion Activities Survey, 1991.)
9. *The Toyota Way*, Liker, p. 141.

10. Robinson & Schroeder, p. 54. (Original source: The Japan Human Relations Association, Summary of Japanese Suggestion Activities Survey, 1991.)
11. TDO Presentation, TWI Lean slide #2, Central New York Technology Development Organization.
12. *The Toyota Way*, Liker p. 21.
13. *The Machine That Changed the World*, p. 53.
14. *The Toyota Way*, Liker, pp. 22–23.
15. *The Machine That Changed the World*, p. 99.
16. Huntzinger, Jim. (Second Quarter 2002) *The Roots of Lean Training Within Industry: The Origin of Kaizen.* p. 15. The Tribune. The Society of Manufacturing Excellence.
17. Robinson & Schroeder, p. 52. (Original source: The Japan Human Relations Association, Summary of Japanese Suggestion Activities Survey, 1991.)
18. *Lean Thinking: Banish Waste and Create Wealth in Your Corporation*, James Womack, Daniel Jones, Simon & Schuster, 1996, p. 10.
19. Womack, Jones; *Lean Thinking*, pp. 10–11.
20. Womack, Jones; *Lean Thinking*, p. 9.
21. *The Toyota Way*, Liker, p. 251.

CHAPTER 4

Characteristics That Made and Sustain TWI's Success

"One must learn by doing the thing; for though you think you know it, you have no certainty until you try."

SOPHOCLES 445 BC

Considering that organizations around the world have continually used TWI for over 60 years, one could say that it has been the most influential training program the world has ever seen. Why is a program that was created over 6 decades ago still in use today while not being substantially changed in all those years? There are two main reasons. The first is that TWI uses basic training material making it timeless in its practicality. The second is that the training material is immediately applicable and usable—it's not just academic and certainly not theoretical in its approach to training people. Let's take a closer look at these two important characteristics.

TWI Depends on Basic Training Material

Improving what you do, instructing others in how to do it, and dealing with people are three skills that most people need and could use on a daily basis. The three "J" programs, Job Methods, Job Instruction, and Job Relations provide the analytical tools to develop these skills. Though these are basic skills, many people may never have had training in them, or may even be unaware of them.

Skill One: Job Methods (JM)

Organizations widely accept that increasing productivity is determined not only by the tools they use, but by how they use them and finding better ways to do whatever it is you do will be a constant challenge if you are to grow. Sometimes it is the lack of new ideas that inhibits improvement, but more often it's employees' inability to break out of unproductive work habits that limits change. Most of us have heard these comments in one form or another: "We've always done it this way." "I'm comfortable doing it this way." "This is the best way to do this." When ideas do arise, organizations often don't have a process in place to capitalize on them.

Often aware of this shortcoming, management will introduce a suggestion system to harvest all the good ideas of the employees. The main difficulty with suggestion systems comes from the fact that the "one making the suggestion" is not usually the "implementer." Most of these types of conventional suggestion systems are at best ineffective and at worst counterproductive. Why? Because whoever makes the suggestion is usually not supposed to implement it; the suggestion is being beyond his or her expertise. This is classic mass-production thinking based on division of labor.

This type of thinking leads to an imperfect system where some employees may play the system like a lottery by submitting an inordinate number of suggestions in the hope of being recognized. Or employees will write suggestions without complete knowledge of the problem in an effort to be the first person to make the suggestion. (The first person gets the reward.) Because of the competitive nature of the suggestion process, many employees may not compete and instead keep their ideas to themselves. They won't even discuss them with other employees for fear that someone else will "write it up" and get the "prize" or even change the way they have to do work. As a result, brainstorming among employees is severely inhibited. JM eliminates all of these possibilities by providing a straightforward method to improve processes. Although token rewards may be involved, employees use JM because it makes their job easier. They use it because they gain from it. Without such an open suggestion process, there is little teamwork, brainstorming, or implementation of improvements that are so critical to continuous improvement and organizational growth.

Skill Two: Job Instruction (JI)

Incorporating a job-methods-changing procedure into employees' lives is an acknowledgement by the organization that that there will always be market, financial, or organizational forces that will necessitate changes and require employees to do their job differently, do them better, or learn new jobs. At any given moment, materials, people, designs, regulations and products all have potential to change for a variety of reasons. Kaizen, as practiced by Lean organizations, is a philosophical work ethic requiring that every time employees report to work, they look for better ways to do a job. More specifically, continuous improvement is a method of making incremental improvements of all kinds, large and small over a long period to achieve the long-term Lean goal of eliminating wastes that add cost but no customer value. Lean organizations apply continuous improvement to operations, equipment, processes, and people and require:

- Using operating practices that expose new opportunities for improvement
- Creating a culture where employees do not fear improvements and changes
- Training employees in practical problem-solving techniques to better implement and sustain improvements

In a mass-production mentality, many organizations believe that formal instruction is not that important. They believe that an employee will learn what he or she needs to do no matter how good the instruction is, if instruction exists at all. This kind of thinking is detrimental even if an organization is immune from competition, such as a government bureaucracy. Having employees (an organization's most valuable resource) learn through trial and error or through shoddy instruction is detrimental to good production. Only by providing proper instruction can employees be productive as quickly, inexpensively, and safely as possible while promoting continuous improvement. An organization also needs to instruct employees on how to teach their skills to others. We need only look back on the TWI Services success in World War II (WWII) to understand this:

"Knowing how to do a job gives no guarantee of ability to instruct someone else to do it. In ordinary times, people learn through mistakes. In war time this could not be tolerated—a worker can do the job right the first time if he is properly instructed."[1]

Although you can usually train someone how to teach, many people are not *inherently* good teachers. Being proficient at a skill does not mean that one automatically knows how to teach that skill to others. Welding, using a software package, and cleaning someone's teeth are all learnable skills, but it's obvious people do not usually become proficient in these skills through trial and error—they need to be taught. The point is, if the instructor knows both the skills of the job *and* the skill of instructing, the learner or employee will reach proficiency more quickly, with fewer mistakes, and in the safest manner possible. This is why TWI requires JI training for all employees responsible for teaching other employees how to perform jobs.

Many fore[men] have had considerable experience in training ... Many such men, while they know that they have succeeded in putting over the training, are conscious that something has not been just right—they have known that while they knew the jobs to be taught (or their instructors knew them), many new men failed to "catch on" readily, seemed to progress very slowly, were "dumb," and often never seemed to get so that they could do a first class job. Sometimes a good many of the men in training would quit before they were trained, giving all sorts of reasons, and so increasing the turnover.

The trouble, of course, lies in the fact that, whether whoever gave the instruction was or was not a first class man on the job, he did not know "how to put it over." He may have known his own game but he did not know the instructing game.[2]

Skill Three: Job Relations (JR)

All of us deal with people every day. It seems reasonable therefore that we should know how to solve interpersonal problems when they arise and even anticipate them before they occur. However, dealing with people-problems analytically is not inherent to most people. This may be partly due to our emotions and personal backgrounds that color everything we do. Human resource professionals understand that using a nonemotional, analytical approach is the optimal way to handle personnel problems. This is not to imply that you must be uncaring, tactless, or offensive in dealing with people; rather the problem-solver should be able to separate his or her emotions from the problem at hand and consider people's opinions and feelings to determine better their motivation and their needs. The goal is to derive a solution in a logical, meaningful way. JR teaches the skill of solving personnel problems using the scientific method and providing methods to avoid the trap of becoming emotional.

TWI Requires Useable Techniques

The three skill areas, JM, JI, and JR address many of the problems and challenges organizations encounter daily. If an organization has a solid grasp of how it can use these three skill areas it will resolve many of its on-site difficulties. This is why the TWI Service concluded that:

> ". . . There was so much evidence that all supervisors did need skill in instruction, in improving methods, and in working with people that very few plant problems were found not to involve at least one of the TWI supervisory programs . . . it became virtually impossible for any manager to name a problem involving people on which TWI could not give assistance."[3]

(*Note:* The TWI material uses the term "supervisor." This book will likewise use this term but the reader should keep in mind that supervisor applies more broadly *to what a person does, rather than as a title.* Also, this book will often use the term "organization" or "company" instead of the TWI term "plant.")

But as discussed in Chapter 2, another factor in the success of TWI is the recognition by the developers that having all this knowledge is ineffective if you don't know how to use it. C.R. Dooley writes in the Preface to the *TWI Report*:

> If there is any single thing that could be stated as "what TWI has learned," it would be that "the establishment of principles, and even getting acceptance by managers alone have practically no value in increasing production." "*What* to do" is not enough. It is only when people are drilled in "how to do it" that action results.[4]

This crucial point makes TWI stand out from most other training. The TWI developers concentrated on results because they saw the training as a solution to a problem. Though there is not a significant amount of new information in the TWI programs distinguishing it from other types of training, the content and structure of the programs do lend themselves to producing great results. As quoted at the very beginning of Chapter 1, "The TWI programs are distinctive, not because of the accepted principles of good management that they cover, but because they are successful in getting these *used*."[5]

Using the Scientific Method to Create Specific Results

The core of the "accepted principles of good management" is based on the scientific method, a method of logic that philosophers view as one of the basic ways people can *know* something. The word "science" originates from the Latin word "sciens," meaning "having knowledge." The scientific method uses objective evidence that anyone can question or replicate. Table 4-1 shows the scientific methods in the first column and terms that are useful to managers in the second.

Table 4-1. Using the Scientific Method as a Principle of Good Management

Steps in the Scientific Method	Steps in Management Principles Used by TWI
1. Observation: Define the problem and its parameters.	1. Define an objective or a problem and translate this into operation terms.
2. Hypothesize: Suggest a possible explanation or solution.	2. Gather facts.
3. Testing: Collect information (data) and test hypothesis.	3. Analyze the facts.
4. Results: Interpret the results of the test to determine if hypothesis is correct.	4. Make and implement a decision.
5. Conclusion: State a conclusion that others can independently evaluate.	5. Test or check the result.

The TWI programs fashioned the scientific method around the principles of good management into a procedure that anyone could readily adopt by staying on the fine line between the abstract and the specific. Note that in the five steps, TWI uses some abstract areas (the problem or objective) and some concrete areas (facts). TWI did this to avoid the situation where the training is too abstract in that it might tell you only what you should do: "Increase morale because happier employees are more productive employees." That makes sense, but it doesn't tell you how specifically to improve morale, or what you need to do when sales are down, costs are up, and you have to lay off people. The same limitation holds true if the training is too specific where you don't tie the training to your organization and culture. Having success with a given method in Company *A* does not guarantee success when that same method is duplicated in Company *B*. Programs such as Management by Objectives, Quality Circles, Total Quality Management, and Lean can fail if not applied correctly. If the people using them attempt to duplicate their use from a company where they were successful without taking into account important differences in the organization such as the culture, the programs will be doomed. TWI said it best in the "Five Needs" Exhibit 4-4 that we cover later in this chapter:

> "Confidence and resourcefulness in how to proceed, not standardized solutions and rules, are [what we] develop[ed.]"

Developing a Four-Step Method for Each Program

The scientific method or the "engineering method,"[6] as it is referred to in the *TWI Report*, is a common thread that runs through all programs. When the developers put the training programs together, they came up with four programs that each used a *four-step method*. They derived the four steps over time mainly from the traditional five-step scientific method (refer to Table 4.1). The Job Relations program was the first program to structure and apply the 4-Step Method to personnel problems:

> "It is followed in legal and military practice, but its application to the personnel field was unique. The steps seem so reasonable and its intuitive use by successful leaders so evident that it is hard to understand why it had never been formulated in the personnel field before this time."[7]

The development of JR took over 2 years to complete because no one had ever quantified the solution of personnel problems in a method before. The method went through ten versions and the number of steps varied from six to

Exhibit 4-1. Comparison of Alternate Job Instruction Steps

Instruction Steps developed by Michael J. Kane	**TWI Job Instruction**
	How to Get Ready to Instruct
1. Show him how to do it	• Have a timetable
2. Explain key points	• Break down the job
3. Let him watch you do it again	• Have everything ready
4. Let him do simple parts of the job	• Have the workplace properly arranged
5. Help him do the whole job	
6. Let him do the whole job—but watch him	4 Steps of How To Instruct
7. Put him on his own	1. Prepare the worker
	2. Present the operation
(Final Report, page 19)	3. Try out performance
	4. Follow-up

(Final Report, page 33)

Instruction Steps WWI Shipbuilders

1. Preparation
2. Presentation
3. Application
4. Inspection (or test)

By Charles R. Allen & Michael J. Kane

(Final Report, page 186)

four.[8] Looking at the four TWI programs now, one could see how the number of steps could vary in each program. For example, Exhibit 4-1 shows the differences and similarities among the 7-step method of Michael J. Kane, the final 4-Step Method of Job Instruction, and the 4-Step Method that was used in shipbuilding in World War I (WWI).

Although the Job Instruction method has more information than Kane's method, it was restricted to four steps. The additional information is an augmentation of the main steps or preparation for the instruction. The point is: Once four steps were arrived at, it seemed very suitable for each program (using different wording) to 1) collect facts, 2) analyze them, 3) make a decision, and then, 4) check or follow up on the decision (see Table 4-2). In fact, a unique aspect of the TWI programs is that the TWI developers made the scientific method accessible to people for everyday use, using a demonstration for each step, and creating a *training card* for each program with the 4-Step Method that people could carry in their pocket (TWI referred to these as *reminder cards.*) TWI encouraged employees to carry these training cards with them at all times after training. These training cards contain the core for each program and we will be referring to them throughout the book. Samples of these cards are shown in Exhibit 5.3 (JI), Exhibit 6.5 (JR), and Exhibit 7.1 (JM).

Table 4.2. Program Wording for the TWI Four-Step Method

TWI Four-Step Methods				
Steps	Job Instruction	Job Job Relations	Job Job Methods	Program Development
1	Preparation	Get the facts	Break down the job	Spot a production problem
2	Presentation	Weigh and decide	Question every detail	Develop a specific plan
3	Try-out Performance	Take action	Develop the new method	Get plan into action
4	Follow up	Check results	Apply the method	Check results

The Four-Step Method in the TWI programs is about developing confidence and resourcefulness for both employees and organizations. It clearly lays out the roadmap on how to proceed with the training programs. This is, I believe, the true legacy of TWI and the principal reason for its success. (As the reader will learn, understanding each program's 4-Step Method is central to understanding TWI). The 4-Step Method provides each program a well thought out, clear, objective, and useful way to solve problems. TWI did not design the training programs for people to understand broad concepts—it designed *methods* that people could apply in practical, concrete, ways to achieve real results. With this approach, employees could learn a skill that enabled them to grow within the objectives of any type of organization. The simplicity and clarity of these programs are a result of TWI distilling the programs to the point that the knowledge gained is just what a person needs, and no more—there is nothing extraneous that would cause a distraction or waste time.

"In looking at the simplicity of TWI programs it would seem that, since they only represent common sense, their development should have been possible without too much trouble. But it must be remembered that a lot of non-essentials had to be eliminated. One real job was streamlining and intensification."[9]

The TWI Service did not think up these programs and skills in a vacuum, but rather they responded to the basic needs of the defense industry that was quickly becoming the largest in the world. TWI's mandate was to train workers quickly so that industry could do more with less and do it faster. This is exactly the Lean thinking recipe for progress today and one reason why Lean is so successful; it taps into people's need for progress, which I believe is "hardwired" in our DNA.

To have a deep appreciation of why TWI has stood the test of time, it is important to understand the importance of the two concepts we've been discussing, 1) basic training material and 2) usable techniques. In the pragmatic and scientific spirit of the TWI Service, these concepts became the twin foundations and identifying characteristics that has given TWI its long-term success. Having a sound theoretical and conceptual foundation is an important starting point for any program, but it is basic training and usable techniques that are the visual characteristics people see and remember when they experience TWI training. In the next section, we will continue to outline these characteristics, among other things.

Three Main Criteria: Simplicity, Usability, and Standardization

Dooley and Deitz were experienced trainers and they gathered other experienced trainers around them. They also looked to experienced people of the past, especially to Charles R. Allen who developed a four-step instruction for shipbuilding in WWI. They were in an emergency situation to win the war, which out of necessity required creating parameters. The first challenge was how to handle the scope of the project. The defense industry included everything that would support a war effort, which meant most industries across the entire country, and most companies within those industries. This meant they had to account for all varieties of personnel, from those who were trained and experienced to those who had never worked in industry, or were not a major part of the workforce, e.g., women. TWI's only solution at the time was to create "one size fits all" programs that were meaningful and beneficial for every level of employee.

The TWI Service was fortunate to have a huge laboratory in which to test its ideas. By the end of the war and after only five years of existence, TWI had conducted training in 16,511 plants. Thus when TWI conceived of a new idea there was a large selection of places to test and develop it. They used a development process that we will discuss in Chapter 5, but at the outset, three main criteria drove the program developers: 1) Simplicity, 2) Usability, and 3) Standardization.

Criteria One: Simplicity

In 1940, TWI had literally millions of people to train in a very short period. The developers understood that: "A national program has to be clear enough and easy enough that it can be handled by average trainers."[10] In order to train a vast number of people quickly, the developers used a concept called "*The Multiplier Principle*," described as follows: "Develop a standard method, then train the people [master trainers] who will train other people [trainers] who will train repeated groups of people to use the method."[11] This meant that TWI personnel would conduct "train the trainer" sessions, called "Institutes." (Institutes are discussed in Chapter 5.) An *institute conductor* or *master trainer* would train candidates. These candidates would then return to their organizations and train the selected employees. As a result, both the training material and the method of training had to be simple enough that an average person could comprehend and use it to train others.

Most employees had never been trainers before, yet for the programs to be successful, the TWI Service had to take potential trainers and turn them into successful trainers after attending one Institute. This was one reason why the material had to be basic and concise. Although some of the potential TWI trainers were already engaged as trainers, the volume of work was so great that many people who were not trainers would have to be pressed into service as trainers. TWI recognized that if they only used experienced trainers the training material might be very different. They also recognized that even among professional trainers, the trainees would still master the training material at varying rates. Because of the different levels of experienced trainers, and the need to recruit inexperienced trainers, the material had to be simple and well organized. Simplicity was also necessary because of the pool of potential trainees. Employers would not readily accept a program that would take employees away from their jobs for any great length of time.

It cannot be stressed too much how efficient the resulting TWI training was and how much time had been spent distilling out extraneous material to arrive at a core of usable information.[12] Abe Lincoln and Stephen Douglas at Gettysburg is a classic example of contrasts in conveying information. Lincoln said everything in about 3 minutes in a great speech that no one would think of altering. Douglas took an hour or so, and no one remembers it. I bring up this example to emphasize that nearly every word in TWI is there because it is deemed important. Dismissing or removing even a few words can be detrimental to the program.

Simplicity and usability work together. The simpler something is the more likely it will have wide applications. If the training is too detailed or involved, it will run the risk of losing its broad appeal.

"This also is in line with TWI philosophy of training supervisors in a pattern which is a thinking and operating process, and which can be used on small everyday problems before they become the big ones which might require paper work."[13]

To make the programs simple, the developers made sure they used language that the average participant would readily understand. They termed it "shop language" as opposed to "academic language." In Job Methods, especially, they changed the language to accommodate the "average" person.

"Established principles of work simplification were cleared of engineering terms, and techniques were clarified so that they could be applied by average supervisors rather than by engineers."[14]

In addition to using shop or common language, TWI recognized that a person can absorb only so much information over a fixed period of time, so they limited the amount of material in the programs to what most people could retain.

The characteristics that relate to "Simplicity'" are the amount of training material and how it is presented. You can provide additional training to employees as required, however, adding additional material to the TWI programs may impair their effectiveness by increasing the time needed for training and the time needed for training the trainers.

Finally, because these programs are simple and concise, a usual reaction among experienced trainers is to want to change or improve the TWI training. However, nothing was written in stone and the TWI developers understood that the programs might readily change and evolve over time. Before contemplating so-called improvements, trainers should understand that TWI evolved out of a blend of *experience*, *necessity*, and *trial and error* that created tested characteristics that make it successful today. If you truly believe you must make "improvements," trainers should likewise do sufficient trial and testing on a large population to assure their changes provide the desired results.

"Work From This Outline—Don't Trust to Memory"

In the early days of the Service, there was a great deal of flexibility in presenting the programs because the developers had no experience in delivering a program on a nationwide basis. After going into large plants and large organizations such as the Armed Service Forces (ASF), TWI learned that the results and the degree of success were uneven and some results were unfavorable. Also, when TWI-trained supervisors were transferred throughout the organization, it became obvious that all trainers were not presenting the same material nor presenting it in the same way. Because of the variation in delivery, some people thought the training was useful and were recommending it while others did not and advised against it. The anecdote in Exhibit 4-2[15] shows the need of adhering to the material and thus the method.

Three further comments regarding Exhibit 4-2 are required. 1) This Exhibit is verbatim from the TWI Report and, as was the custom of the time,

Exhibit 4-2. Why It Is Important to Follow the Manual Exactly

---

"Following the Manual"

A railway engineer on the "City of San Francisco" does not ever consider the possibility that, just because he has made the run on a particular passenger division between Chicago and San Francisco hundreds of times, he might now leave the track. But trainers, as their experience increases, are often tempted to introduce innovations.

Incidents like the following selection from a district report show why following the outlines is important:

In a Job Methods session, a foreman was demonstrating a present method breakdown which was only fair. The job was a slitting operation in heavy sheet metal, performed by a girl operator on a homemade slitting machine. She went as far as she could on the machine, and finished the slit by hand with a hack-saw to a tolerance of 1/64 inch. The foreman's improvement was to put an adjustable stop on the machine-table, so the work could all be done on the machine, to a tolerance of .003 inches.

The day shift superintendent was "kibitzing" the group. One detail of the breakdown was "Start the machine." The trainer asked, "How do you start the machine?" Before the foreman could answer, the superintendent cut in: "What difference can that possibly make? The man has already made his improvement."

"I don't know what difference it might make, because I don't know anything about this machine," said the trainer. "But I do know this program, and we are following the program. To follow the program, we have to have every detail, and we do not have the details of starting the machine." He turned to the foreman and asked him how the girl started the machine.

Exhibit 4-2. (*Continued*)

The foreman, who had been through J.I., told and showed and explained: "She takes two steps to the right, like this, and then she jumps into the air, like this, and swats the starting lever." The trainer got all that down on the blackboard as the man did it. Then he checked the "Stop machine" detail. The foreman told him the girl took the same two steps, jumped, and hit the lever again, except that she knocked it the other way. The trainer put all that on the board.

Then he turned to the superintendent and said: "Does this operator have to start and stop the machine for every piece?" "Sure." "And how many pieces a day will this operator slit for you?" "Forty an hour, 320 a day," said the superintendent. "So, this girl has to jump and hit that lever twice for each of the 320 pieces, making 640 jumps a day?" asked the trainer. "Now, Mr. Superintendent, will you please go over there in the corner and jump as high as you can 640 times, and swing your arm as far as you can on every jump, and then let us know if it fatigues you at all?"

The result was that, in addition to the initial improvement, 640 jumps per day were eliminated by extending the lever so the girl could reach it easily. The superintendent ordered method breakdowns made on every job over which he had jurisdiction.

---

it used the word "girls" instead of "women." 2) Although TWI did not state whether the superintendent was participating in the class or just observing, he was probably just observing. From page 198 of the TWI Report: "Trainers were warned against having executives just "sit in" on sessions. Full participation of executives was encouraged, but too many did not bother to put on a demonstration—just contented themselves with giving advice." 3) This may seem like an extreme example of a job method because it does not seem possible that a deficiency in a machine (short lever arm) would stay uncorrected for very long. Sadly, such deficiencies are around us all the time and we get so used to them that we do not see them.

Again, the object of the training is to learn the method and not to solve a problem. It wasn't long before the developers realized that to get consistency in results they needed consistency in the process.

"Gradually it was brought home that everyone must positively "Follow the Manual." This proved to be a strong selling point as TWI work has been recommended by one employer to another or one part of a company to another part.

"Nobody pretends that the TWI programs can be handled in only one way, but it is known that the programs as outlined in the manuals can be handled safely with good results by an average trainer. A deviation may be one that one specific trainer can handle. If another trainer sees him and tries to follow his example, he may fail. Also, the second trainer might think of deviations of his own and not be able to handle them.

"Ideas about technique do not occur just once. In fact, they occur over and over again. The thing that one trainer may experiment with may have been tried already and found not up to the standard of usability by all trainers. Efforts may be wasted on something which has already been thought of, tried out, and rejected for cause."[16]

TWI applied this approach to all three "J" programs. The Job Instruction Manual was the first manual in use and at the bottom of each page is written: "WORK FROM THIS OUTLINE—DON'T TRUST TO MEMORY." The Job Methods Manual was the next manual in use and the developers used the same phrase, but this time it was restricted to the trainer's instructions, which preceded each session outline. The Job Relations Manual includes reference material at the end of the manual. In the reference material, there is the following statement: "Job Relations is to be put on *exactly* as outlined in the manual."[17]

These strict instructions for simple material led to a paradox about how the trainer could deliver the material. The paradox is that "simple" material can be difficult to deliver effectively. The reason for this is that the training material is very concentrated, leaving only its essence to be delivered in the shortest amount of time. TWI deleted side comments, interpretations, and material not specifically tied to this goal. If the instructor was not completely familiar with the training material or the meaning and intent, he or she had two choices. Read the manual or paraphrase the material, which experience showed actually took the instructor over the 2 hour limit. Reading the material when you are unfamiliar with it can be deadly to your audience, either putting people to sleep and/or causing the trainer to lose all credibility. Paraphrasing may seem like a quicker route than reading the material verbatim, but not only did it take much longer, it also led to omissions and/or inclusions of extraneous information, which derail the whole idea of simplicity and actually confuse the participants. In either case, it becomes more difficult for proper learning to occur.

The developers of TWI knew it was imperative that the trainer or instructor be familiar with the manual's structure and contents. Being familiar meant knowing the manual like a director would know every line in a play's script (and how the performance is intended to be received), and then deliver them like an actor.

"Following the Manual" does not mean sitting down and reading it. *Learn it*—Then check yourself constantly.[18]

Because TWI wanted its trainers to deliver the exact content of the manual *without* reading the manual and only having to memorize parts of the manual (the verbatim sections and work on a blackboard), they developed a typographical style for the working versions, which allowed a trainer to present material directly from the manual.

"It was decided that a manual should be readable from a distance of from four to five feet, and that a glance should be enough to show the exact kind of thing that the trainer should be doing—what he must put on the board and the few parts which were to be stated verbatim. The typographical scheme employed was for printing in large (14 point), clear type, widely spaced (4 point leaded), according to the typographical code shown in Exhibit 4-3)."[19]

Exhibit 4-3. Making the Manual Readable from a Distance

CAPITALS	Section Heads
Horizontal line across page	Encloses section for timing
Plain type	Trainer says in own words
* Star in front of line	Trainer says verbatim
Material between lines	Board work
[Bracket]	Instructions to trainer

Because the programs are scripted, experienced trainers (especially those with instructional design experience) in today's world may feel frustrated because there is little room for variability in the content or delivery. It would seem one's creativity, style, or personality is being hampered. The TWI Programs are, if anything, substance over style. On the other hand, novice trainers will find that with some effort they can be very successful with the programs.

Criteria Two: Usability

Previously stated, but worth repeating, the focus for the TWI developers was on getting immediate results from the programs and this meant organizations had to apply what employees were learning if they were going to get those results. Consequently, much of the development around these programs was to ensure usability.

Because these programs are skill based, the developers used the principle of "Learning by Doing." A person can know something to the extent that he can intelligently discuss the subject and can even answer questions about it. However, one cannot determine whether he can actually perform the task until he actually does it. Consider any skill-based activity such as playing a violin or playing tennis. If you want to learn how to play tennis, you might start out by reading a book to learn the object of the game, rules, equipment, and so forth. It may also describe techniques of holding the racquet, and hitting ground strokes, overhead smashes, and serves. Visualization may help a lot, but you will never really learn tennis until you practice—*a lot*! After days or weeks of practice, you will be up to a certain level of competency. TWI training works in much the same way as learning how to play tennis, which means the trainee is required to practice the skills in each program. The developers of TWI knew that the best learning was experiential (studies have since been conducted that confirm this premise) and learned two ideas through the developmental experience. These characteristics have not been altered since and are critical to the success of the program.

1. *Each participant should practice as much as possible.* Therefore, each participant will solve at least one sample problem regardless of the program in which he or she is enrolled with the instruction limited to the first session and parts of later sessions.
2. *Select problems from the participant's work area.* The sample problems must be related to what the participants do and the type of problem they would encounter if the participant was fully skilled in the TWI method and using it on his or her own. There are several reasons for working on problems from one's own workplace. First, acceptance will be better since the participant will see the relevance and applicability of the method. Understanding will improve because the person must learn only the method and not all of the peripheral parts of the problem. Secondly, the employee will retain more of the training than if he or she used a made up problem because it will have immediate relevance. The U.S. government formed Training Within Industry specifically to "[train] industrial people to handle their own production

problems through training."[20] Finally, at the end of the training, the participants will not only have learned a skill, but they will also have completed a useful project in their workplace.

Differentiating Between Training and Education

The name of the service, TWI, has a very specific meaning, which further emphasizes usability. It differentiates between training and education.

- *Education* is for the rounding-out of the individual and the good of society; it is general, provides background, and increases understanding.
- *Training* is for the good of plant production—it is a way to solve production problems through people; it is specific and helps people to acquire skill through use of what they have learned.[21]

"Within Industry" means that you must do the training within an industrial setting and those involved in that industry must do the training. You cannot delegate this duty to another organization. Other learning organizations such as vocational schools and colleges cannot prepare a worker for work done "on the job." Therefore, universities and vocational schools should do the educating and workplaces should do the training.[22] Further, TWI found that to guarantee a sufficient amount of practice and still be efficient in training, you should have no more than twelve participants in a class. The ideal number is ten and there should be no fewer than eight. Participants learn from the other example problems demonstrated in the class, but less than seven diminishes the quality of learning and more than twelve expands the time beyond ten hours.

TWI Format for Delivering the Training Sessions

The proper structure for the training sessions is another characteristic responsible for TWI's success. Each "J" program has five 2-hour sessions each day for a week. (The forth TWI training, Program Development, is structured differently and consists of more hours of training per day, but the training principles are the same.) This format helps the participants better absorb and reflect on the information between sessions. Studies show that people's retention drops off after 2 hours. In addition, it is easier to schedule a 2-hour session so that employees can more easily work this into their workday without disrupting production.

In the first session, the trainer presents a real-world problem that everyone can easily relate to, shows how people usually handle these problems, and then introduces the 4-Step Method. The trainer spends the last four sessions having the participants practice the 4-Step Method on actual and current problems they bring to the training. There is some teaching done in the last four sessions, but it's reinforcement of what the trainer has already presented. There is some new material presented on the last four days, but it's in addition to the 4-Step Method. You can stretch the five 2-hour session format over a weekend if necessary but it should not continue beyond a 2-week period because in the early stages of learning a skill, people need more immediate reinforcement. The principle here is that of "distributed practice" where, even if a person is not consciously thinking about the program, their mind will continue to work on the material. This interim period between sessions also gives the participant time to formulate questions, which further enhances the learning process. Since "learning by doing" is fundamental to the TWI programs, this period also gives the participants time to formulate, analyze, and solve their specific sample problems.

The Five Needs of a Supervisor

TWI developed a significant characteristic, the concept of "The Five Needs of a Supervisor" (see Exhibit 4-4). TWI did not set out to define this but as the developers responded to the needs of industry, this concept arose as a way to discuss the needs of a given business and also TWI's role in meeting those needs.

Discussing the "Five Needs" is important to the success of the programs because it helps the participants understand how and why the programs fit into what they do, which encourages acceptance and acceptance leads to a motivation to learn. The three "J" Programs, JI, JM, and JR, directly address the three "skill" needs (numbers 3, 4, and 5). Although each program is independent of the other two and it is not necessary to include all three in a training program, I recommend organizations do so because they reinforce each other. You use JM to make changes and then use JI to reinforce those changes by making everyone competent in them and then use JR to enable both JM and JI to operate more effectively.

When management uses all three programs, there is usually some discussion of which one to start with. The reasonable answer is to start with the one most needed. If employees appear to be ineffective, if there is a large amount of scrap or mistakes, or if many employees seem to be doing the same job differently, JI would be a good place to start. If an organization does not meet production schedules routinely or if completing tasks seem to take longer than they should, JM would be a proper starting place. If morale is low, employees do not seem to get along well with one other, or if there are many grievances or complaints, JR would be an appropriate first program. Each of these

Exhibit 4-4. Five Needs of a Supervisor

THE FIVE NEEDS CONCEPT

While Program Development was being tried out, TWI discovered a way of talking about supervisory needs that proved useful in outlining what TWI was prepared to do, and making clear the fields in which the plant would have to develop its own programs. It proved effective in discussing the special needs of a plant, and made "our business is different" concepts clear in relation to basic needs of all supervisors. The statement, which has become a standard part of TWI thinking and publications, is:

EVERY SUPERVISOR HAS FIVE NEEDS

1. *Knowledge of the Work*—materials, tools, processes, operations, products and how they are made and used.

2. *Knowledge of Responsibilities*—policies, agreements, rules, regulations, schedules, and interdepartmental relationships.

These two knowledge needs must be met currently and locally by each plant or company.
   Such knowledge must be provided if each supervisor is to know his job and is to have a clear understanding of his authority and responsibilities as part of management.

3. *Skill in Instructing*—increasing production by helping supervisors to develop a well-trained workforce which will get into production quicker; leave less scrap, rework, and rejects; fewer accidents, and less tool and equipment damage.

4. *Skill in Improving Methods*—utilizing materials, machines, and manpower more effectively by having supervisors study each operation in order to eliminate, combine, rearrange, and simplify details of the job.

5. *Skill in Leading*—increasing production by helping supervisors to improve their understanding of individuals, their ability to size up situations, and their ways of working with people.

These three skills must be acquired individually. Practice and experience in using them enable both new and experienced supervisors to recognize and solve daily problems promptly.

   Training Within Industry Service assists companies in giving their supervisors a start in acquiring these skills through three 10-hour programs: Job Instruction, Job Methods, and Job Relations.
These skills, acquired through this training, must become a part of day-to-day operations. In no other way can production be so quickly influenced and manpower conserved.

Confidence and resourcefulness in how to proceed, not standardized solutions and rules are developed. These enable supervisors to get good teamwork, to give better service, and to get out more production. (my emphasis) **From: Final Report; pages 48–49**

---

programs will help relieve all of the above problems. What is most important is just to start using any one of the three.

The TWI developers recognized that there was a great deal of variability among companies and even the departments in them. For example, a supermarket will have a different accounting system than will a steel mill. Engineers in a fabrication plant will perform different work than those in a chemical plant. The work will be different from company to company and from department to department, and so will the rules and responsibilities. Safety rules in the supermarket are different from those in the steel mill. These differences are reflected in the two knowledge requirements: *Knowledge of the Work and Knowledge of Responsibilities*. TWI addressed these two needs through Program Development, an analytical method used to create a training program that addresses a specific, unique need. The first step is performing a Needs Analysis and then determining if the organization can resolve the need through training, followed by the development of a customized training program. TWI intended the Program Development program for personnel who are responsible for developing training programs. However, since Program Development uses the basic scientific method, it is applicable for anyone dealing with problem solving.

Criteria Three: Standardization

The TWI development team realized that training one part of an organization or even an entire organization is not necessarily an insurmountable task. Getting the entire defense industry trained in a short period, however, required standardizing the training material. Since there were many ways of delivering the same material, the Service spent a great deal of time finding the way that would be best for the greatest number of trainers and participants. They ended up focusing on three areas: facilities, participants, and trainers.

Standardization Area One: Facilities

Naturally, training facilities are a critical part of running the training programs and TWI had to give consideration for all types of venues. Though not to the extent today, in the 1940s there were a variety of audio visual aids to choose from for presenting the material. It was important to have the proper equipment. TWI ruled out film and filmstrips because not everyone might have access to projectors. Sticking to the theme of keeping everything simple, the TWI developers made the blackboard the only required A-V accessory.

"Because TWI programs had to be standard and because the circumstances under which they were used varied so widely, it was necessary to eliminate practically all gadgets and aids. It was found that a blackboard was essential. A number of points have to be illustrated, and a blackboard is the most effective standard device which is readily available."[23]

As it turned out, this was a wise decision in at least one case where loggers were being trained.

"Some sessions for the Kirby Lumber Company, the largest logging and milling company in the South, which operates over many hundreds of square miles in East Texas and Louisiana, were held right in the pine forest, with the blackboard nailed on a tree, the men seated on logs, and the trainer's equipment resting on a stump. In other companies, sessions were held in railroad cars and even in tents."[24]

Today, contemporary trainers make use of aids such as LCD projectors or overhead projectors, but in terms of keeping the presentation simple and clear, it is debatable how much these devices add to the success of the presentation.

Standardization Area Two: Participants

To achieve the great strides in productivity that was necessary during wartime, companies had to employ millions of people even though many of these people had no industrial experience at all.

"The tremendous increase in gross national product at a time when manpower was being steadily drawn into the armed forces would not have been possible if we had not called on the housewives of the nation, the youth of school age, the oldsters who had earned retirement, and the physically handicapped to supplement, and in part to replace, those who would normally have staffed our industries, trades, and services. The labor force increased in five years from 54,000,000 to 64,000,000—up almost 20%. Out of these 10,000,000 new workers, plus all but a few hundred thousand of the 9,000,000 unemployed of 1939, came the manpower—and womanpower—to replace the 10,000,000 added to the military services and to add 7,500,000 to civilian employment. Most of this addition went into manufacturing plants. Agriculture, and later, construction actually lost workers."[25]

As companies added new workers, the more experienced workers were pressed into supervisory positions. Although there was no alternative, the result was that inexperienced supervisors lacking job and training knowledge were now leading inexperienced workers. As would be expected, this resulted in frustration to both the supervisors and the workers. The TWI staff received the following stories from various defense contractors in the fall of 1940:

> "Some of the new workers do not know which end of the drill to chuck up.
>
> "In some way, a hole had gotten into the skin of the wing. A worker had put a 'dummy' rivet into the hole. The lead-man was interested in ascertaining the character of the hole, and its size. He told the new worker to drill out the rivet. The worker proceeded to drill a circle of holes around the rivet and then knocked out the piece of skin.
>
> "In an induction talk, a Safety Engineer asked a group of 20 new people: 'How many of you know the difference between a drill press and a sewing machine?' Four of them had never in their lives seen a sewing machine."[26]

As noted, at least one employer was happy to employ "theater ushers, musicians, and manicurists" because they could quickly become productive as a result of TWI training.

Standardization Area Three: Trainers

One objective of the program was to get the trainers (and subsequently the participants) to agree that it would help them; otherwise, they probably would not use the training after the session was over. Because TWI was dealing with many new supervisors, they often did not know what their problems were and thus it was difficult to determine the type of training that would help them. For example, each program used the sample problems to demonstrate the respective method. Each of these problems had been thoroughly tested and screened for applicability and usability. The demonstrations had to be sensible to all participants so that they would understand the method in question. At the same time, TWI had to include all of the method's concepts.

Development details are included in subsequent chapters so it suffices to say here that TWI refined the programs to where the average trainer would have no difficulty with them. After many reiterations and changes, what emerged was called "The 'Package' Idea." (This is the principle of using 10 hours of training for 10 individuals, using a 4-Step Method, demonstration, and practice.) It is actually attributed to one man, Glenn L. Gardiner, Vice President of Forstmann Woolen Company and the Director of TWI's New Jersey activities.[27] As noted, much of the material was not new; and people had especially used the material in Job Instruction in various forms for many years. However, the TWI developers believed that standardizing training material was as an important a factor in increasing productivity as it was in using automation in production. If volume were low, the training could be variable. High volume necessitated and benefited from this standardization. Standardization meant that there was now a repeatable and reliable package or module for training that could easily be transported and delivered around the country and presented as intended, it would be successful no matter who the participants were or at what company they were employed.

Summary of Essential TWI Characteristics

The three criteria of the programs—simplicity, usability, and standardization—are a common thread that runs through all the TWI programs. Many points were determined in advance, but others "happened" once, and proved so successful that TWI turned them into ten musts (see Exhibit 4-5).[28]

Exhibit 4-6 further summarizes six essential characteristics that made TWI so successful. As with the ten musts, these particular characteristics are what continue to make TWI successful today, and more specifically are the very aspects of the program that organizations should not arbitrarily change.

Quality Control and Management Involvement

This chapter has focused on the characteristics of the course design that made the TWI programs successful. However, two other factors supported the success of the programs that bear repeating. The first is instituting a program to track *quality control*, which keeps the integrity of the course design while allowing for development. The second is *management involvement*, having top management sponsor, participate and demand results in using the skills so that an organization can realize its benefits. As discussed in Chapter 2, TWI held meetings called *Management Contact Approach* and formed the nucleus of five concepts which management needs to follow to assure the training is used; and results, achieved.

"... TWI has learned that development of a good program is not enough, standardized presentation alone gives no guarantee of results, and not even the acquiring of some skill is enough. Only when top management understands, sponsors, participates, and demands results, can full usefulness of the program be obtained."[29]

Once the training is complete, organizations must have a program in place that requires the participants to submit results of their activities that related to the training. Organizations can deliver TWI flawlessly, but they will not

Exhibit 4-5. TWI's Ten "Musts" Points

Fundamentals of TWI

1. It is necessary to have a specific method or pattern that the plant man can follow in solving his own problems. The method must be simple, and it must be briefly stated. Each of the four TWI programs has a 4-Step Method.

2. The method is to be applied as a production tool. Therefore, it should be stated in shop terms, not in academic language.

3. Technical perfection alone is not enough. There must be something in the program that gets acceptance and use. Advertising men talk about believeability. Training designers have to watch for believeability, acceptability, and usability.

4. In order that members of training groups can "learn by doing," groups must be kept small enough to permit time for guided, individual practice of the method on their own everyday problems. There is no substitute for practice.

5. There must be a definite outline of exactly what will be covered, how much time will be given to each point, and how it will be done in order that there will be a recognized universal standard for the training sessions.

6. Ten hours of content is best put across in five 2-hour meetings. A 2-hour session does not need to be interrupted by an intermission. Time spent in opening and closing the meeting is no greater for a 2-hour session than for a 1-hour meeting.

7. Five meetings should be spread over no longer an interval than two weeks. When new material is being learned, progress in acquiring skill is most rapid when the subject is fresh. Compact scheduling means that operating people are not tied up over long periods.

8. Since training is an operating tool, it is wasteful to conduct it on a voluntary basis. Management must select the supervisors who are to be trained. Since training is a technique that is designed to improve production, training should be conducted on company time, at company expense.

9. When a program is being operated nationally, quality control is necessary so that there can be a guaranteed quality standard, nationwide, and so that poor local results will not have an unfavorable reaction on the national program.

10. The trainer who conducts each of these TWI 10-hour programs has been prepared in a two-weeks Institute (one week spent in group work, and one week of practice under observation and coaching). In order to make economical use of TWI staff time, it was specified that no prospective trainer would be admitted to an Institute unless he were going to conduct at least five supervisory groups. It was also required that the trainer conduct at least one group in every 90-day period in order to remain qualified for active service.

Exhibit 4-6. Six Essential Characteristics for a Successful Program

Characteristics of the TWI Programs
That Make Them Successful

1. A Quality Control procedure to insure that the programs are delivered as they were designed.
   a. Follow the manual
   b. Do not add or delete material
   c. Use certified trainers
   d. Include '5 Needs of Supervisors'

2. A simple, 4-Step Method

3. Learn by Doing
   a. Each participant selects a work-related problem to solve
   b. Include as much "hands-on" practice as possible

4. Ten hours per program
   a. Two hours per session
   b. No more than one session per day
   c. No more than a two-week time span for the five sessions

5. Ten participants per session
   a. No more than twelve participants
   b. No fewer than eight participants

6. Create a system to ensure that the training is used

achieve the desired results if they do not use it immediately. The program need not be formal. As described in the story in Exhibit 4-2, once the manager understood the possibilities that could result from the Job Method activity, he requested job breakdowns for every job under his control. If the organization did this within a schedule, by the time all the breakdowns are complete, not only would it realize savings, but also employees may have gotten into the habit of practicing the Job Method skills. You can use any device to keep the method in use.

Finally, to gain a deep appreciation of TWI's efforts in developing these programs, and to understand the "mantra" about following the program exactly or risk altering it to your program's detriment, Part 2 (Chapters 5–8) outlines the development history as well as the how and why behind each version of the four TWI programs. Though I would highly recommend reading Part 2 to learn, among other things, how the 4-Step Method evolved for each program, the reader can jump to Part 3 (Chapters 9–12) for a direct discussion on how trainers deliver each TWI program. (*Note:* The beginning of Chapter 5 covers some specific methods TWI used in creating all of the TWI programs.) Or, you can read the chapters in pairs, Chapter 5 and 9 for JI, Chapter 6 and 10 for JR, Chapter 7 and 11 for JM, and Chapters 8 and 12 for PD.

1. *TWI Report*, p. 201.
2. *TWI Report*, pp. 188–189; from Charles R. Allen; The Instructor, the Man, and the Job, page 361.
3. *TWI Report*, p. 60.
4. *TWI Report*, p. xi.
5. Robinson and Schroeder, p. 36.
6. *TWI Report*, p. 179.
7. *TWI Report*, p. 40.
8. During trial periods, it was found that Step 2 (Evaluating) and Step 3 (Making a Decision) were often hard to separate. So the developers decided to join them into one step—Weigh & Decide. The preparation for Job Relations is to "Define Your Objective," which could easily be considered a fifth step.
9. *TWI Report*, p. 261.
10. *TWI Report*, p. 180.
11. *TWI Report*, p. 6.
12. Creating well written, concise training can be a detriment when it is being used by an experienced trainer. This was true in 1940 and it is still true today. "Some panel members who the District Directors counted on to "sell" this new program to their own companies suddenly became lukewarm; often they became positively cold to this threat to their personal prestige as training directors who had always devised their own training programs." *TWI Report*, page 53.
13. *TWI Report*, pp. 184–185.
14. *TWI Report*, p. 37.
15. *TWI Report*, pp. 182–183.
16. *TWI Report*, p. 163.
17. Job Relations Manual, p. 97.
18. Job Relations Manual, p. 103.
19. *TWI Report*, pp. 183–184.
20. *TWI Report*, p. 16.
21. *TWI Report*, p. 17.
22. Many schools recognize this and require internships or "work blocks" as a prerequisite for graduation.
23. *TWI Report*, p. 184.
24. *TWI Report*, p. 134.
25. *TWI Report*, p. 95.
26. *TWI Report*, p. 21.
27. *TWI Report*, p. 30.
28. *TWI Report*, pp. 177–178.
29. *TWI Report*, p. 185.

PART 2

The Evolution of Each TWI Program

CHAPTER 5

How TWI Developed the Job Instruction Program

"The trouble, of course, lies in the fact that, whether whoever gave the instruction was or was not a first class man on his job, he did not know "how to put it over." He may have known his own game, but he did not know the instructing game."[1]

A major objective of the TWI programs was to create programs that would be universally accepted and valued across the country. That meant they had to be successful in well-run plants, plants that contained much confusion, and in large or small organizations. The programs had to work for all types of employees: experienced and inexperienced, older and younger, male and female, production and office.

The developers understood that the TWI trainer should have a deep understanding of TWI programs to deliver the programs effectively to industry. That understanding would come, in part, by knowing why certain information was included and/or excluded. It would not be possible for the *master trainer or institute conductor*, who conducted the "train the trainer" sessions, to convey all the relevant ideas to prospective TWI trainers during these sessions. However, as prospective trainees became more familiar with the material, they would ask questions to increase their understanding. (We will discuss "train the trainer" sessions, called "Institutes," later in the chapter.)

Explaining the how and why behind the development of the TWI programs can shed much light on the structure of the material which can provide the necessary understanding at the outset to improve presentations and more importantly provide better trainee learning. The purpose of this chapter and chapters 6, 7, and 8 is to accelerate this understanding, as well as show why these development procedures enabled TWI to create timeless and universal programs for such a wide variety of organizations. Before discussing in detail the JI program, we will cover some of the specific methods TWI used in creating all of the TWI programs.

Procedure for Creating a TWI Program

As discussed in Chapter 2, the developers spent the first year exploring content, techniques, and training methods and concluded that consulting or disseminating of information was not sufficient for helping industry address the challenge of quickly training workers and increasing production. Through experience, they discovered that just telling people "what" to do was not sufficient; it was important to create a cohesive program to tell them *how* to do it.

When confronted with the first definitive challenge with the lens grinders, TWI's solution was to create a training program for job instruction or "how to break in a new person." The developers devised try-out sessions for various programs. They would follow up with revisions, which led to a cycle of try-out, evaluation, and revision. The developers would never accept programs "as is, except for a small change," because they would never know what effect that "small change" would have on a presentation. This meant that the cycle of try-out, evaluation, and revision would repeat until the evaluation did not prompt them to make any more revisions. Of course, being in an emergency, the TWI Service had a ready-made laboratory, delivering programs to 16,000 companies over a 5-year period that gave them an opportunity to distill many ideas into succinct programs. The general procedure for creating a program was as follows:[2]

1. *Drafting the program.* One individual would be selected to draft the program, which the group would review. Note that in addition to possessing competence in a field, this person had to have the ability to view problems with an open mind and be willing to accept new ideas since many people would have input to the final product.

2. *Submit trial to training groups.* When the group arrived at a point where they believed they had a final version, they would submit it to trial-training groups. They needed more than one group because they wanted to see the effect of variety in both the trainers and the participants. For example, an experienced trainer might make any material successful, while an inexperienced one might get good results with only particular material. The same was true for the participants: Both experienced and new supervisors must accept and gain from the programs.

3. *Evaluation.* Evaluation of the programs was based on "suitability of content, effectiveness of techniques and methods, and checking the results against the problem which was identified or the objective which was to be met."

4. *Program try-outs.* Most program try-outs had two observers present. One was from the TWI development group and one was from the

plant's staff. The observers did not comment during the session, but evaluated how effectively the material was being presented.

5. *Revisions.* "The steps of revision, try-outs, and evaluation were repeated until the group accepted the training session outlines exactly as used.

Through this process evolved the three "J" programs. Even though the developers went through many trial presentations with numerous evaluations and revisions to create these programs, they knew that improvements were still possible, especially once they received feedback from the *field instructors (trainers).* To allow for improvements while at the same time preserving the quality of the programs, the developers used a revision procedure once they released a program to the field. If a field instructor had an idea for a change in the program, he or she would first discuss it with the district *headquarters field representative.* Each of the 22 districts had a headquarters field representative who had contact with the field instructors. If the headquarters field representative thought that the idea had merit and was new, he or she would send it to the *associate director* of the headquarters development group. The associate director would arrange for try-outs using the same procedure that was used for the initial programs.[3] Although not stated in the report, it would become the tradition of TWI to explain to the person making the suggestion why an idea was not accepted. The answer could be as simple as, "This is a good technique, but we believe that all trainers would not be able to do it effectively."

Three Objectives for Each "J" Program

The word *job* has a very specific purpose and meaning in the three "J' programs. The developers knew that the material had to be fundamental and simple and be applicable for everyday use by employees. TWI wanted people to know and understand that they designed these programs for the "job level," were pragmatic, and easy to use.

"This was a very important factor in determining the content of the programs and outlining the whole approach. For that reason, each of the programs carries the word "Job" in its name as a promise to plants and a reminder to training people of this down-to-earth philosophy."[4]

The developers agreed that for TWI to achieve its objects, the TWI trainers would have three objectives for all TWI programs:

1. To interest people in learning the method
2. To help them learn the method
3. To get them to *want* to learn the method[5]

One might think that TWI would have given the TWI trainer a great deal of latitude for succeeding in delivery of these three objectives, but it soon became apparent that to achieve these three objectives, the TWI trainers had to deliver the TWI method as it appeared in the manual. Therefore, as discussed in Chapter 4, constraints were included that prevented the TWI trainer from straying too far from the manual, though he or she could add a few anecdotes or other information to enhance the material. However, any material deleted from the manual tended to decrease the effectiveness of the program. To achieve the three objectives, the developers created five common points for each of the three "J" programs:

1. *Show why the programs worked.* The trainer gave the participant the reasons and the advantages of using the program and why it worked. This way, the TWI trainer would get the participants interested in learning the program's 4-Step Method before even presenting it.
2. *Help participants apply their understanding of the programs.* The TWI trainers would work on getting the participants' involved in the programs by helping them apply their new understanding of the TWI principles.
3. *Provide group problem-solving activities.* The trainer and participants would select a problem and the group would work on it together.
4. *Provide individual problem-solving activities.* The trainer would ask each participant to work on another problem individually.
5. *Provide positive feedback.* The trainer gave credit for good results and good effort.

The TWI trainer covered the first three points in the first sessions, which were referred to as the "famous firsts." It was important to sell the participants on the method so they would be more apt to use it. The trainer accomplished selling points 1–3 by showing the participants that their habits were like those of other people in similar positions and they were not particularly effective. Then the TWI trainer used points 4 and 5 to show them as well as to engage them in another proven method that provided better results.

Finally, as discussed in Chapter 4, the TWI developers used the scientific method to develop the 4-Step Method of 1) collecting facts, 2) analyzing them, 3) making a decision, and 4) checking or following up on the decision when putting these programs together. (*Note:* when referring to the 4-Step Method, I will designate if it is for JI, JM, JR, or PD, e.g., JI 4-Step Method.)

We will now look at the circumstances that helped create all four TWI programs. We will cover the Job Instruction Program in this chapter and Job Relations, Job Methods, and Program Development in Chapter 6, 7, and 8, respectively. Because of the different terminology between this book and the

TWI manuals, as well as the subtle differences in terminology and roles between programs, I have provided Table 5-1 to help define the various roles in TWI training and Table 5-2 to define the participants participating in a specific program.

Table 5-1. Defining Roles of the Trainer and Participants

	Key to Identify Roles in TWI Training	
	Role	**Responsibility**
1	Master Trainer or Institute Conductor	Conducts the "train the trainer" sessions (trains the trainer) in the TWI programs and in the TWI method. These training sessions are called Institutes. The trained participants then return to their organizations and train the selected employees in TWI.
2	TWI Trainer or Trainer	Conducts one of the four TWI programs to teach participants, supervisors, or employees the TWI method. The trainer teaches TWI.
3	Participant/Supervisor/Trainees	The person being trained in the TWI method by the TWI trainer.
4	Instructor	For the JI program, this is the trained participant or supervisor that instructs (trains) employees in a job at his or her workplace. The instructor teaches the specific "job" not the TWI JI method.
5	Training Director	In PD, training directors are the people responsible for solving production problems, specifically by creating and directing training programs at their workplace.
6	Workers or Employees	People at the workplace that the instructor is training.
Note: Supervisors can also mean manager, director, team leader, VP, etc.		

Table 5-2. Defining What Participants Are Taking What TWI Programs

Key to Identify Participants Taking the TWI Program	
TWI Program	**Participants Taking Program**
Job Instruction	Anyone who instructs another person in how to do a job, usually this is a supervisor or experienced employee.
Job Method	Supervisors or any designated employee.
Job Relations	Anyone whose job responsibility includes reaching objectives that are dependent on the efforts of other people, especially any level supervisors and union officers.
Program Development	Individual (supervisor) with assigned functional responsibility for identifying production problems and for planning training to meet those needs.
Note: TWI defines a "supervisor" as anyone who directs the work of others. This can include manager, director, team leader, VP, etc.	

Developing the Job Instruction Program

Throughout the summer of 1940, there were many discussions about the lack of skilled workers. As soon as Dooley & Deitz arrived in Washington, they were given their first challenge: Government arsenals and navy yards needed a total of 350 properly qualified lens grinders as quickly as possible. The problem was that it took about 5 years to master the art of lens grinding.[6] The directors called together representatives from several national companies, who had a special interest in this problem. These were:

1. Sperry Gyroscope Corporation
2. Leeds & Northrop
3. Bausch & Lomb
4. General Electric Company
5. Eastman Kodak Company
6. American Telephone & Telegraph Company

It was agreed that TWI could borrow M.J. Kane from AT&T, who had been a member of the group that had trained shipbuilders during World War I (WWI), to head the project by visiting plants and collecting data to review the situation. When the developers studied the lens-grinding process, they identified that it actually consisted of 20 jobs (see Exhibit 5-1).[7]

Exhibit 5-1. Skills Required for a Qualified Lens-Grinder

Twenty Skills Required of a Fully Competent Lens-Grinder

1. Cut Optical Glass	11. Etching
2. Grind Lenses	12. Etching (General)
3. Grind Prisms	13. Polishing (Prisms Blocks)
4. Grind Reticles	14. Polishing Small Lenses
5. Grind Windows or Covers	15. Polishing Large Lenses
6. Correct Prisms for Polish	16. Polishing Repairs
7. Blocking Prisms	17. Centering
8. Blocking Reticles	18. Cementing (Lens)
9. Silvering (Ordinary)	19. Cementing (Ocular Prisms)
10. Silvering (Oculars & Cutting)	20. Roof Prisms (Correction)

The developers first broke the 20 jobs down into various types of processes and then the processes into operations. Thus, grinding a prism (the process) is one of the skills required of a fully competent lens grinder, and grinding a prism consists of 14 operations. One of those operations is grinding two 90° angles, which consists of six steps (see Exhibit 5-2).[8] Therefore, although it would take years to learn the entire skill set of a fully competent lens grinder, it would take a much shorter time (perhaps a day or two) for someone to learn the six steps of grinding two 90° angles onto a prism.

Exhibit 5-2. One Operation for Grinding Two 90 Degree Angles

Production of the M-1 Circle Aiming Instrument
(Consisting of Poro Lenses, Lenses and Reticles)

PROCESS

1. Cut Glass
2. Block Lenses for Grinding
3. Grind Lenses
4. Edge-grind Reticles
5. **Grind Poro Prisms**
6. Grind Compass Covers
7. Block Prisms for Polishing
8. Block Reticles for Polishing
9. Block Lenses for Finish Grinding
10. Block Polishing (Prisms and Reticles)
11. Etching Reticles
12. Lens Polishing
13. Lens Centering
14. Cementing Lenses

OPERATIONS FOR ITEM #5: GRIND PORO PRISMS

1. Grind one side (individually by hand)
2. Block on plano tool preparatory to grinding for thickness
3. Grind to thickness
4. Remove and clean
5. Block prisms for grinding 90° angles
6. **Grind two 90° angles**
7. Block for hypothenuse grinding
8. Grind hypothenuse
9. Grind top bevel
10. Grind ends to size
11. Rough radius (lathe)
12. Fit by hand to gauge
13. Bevel
14. Hand Correction

STEPS FOR OPERATION #6: GRIND TWO 90° ANGLES

Steps	*Key Points*
a. Select wax for the job	1. Be sure seating is good (air bubbles)
b. Using wax, group several prisms into a block about 3" in length	2. To save production time, work on all errors in rotation, reducing each gradually
c. Identify and clean one side to use as a base in squaring	3. Even distribution of pressure to insure that the four corners are bearing.
d. Use square (rough) on two lengths and index	4. Pulling and wheel direction
e. Select and mark error on two lengths	5. Count – turn – count – turn, etc. until ready to square
f. Grind on wheel to an accurate surface	

In addition, the developers recognized that the order of operations for learning should not necessarily be the same order for production. The operation "grind one side of a lens" is easier to learn than "grinding to thickness," and therefore the developers determined it should be learned first even though the operations are different in the order of production (see Table 5-3).[9]

Table 5-3. Sequence for Production vs. Sequence for Learning

PORO PRISMS	
Sequence in Which Work Must Be Done *(For Production)*	*Sequence for Upgrading* *(For Learning)*
1. Grind one side (individually by hand)	1. Grind one side (individually by hand)
2. Block on plano tool preparatory to grinding for thickness	4. Remove and clean
3. Grind to thickness	2. Block on plano tool preparatory to grinding for thickness
4. Remove and clean	7. Block for hypothenuse grinding
5. Block prisms for grinding 90° angles	5. Block prisms for grinding 90° angles
6. Grind two 90° angles	13. Bevel
7. Block for hypothenuse grinding	3. Grind to thickness
8. Grind hypothenuse	8. Grind hypothenuse
9. Grind top bevel	9. Grind top bevel
10. Grind ends to size	10. Grind ends to size
11. Rough radius (lathe)	6. Grind two 90° angles
12. Fit by hand to gauge	11. Rough radius (lathe)
13. Bevel	12. Fit by hand to gauge
14. Hand Correction	14. Hand Correction

Although the developers did not simplify the job, they did break it down into its component parts so that it would be easier for someone to learn. The developers decided that experienced lens-grinders should do this "break down" since they knew the complete job. To capture the actual work in every step, TWI asked the experienced lens-grinders to note other best practices that enabled them to perform certain operations. For example, there are six steps in the Operation "Grind Two 90° Surfaces," but a person would need to know that they need to remove air bubbles from beneath the prism so that it seats well on the wax. Experienced lens grinders learned through trial and error that it was faster to "work on all errors in rotation" at the same time and that one must put "an even pressure distribution on the prism so that all four corners will equally bear the load." These "tricks of the trade" enabled them to achieve their productivity because they knew not just *what* to do but also *how* to do it. Furthermore, knowing *why* it should be done in a particular way helped them remember how to do it.

Combining Key Points With the JI 4-Step Method

The "*how*" became known as "Key Points" and a component of Job Instruction that took training to a higher level. Most every type of instruction includes telling people "what" to do, but not "why." Although employees may do their best to mimic or copy the instructor's actions, variations in jobs occur, and merely *copying* motions can lead to problems. Furthermore, there are many times when the instructor does something he or she is not even aware of. This occurs when someone knows a job so well that they don't even think about what they are doing. Alternately, they may *think* they know the job, but when they try to explain it, they realize they don't know it as well as they thought they did. These are *actions* that are not immediately obvious and that separate experienced workers from inexperienced ones. These particular actions are *Key Points* and fall into three categories. They are actions that:

1. Make the job easier to do,
2. Are critical to the success or failure of the job, or
3. Might prevent injury to the worker.

An operation step tells a person *what* to do, but a Key Point tells him *how* to do it. There is always a reason for a Key Point and thus the instructor must state *why* the worker should be doing it. This not only increases understanding of the job but also leads to better retention. When the trainer uses the Key Points along with a program's 4-Step Method, the participant will almost surely perform the task correctly the first time by himself. We will discuss Key Points in Chapter 9.

We already discussed the alternate JI steps in Chapter 4 (Exhibit 4-1) and how Charles R. Allen & Michael J. Kane developed the 4-Step Method. This method can be traced back even further to Johann Freidrich Herbart (1776–1841), a German educator and philosopher. He stressed the importance of creating and maintaining a student's interest and cited four steps in teaching:

1. Present the information to the student.
2. Help the student analyze the new material and compare and contrast it with ideas they have already learned.
3. Develop a new rule or principle.
4. Help the student to apply the new information or the new rule to solve another problem.[10]

Charles R. Allen was a vocational instructor under the Massachusetts State Board of Education before WWI, and during WWI, when he was the head of the group that set up the shipbuilding training, he took these four instruction steps and succinctly stated them as:

1. Preparation
2. Presentation
3. Application
4. Inspection (or Test)

Allen's four steps of instruction were published in various forms. In 1940 M.J. Kane took the concept of Allen's four steps and combined it with the concept of Key Points, fashioning the following TWI seven-step instruction:

1. Show him how to do it.
2. Explain Key Points (how and why).
3. Let him watch you do it again.
4. Let him do the simple parts of the job.
5. Help him do the whole job.
6. Let him do the whole job—but watch him.
7. Put him on his own.

In November 1940, these steps, along with the "Key Point" concept, were incorporated in a bulletin, "How To Instruct a Man on a New Job (see Bulletin 19)."[11] This was the program TWI ultimately used to train people to be lens-grinders.

> "As a result of this work, the training of people for the separate jobs involved in lens-grinding was reduced from approximately five years to a matter of [4–6] months."[12]

TWI issued the bulletin "How to Prepare Instructors to Give Intensive Job Instruction" (see Bulletin 7) in December 1940 when TWI had all the basic knowledge for JI but had not yet perfected the method. The bulletin includes information on *what* to do, but after reading it, one might not be sure of *how* to do it. A comparison of that document with the final JI program should give the reader a good understanding of the difference between "education" and "training" cited earlier. Even today, participants in many excellent contemporary training programs struggle with implementation–the *how* to do it aspect.

Later the TWI developers refined the M. J. Kane seven steps to four and created a training card (reminder card) for the JI 4-Step Method that covered "how to get ready to instruct" and "how to instruct." Exhibit 5-3 introduces the two-sided training card for the reader to see at-a-glance the JI-4 step method. Chapter 9 discusses the contents of the JI training card in more detail.

Exhibit 5-3. JI 4-Step Method Training Card*

How to Get Ready to Instruct	**How to Instruct**
Have a timetable— How much skill you expect to have, by what date Break down the job— List important steps Pick out key points (Safety is always a key point) Have everything ready— The right equipment, material, and supplies Have the workplace properly arranged— Just as the worker will be expected to keep it ─────────── Job Instruction Training TRAINING WITHIN INDUSTRY Bureau of Training War Manpower Commission ─────────── KEEP THIS CARD HANDY	Step 1—Prepare the worker • Put him at ease. • State the job and find out what he already knows about it. • Get him interested in learning the job. • Place in a correct position. Step 2—Present the operation • Tell, show, and illustrate one IMPORTANT STEP at a time. • Stress each KEY POINT • Instruct clearly, completely, and patiently, but no more than he can muster. Step 3—Try out performance • Have him do the job—correct errors • Have him explain each KEY POINT to you as he does the job again. • Make sure he understands. • Continue until YOU know HE knows. Step 4—Follow up • Put him on his own. Designate to whom he goes for help. • Check frequently. Encourage questions. • Taper off extra coaching and close follow up. ─────────── If the worker hasn't learned, the instructor hasn't taught.

*Dietz, *Learn by Doing*, p. 16.

Dilution of a Job

Critical to the success of JI was a concept known as *dilution* of a job. The term "dilution" caused some confusion since some people believed that a diluted job meant one with a lower skill level. Actually, "dilution" or what we today call "specialization," merely meant reducing the number of the required skills, while leaving the remaining skills at the same level. This concept was discussed in J.C. Furnas' article, "Battle for Skills" which appeared in the May 10, 1941 issue of the *Saturday Evening Post*.

> "The all-around master mechanic—as scarce these days as a hotel room in defense boom Washington—went through years of apprenticeship and years more in a shop to become virtuoso on a turret lathe, a milling machine, a boring mill and twenty other gigantic gadgets. He knows what makes them tick and, in a pinch, could both repair and build them. He is indispensable and any nation with an ample supply of him owns a military asset equal to Napoleon and Alexander the Great rolled into one. In the present emergency, however, it is wasteful to keep him on machine jobs in any plant that will adapt itself to upgrading as most plants will. His spot is supervising the work of men not quite so good as he is.
>
> "So he is firmly escorted upstairs–"upgraded," in fact. The places left vacant by the upgrading of the Grade-B mechanics who take over from him are filled by a crowd of single-skill youngsters – boys who look like likely candidates for eight to twelve weeks of intensive training in handling one kind of machine. When the objective is not all-around training but single-skill competence, it is surprising to see how rapidly those weeks enable a green but apt youngster to turn out respectable work with a riveter or a welding torch or a grinding gadget. It is unorthodox in many industries. But it is the only way to boom a plant from 300 men to 3000 inside a year. And it seems to be working in most places."[13]

Breaking down a job into its component parts was a different, radical way of thinking, so the TWI Service had to clarify the concept. Just saying that training people in individual skills would allow more people to be useful faster apparently did not work. The developers believed that if a person has several skills and uses only one of them all the time, the other skills are wasted. In an "emergency" it is not appropriate to waste resources. So it was important for a worker to do a job requiring all of his or her skills and if not, the worker should be replaced by another worker that had just the required skill for that particular job.

"Using a man with wide skills on a production job which requires only one or two skills is a waste of skills. Often the single-skill operator can perform more quickly and more accurately his one operation than can the all-around craftsman. Skill therefore is not diluted, and misunderstandings are saved when people talk about "engineering a job" and developing specialists rather than about "dilution."[14]

This didn't mean that a worker should learn only one skill and stay static for the rest of his or her life. It meant not wasting anyone's skills in order to make the best use of the workforce at hand. When the Job Relations Program was later developed, TWI further explained the concept this way:

"Make best use of each person's ability. Look for ability not now being used."

The developers intended for the supervisors to keep track of their employees' skills to determine who knew the various jobs in the department, who should be trained, and when they should be trained to optimize production.

"This idea had been inherent in the program from the beginning, but again, too much had been assumed about what the supervisors would just naturally do."[15]

To make this intent explicit, TWI added a timetable to the program so that supervisors would have a plan of when their employees needed training based on production requirements (see Table 5-4 for an example).[16]

Table 5-4. Job Instruction Timetable

Simple Job Instruction Timetable							
	Drill	Bore	Ream	Race	Taper Turn	Burr & Burnish	Etc.	Etc.
White	✔	✔	✔	✔	✔	✔		
Nolan	✔	✔	✔	11-10	—	—		
Smith	11-1	11-20	—	✔	✔	12-1		
Jones	—	—	✔	11-15	12-1	12-8		
Etc.								

✔ means the worker can already do the job.
— means the worker doesn't need to know the job.
11-1, 11-15, etc., indicates the dates the supervisor has set to have workers TRAINED to do the jobs required.

Job Instruction in New Jersey—The 10-Hour Course

In the spring of 1941, the New Jersey District group met and developed a 10-hour course in "How to Instruct" based on Allen's 4-step procedure. They created a rough outline of the course and included a training demonstration, using different techniques to teach participants (future instructors) how to tie the fire underwriter's knot to make the point that there is a proper way to instruct workers. (Additional information on the fire underwriter's knot is in Chapter 9) The New Jersey Vocational Education Staff had used this demonstration for many years and it was thought to be "both the most dramatic and the most practical."[17]

The group broke down the 10 hours into five 2-hour sessions using 40 *vocational instructors* paid by the federal government who were free for the summer months. Since the Extension Department of Rutgers and the NJ State Department of Vocational Education had also been offering instructor training courses, all three programs were combined into one program so that all organizations would be offering the same course.[18]

The first group of ten participants was instructed at American Steel Castings Company in Newark. The instructor was a professional trainer and trained without the benefit of any written material. The company was pleased with the first group and made a request to have all of its supervisors trained. The TWI panel convened to discuss the results and came up with the following changes:

- The demonstration could be limited to the first session, which would leave the remaining four sessions for practice.
- The demonstration included the "correct" way to train and the "incorrect" way to train. It was decided that the "incorrect" way should be shown first.
- Job breakdowns were done in two columns: "Do" and "Know" rather than "Steps" and "Key Points."
- A slogan "If the worker hasn't learned, the teacher hasn't taught" was adopted.[19]

The purpose of the slogan was to emphasize the supervisor's responsibility in getting employees productive as quickly as possible. This is a controversial statement because it does seem to put all the responsibility on the supervisor. The underlying assumption is that the employee wants to be productive and thus will be exerting necessary effort to do so. It also assumes that the employee has the capability to understand the job in question. Usually, these assumptions are valid. Within a month of the first program, industries in New Jersey were asking to have their own employees trained to offer the course. It was soon apparent that this would not be just a summertime event, and additional trainers had to be found.

Job Instruction Goes National

In August TWI district leaders met in Washington and decided to move away from consulting and bulletins and instead offer New Jersey's job instruction program nationally. TWI listed four requirements for the national JI program:

1. The program should be simple.
2. It must have a set outline, utilizing a minimum of time.
3. It must be built on the principle of demonstration and practice of "learning by doing" rather than on theory.
4. It should use the multiplier effect so that the training can be spread as quickly as possible.[20]

The New Jersey group had used their program successfully in 70 plants, so TWI felt confident in adopting it immediately. But because the New Jersey program had used professional trainers, the materials were only in brief outline and needed further development. Also, TWI didn't want to lose the concept of Key Points, so the developers combined M.J. Kane's 7-step instruction method with another 4-step method developed by Glenn Gardiner, who wrote most of the New Jersey program. This then became the basis of instruction for the national JI program. To make it acceptable to inexperienced trainers, TWI created a detailed manual that delayed the launching of the program until November 1941. By January 1942, TWI had certified enough people to collect data. Table 5-5 shows how the cumulative numbers of people certified in Job Instruction grew throughout the years.[21]

As TWI was spreading JI nationally, the people selling it used whatever tools they could find to describe the program. The Los Angeles district created

Table 5-5. Cumulative Number of People Certified in JI

Job Instruction Certifications					
Quarter ending	Per quarter	Cumulative	Quarter ending	Per quarter	Cumulative
Jan. 1, 1942	15,767	15,767	Jan. 1, 1944	82,565	767,892
April 1, 1942	32,874	48,641	April 1, 1944	64,892	832,784
July 1, 1942	76,365	125,006	July 1, 1994	52,565	885,349
Oct. 1, 1942	93,730	218,736	Oct. 1, 1944	32,404	917,753
Jan. 1, 1943	147,028	365,764	Jan. 1, 1944	27,614	945,367
April 1, 1943	107,113	472,877	April 1, 1945	25,773	971,140
July 1, 1943	119,983	592,860	July 1, 1945	20,978	992,118
Oct. 1, 1943	92,467	685,327	Oct. 1, 1945	13,752	1,005,870

a checklist that a company could use to determine the quality of their instruction (see Exhibit 5-4).[22] (I added questions #14 and #15.) A discussion of these questions leads one to think about how instruction is conducted in their organization and may then lead to the conclusion that JI training is needed. This checklist could be used today for the same purpose.

Improving Job Breakdowns

TWI launched the program in 1941 and modified it several times until 1944. A major change occurred in 1942 because of problems with job breakdowns (the listing of the important steps and Key Points in a job). TWI knew that the instructor had to be prepared before beginning to instruct and, in 1941, had included three "Get Ready" items in the programs:

1. Decide what the worker must be taught in order to do the job efficiently, safely, economically, and intelligently.
2. Have the right tools, equipment, supplies, and materials ready.
3. Have the workplace properly arranged, just as the worker will be expected to keep it.

As it turns out, job breakdowns are probably the most important and the most difficult concept to get across to most people when they see the program. The New Jersey program recognized its importance and made the participants aware of this challenge in the training groups but did not take any official action to remedy it. After the national program was out for several months, TWI determined that it needed to add the "Break Down the Job" to the "Get Ready" points and thus it became an official part of the program.

After TWI specifically added the Job Breakdowns to the program, TWI further determined that the standard presentation of how to do a "breakdown" using a blackboard was insufficient. The heart of Job Instruction is "learning by doing;" and at this point, participants learned job breakdowns by trial and error. Thus, each institute conductor was required to assemble a kit of tools and materials so at least 13 sample jobs could be broken down. The institute conductors would first break down these jobs, then their trainers would practice breaking them down, and then a discussion would ensue. This discussion helped the trainers formulate a better idea of what constituted a good breakdown, since you can break down a job in more than one way. TWI determined that job breakdowns were the weakest part of the program, so they directed all of the institute conductors to call in all existing trainers to take this remedial training.[23] Although other refinements were made, job breakdowns were the last major change to the JI program.

Exhibit 5-4. Quality Job Instruction Checklist

Job Instruction Checklist

1. Do you "break down" the job you are showing into simple, easy steps, and show the easiest things first?

2. Do you give a general picture of the whole job, before starting off on some small part of it?

3. Do you tell them what they should know clearly and simply?

4. If the person you are training repeats the same mistakes, are you sure it is not your fault because you did not explain how to do it so the person understands it?

5. Do you make sure the person understands the words you use in explaining certain jobs—especially the "terms of the trade" that are new?

6. Do you know, and tell the person, exactly how many different operations there are to the job?

7. Do you impress the need for accuracy first and speed later?

8. What do you do to keep the person interested in learning more about the work?

9. Do you encourage the person if progress is satisfactory or rapid?

10. Do you ever get angry with the person, or think they are "dumb" because they do not know as much about it as you do?

11. Are you sure the worker feels perfectly free to ask you any and all questions that come to mind?

12. Do you point out the harmful results of the person's mistakes and *why* they happened?

13. What do you do about problems like these, which a trainee can encounter?
    a. Getting the one or two tricky points, or "knacks" of the job.
    b. Trying to get the "feel" of the whole operation.
    c. Understanding *why* certain things must be done in certain ways, or done "just so."
    d. Breaking old work habits, or wrong work habits.
    e. Catching on to a new or extra tough problem.
    f. Getting speed with ease.

14. Do you specify what parts of the job affect safety?

15. Do you give the person more information than can be absorbed at one time?

16. Do you think carrying out the best answers to these questions would help you do a better and faster job of training?

17. Do you think a few hours of training along these lines—that is, in learning how to put ideas over more easily—would help in doing a better job of it?

Three Situations Supervisors Might Confront When Training Workers

Many supervisors who were trained were very inexperienced and the likelihood was that once they left the JI training program they would not be prepared for the kind of problems they would face at their companies.[24] TWI added references at the end of the manual to deal with three situations that they might encounter. These were:

1. *Handling very long operations.* How does one instruct someone in a job that might take 6 hours or more to do?
2. *Handling a noisy environment.* How do you instruct someone in a noisy environment when ear protection is required and you cannot easily talk with the trainee?
3. *Explaining a feel for the work.* How do you convey the "feeling" of tightening a micrometer on a work piece? If it's too tight or too loose, the measurement will be incorrect.[25]

These three situations are explained in Chapter 9. The training's effectiveness was further hampered by the tendency of workers to imitate the motions of the instructor (supervisor) instead of really understanding the reason why they had to do it that way. TWI corrected this tendency by having the worker explain to the instructor what he or she was doing, how they were doing it, and why it was done that way the first time they practiced the job.[26] That is, they would repeat the job step (*what*), the Key Point (*how*) if there was one, and the reason (*why*) for the Key Point.

The Importance of Institutes—Train the Trainers Sessions

A premise for the TWI programs was to spread the training through a multiplier effect of *training the trainers.*[27] An extremely important step in that direction was having an institute conductor hold "train the trainer" sessions called "Institutes." Initially, the trainers merely received a demonstration of the material they were required to cover and practiced how to put a group at ease and how to get group members to talk and participate actively. The first two Job Instruction Institutes were scheduled for three 6-hour days and had a total of 25 participants. Two separate but similar Institutes were held instead, because it was felt that 25 people would be too many for one group. By the fourth Institute, TWI broke down the hours as follows:

- First 10 hours: the JI Program was presented
- Next 2 hours: questions about the duties of the trainers
- Next 5 hours: practice in opening the first session

- Last hour: discussion of how to handle a group of this [nature][28]

The TWI developers made gradual changes to the Institutes and by 1944 they required prospective trainers to attend a 10-hour session first, to experience the program and become certified. Only after they were familiar with the program would they attend a 40-hour Institute. The 40 hours consisted of the following:

- The first 1½ days: drill on timetable, job breakdown, instruction according to the 4-steps
- The last 3½ days: drill of actually putting on the 10-hour program

In addition to drilling the trainers in what to do and say during a training session, TWI found that it was also necessary to tell them the reasons for these actions—i.e., the *why* or the strategy behind the content.[29] This concept is used in the JI program (Key Points) and also valid for train-the-trainer sessions. Note that after the first day and a half, the Institute conductor could tell whether the participant was considered good enough to be a trainer and some men [and women] were dropped at this stage.[30] As mentioned, a TWI trainer must know the program like a director of a play and deliver it like an actor. In addition, the actor has a stage director who gives feedback so that as he or she practices (rehearses) he or she continues to improve. Without feedback there is no learning.

Knowing a TWI program as thorough as the director analogy above was not usually possible with only the initial 50 hours of training. The person spent the first 10 hours as a participant in a "J" program. Once a person left that session, he/she should be capable of using the respective method. The goal was that after a trainer completed a 40-hour Institute, the person would be able to adequately deliver the "J" program in question. The TWI developers realized that these 50 hours were not sufficient to create proficient trainers all the time. To fine-tune their delivery, TWI increased the Institutes to 2 weeks. The prospective trainer spent the first week in group work and the second week practicing under observation and coaching. The developers realized that in order to achieve the required proficiency, the trainers needed feedback, which required their coaching. (I believe that the observation and coaching would be best done by delivering four 10-hour sessions under the observation of a Master Trainer.) Because TWI recognized that training delivery is skill-based, the trainer had to put on at least one program every 90 days to remain qualified.[31]

TWI developed the JI program with the intent of instructing workers in how to do a specific job in a shop environment. If the job were complicated or long, it would be broken down into smaller parts so that workers could easily digest it. TWI quickly realized that they could use JI for clerical jobs. As the above discussion of the Institutes shows, you can apply the principles of JI anytime you are trying to show someone how to do something. That "something" could be drilling a hole in a piece of wood, shooting a basketball, writing a business letter, or solving a math problem. People show other people how to do things almost every day, which is why JI can be used every day. When you use the JI method to teach someone how to do something, the person is more likely to absorb the material faster, retain it better, and (if applicable) do it more safely.

We will now move on to discuss the development of the second TWI Program, Job Relations.

---

1. Allen, Charles R., *The Instructor, The Man, and The Job*, J.B. Lippencott, Philadelphia, 1919, p. 361. (as seen in *TWI Report*, p. 189).
2. *TWI Report*, pp. 179–182.
3. *TWI Report*, p. 165.
4. *TWI Report*, p. 178.
5. *TWI Report*, p. 165.
6. *TWI Report*, p. 18.
7. *TWI Report*, p. 271.
8. *TWI Report*, pp. 272, 273, 275.
9. *TWI Report*, p. 273.
10. *Worldbook Encyclopedia*, vol. 9, p. 198.
11. *TWI Report*, p. 19.
12. *TWI Report*, p. 20.
13. *TWI Report*, pp. 25–26.
14. *TWI Report*, p. 27. Note also the use of the concept of "waste," which is central to Lean Thinking. Waste of employees' skills is sometimes referred to as the eighth waste cited in Lean literature.
15. *TWI Report*, p. 199.
16. *TWI Report*, p. 200.
17. *TWI Report*, p. 192.
18. TWI initially thought that they'd put the programs on during the summer and be done with it. They found out there was a large demand and so had to hire additional trainers and continue the program after the summer sessions ended.
19. *TWI Report*, p. 193.
20. *TWI Report*, p. 32.
21. *TWI Report*, p. 35.
22. *TWI Report*, p. 191 (plus additions #14 & #15).

23. *TWI Report*, p. 200. Even today, it is highly recommended that additional practice doing job breakdowns be done after the 10 hours of training. The group is encouraged to join together in twos or threes and continue making job breakdowns until they feel comfortable with the process. It could be a formal assignment where the groups are tasked to breakdown each job in the department.

24. Most of the people who received TWI training in the '40s were first-line supervisors. They were responsible for direct workers. Note that I used the term "most" not "all." Also, many were inexperienced supervisors so they had not encountered all the problems that typically occur. Thus, they didn't know what questions to ask when they were in class. One question might be: "Everyone in our department wears hearing protection, so how am I supposed to teach him a job?"

25. *TWI Report*, p. 197.

26. *TWI Report*, p. 199.

27. A participant in a TWI program could be a worker or a supervisor or a manager—I even had a VP once. These people would be taking the course so that they would use it directly. A "future trainer" would be a participant in an Institute. In that case the person would be someone who would intend to go back to their workplace and then put on training sessions for employees in their organization. If the organization is small, this person could be a worker who puts on a TWI session once a quarter. If the organization is larger, the person could be a full time trainer—maybe a training director. This is the multiplier effect and the reason that the training was able to spread so quickly.

28. *TWI Report*, p. 193.

29. *TWI Report*, p. 187.

30. *TWI Report*, p. 202. Because the training was designed to be used by almost all types of people, I surmise that the main reason some potential trainers were asked to leave the training program is that they did not want to be there. A person's ability is related to his or her desire.

31. *TWI Report*, p. 178.

CHAPTER 6

How TWI Developed the
Job Relations Program

"Good human relations are good business practice."[1]

In the last chapter, we covered the development timeline of the Job Instruction program. We will continue covering the remaining three programs in a similar fashion by looking more closely at the various versions they went through. Aside from documenting a historical record of these programs, the main reason I am highlighting their evolution is to provide trainers and trainees an insight and deeper understanding of them. A thorough understanding is required for optimal delivery and learning because their apparent simplicity masks their power. In addition, it should give the reader an appreciation of the timelessness and universality of these programs.

In January 1941, the National Academy of Sciences received the following request from Sidney Hillman, Commissioner of the Division of Labor in the Advisory Commission to the Council of National Defense: "What can be done to increase knowledge and improve understanding of supervision at the work level?" The National Academy of Sciences sent the request to the National Research Council's Committee on Work in Industry, which made a thorough report. The report stated three problems:

1. Selection of supervisors.
2. Training and development of supervisors.
3. Intensified problems of supervision arising from the emergency situation.

Item 1 was addressed to a degree by the bulletin, "How to Select Supervisors," (Bulletin 17)[2] while Item 3 was later addressed by Program Development (Chapter 8). However, the committee recommended that training be directed toward "improving and accelerating the training of supervisors in handling the human situations under their charge so as to secure maximum cooperation."

Mr. Hillman subsequently asked TWI to come up with an appropriate training program to address this need.[3] TWI conducted a survey among several hundred supervisors and their bosses and found that the biggest weakness among supervisors was in handling personnel relationships. That is, the supervisors seemed to be competent with the technical aspects of their jobs (the hard skills), but were somewhat lacking in the personnel aspects (the soft skills). This was confirmed during plant visits.

Although there were many successful supervisors, when it came to dealing with personnel issues there wasn't any existing training program that provided the basis for their success. Instead, their success was predicated on their innate abilities, opportunities, and particular circumstances and challenges. Unlike an engineer learning engineering principles in school and then applying them at work, successful supervisors or managers usually learn personnel methods on the job through trial and error. Consequently, every supervisor developed a different method to solve personnel issues. No one, however, had formalized his or her method. As a result, many otherwise qualified people avoided or could not enter into management because they were not able to learn personnel fundamentals on their own. Or when people did enter management, they performed at a suboptimum level. Therefore, when it came time to develop a universal program for personnel issues, TWI had to "go back to the drafting board."

Having a background in personnel relations, the staff at TWI believed they knew the content that was necessary, but they were not confident in their ability to develop a method for delivering it. In October 1941, they asked trainers at companies with respected training programs about delivery methods. The replies were all quite similar and usually advised that lectures or conferences were appropriate. However, TWI turned to the success of the Job Instruction Program and decided to borrow that successful format, using the 10-hour program stressing demonstration and practice.

Because there was no preexisting model to follow as with Job Instruction, the JR developers took 2 years to develop the Job Relations program and went through approximately ten versions. The only concept that remained from the first version of the Job Relations program compared to the last was that people are involved in each area of a supervisor's responsibilities and thus people must be taken into account for just about everything a supervisor does. TWI was also cognizant of the many personality types of the supervisors and managers.

> "TWI had to have something which could be passed on and something which would work whether the user was a quick or a slow thinker, had a friendly or less acceptable personality."[4]

Like the evolution of the Job Instruction program, understanding the various versions of the Job Relations Program provides a good example of why organizations need a slow, thoughtful, and thorough approach when making any type of change to TWI's methods.

Ten Versions of the Job Relations Program

This section provides a summary of the development of Job Relations collated from selected items from various versions. Table 6-1[5] shows the timeline of versions. From the initial request in January 1941 to the national launch of the program 25 months later in February 1943, TWI continually proposed, modified, discarded, and finally accepted ideas for the program.

Table 6-1. Ten Versions of the Job Relations Program

Evolution of Job Relations	
Version	**Date**
I	Fall 1941
II	Late 1941 (est.)
III	February 1942
IV	April 1942
V	May 1942
VI	May 1942
VII	August 1942
VIII	October 1942
IX	November 1942
X	December 1942
XI	February 1943, official national launch date

Most versions were successful on their own merits, but the JR developers knew they needed to fine-tune the program so it could work as a national program. Therefore, their development process consisted of many sessions with many trials and many errors.

"Conditions were constantly varied in order to develop material which could be used under differing circumstances. The plants themselves ranged from established units of recognized organizations which were continuing to do the same kind of work as in peacetime, to plants with rapidly expanding staffs being put into production by new companies which had been set up to handle production of materials and equipment developed for current war needs. In the plants, the groups themselves were variously made up of "green" supervisors, experienced supervisors, supervisors of the same organization level, supervisors of different levels (including those who reported to each other), groups of men, groups of women, groups of men and women, groups containing union representatives and groups made up of representatives of more than one company."[6]

Job Relations Program Versions I and II—Fall 1941

In Version I, JR started out as a discussion of case studies of actual job relations problems selected from a variety of plants. The trainer handed out case studies to the participants and then read them aloud. The trainer used three main ideas to guide the discussion:

1. Employees are human beings.
2. They are all individuals.
3. It is important to find out how they feel.[7]

The participants compared and contrasted properly and improperly handled personnel cases to clarify the above points. Later there was additional discussion about the supervisor's relationship to all personnel under his or her supervision. The trainer would also use additional, shorter cases that were of specific interest to a particular group.

Version II did not contain any lengthy problems. TWI gave shorter personnel problems to the participants to take home and prepare comments for the next day's discussion.

Job Relations Program Version III—February 1942

Representatives of seven plants that had used both of the first two versions met in Washington with the TWI staff. The participants had appreciated talking about the case study problems, but they said they had their own personnel problems they wanted to discuss. So TWI asked participants to bring in their own problems. The participant would role-play as the employee and another participant would act as the supervisor. The participants were cautioned to avoid bringing in union problems or problems in which feelings in the plant ran high. Emphasis was placed on "sizing up a situation" and six steps were recommended and put on a "reminder card" (training card).[8]

Size Up Before You Act
1. Look over the situation.
2. Listen for personal slants.

3. Line up the factors in the situation.
4. Weigh the factors.
5. Take action.
6. Follow up.

Job Relations Program Version IV—April 1942

People using Version III met with TWI representatives in Chicago in April. TWI abandoned the role-playing exercise because it made the supervisors uncomfortable. TWI abandoned an attempt at having two supervisors read the parts of a case study because reading it without any preparation caused the point of the case to be lost. TWI created a new JR training card with five new points in an attempt to be more helpful to any organization.

1. Be sure that each person knows what his job is.
2. Be sure that each person understands the basis for his pay.
3. Be sure that each person understands the conditions under which he is working.
4. Make each person feel that he is sharing in the war production effort.
5. Watch for significant changes in each person's output, attitude, or relationships.

Although these were good personnel concepts to know and follow, it was determined that there should be some actual steps listed in order to handle day-to-day problems as they occurred. The developers formulated these and put them on a separate worksheet.

1. Get and consider the facts.
2. Get the employee's viewpoint.
3. Make a decision and take action.
4. Follow up.

The worksheet was used for only one trial session because it made handling a job relations problem too much like paperwork,[9] which the JR developers thought would discourage its use.

Job Relations Program Version V—May 1942

The main change in this version from the other four was that the JR training card now had two sets of items called "foundation points" and four "action points" or steps. The foundation points were:

- Be sure that each person understands what his job is.
- Be sure that each person understands the working conditions.

- Be sure that each person understands what affects his earnings.
- Be sure that people on the team work together.

The four steps were:

1. Find out what is important to the individual and why.
2. Consider the whole background.
3. Make a decision and take action.
4. Follow up and watch for changes.

Job Relations Program Version VI—May 1942

TWI held this meeting in May to make some slight changes to the JR training card. The developers removed one foundation point and changed the wording on the JR 4-Step Method.

- Be sure that each person understands what his job is.
- Be sure that each person understands the working conditions.
- Be sure that each person understands what affects his earnings.

TWI modified the four steps to read:

1. Get the facts about the person.
2. Size up the whole situation.
3. Decide and take action.
4. Follow up.

Job Relations Program Version VII—August 1942

When the TWI Directors met in May to discuss the status of the JR program, there was a "marked difference of opinions." Most members of the group wanted the program to contain rules instead of a method. So they agreed not to release Job Relations [on a national basis] until it had the complete endorsement of TWI Headquarters and until the opinions of some plant managers had been solicited."[10] Accordingly, a group consisting of some of the headquarters staff and industrial representatives gathered in June and came up with the following:

- Reduce the number of problems (case studies) presented by the trainer to three.
- The discussion of the relationships that supervisors have was repeated in the fifth session to emphasize that the JR principles could be broadly applied.

- Set up the outlines for the sessions in "Steps" and "Key Points," two-column style.
- The foundation points and the steps were modified as follows:
  - Remember—everyone wants . . .
    - Recognition as an individual.
    - To know how he is doing.
    - Some "say" about things which affect him.
    - Credit when due.
    - To make the best use of his ability.

The five steps for handling a job relations situation were:

1. Get the facts.
2. Evaluate.
3. Make a decision.
4. Take action.
5. Check results.[11]

Job Relations Program Version VIII—October 1942

The developers tried out Version VII in Chicago and Indianapolis and it was well received, although some changes were required. Step 2 (evaluate) and Step 3 (make a decision) could not easily be separated and it was difficult to determine where the one ended and the other began. So the developers combined these two steps into a single step: *Weigh and Decide.* The developers also added a fourth case study on the effects of change. Since there were now four steps, each of the four case studies could focus on or emphasize an individual step.

The JR developers added an extremely important point, which, in effect, turned the JR program into a model of the scientific 4-Step Method adapted to personnel issues. Before engaging the JR 4-Step Method, the supervisor would now have to formulate and state the objective that he or she was trying to achieve. This changed the emphasis from one of disciplining an employee to that of increasing productivity, making supervisors more focused on their goals and less emotional about personnel decisions. This, in turn, had a tendency to raise morale since any subsequent disciplinary action was more easily justified on productivity terms, making personnel actions more consistent. The developers amended the foundations and steps as follows:

Foundations of good supervision
- Everyday recognition of people as individuals.
- Letting people know how they are getting along.

- Giving people a chance to talk over in advance the things that affect them.
- Giving credit when due.
- Making best use of people's ability.

The four steps of dealing with a personnel situation were:

1. Get the facts.
2. Weigh and decide.
3. Take action.
4. Check results.

"Version VIII was tried out in Baltimore and that version convinced the TWI staff members that a working model had been achieved."[12]

Job Relations Program Version IX—November 1942

Now that a final version was in sight, TWI conducted a training institute to prepare for the national launch of the program. [On] Monday, October 26, a training institute was held in Washington where several TWI field staff members were trained in the current JR program. The following week they each delivered two sessions a day at a wide variety of plants in Philadelphia. Members of the headquarters staff attended each session, observed the activities, and took notes. At the end of the week, all compared notes about the effectiveness of the training. "Special attention was given to the technique of handling the problems brought in by supervisors for practice of the method."[13] The members made only minor changes to the trainers' outlines.

Job Relations Program Version X—December 1942 (Final Version)

TWI released Version X nationally in 1943 which had three main changes from Version IX.

1. *Action items.* The developers thought that the fundamental concepts would have more impact if action statements accompanied them. This goes to the heart of "tell them what to do and then tell then *how* to do it." Thus, the fundamental "Give credit when due" is followed by "Look for extra or unusual performance" and "Tell him while it's 'hot'."
2. *Clarify supervisor–people charts.* TWI expanded and clarified the charts explaining the relationships a supervisor had with other people. A supervisor has daily contact with peers, his or her boss, people at many levels in other departments, and people outside of the organization. Having good relations with all these people will improve the supervisor's performance. The JR program can help the supervisor create good relationships with all of these people.

3. *Describing participant's problems to the group.* This change dealt with how the participant described his or her problem to the group. The participant would first explain the problem and then describe all the facts as he or she knew them. Then, the participant would discuss how he or she had analyzed the facts and had come to a decision. It was determined that the participant should stop immediately before he or she was about to tell the final action, so that further discussion of the problem would not be influenced by that decision.

Exhibit 6-1 shows a JR 4-Step Method training card (reminder card) covering "Foundations for Good Relations" and "Determine the Objective." In Chapter 10, we will discuss the contents of the JR training card in detail.

After all the experimentation with all the versions, the TWI staff had learned much about human relations problem solving. Initially, they had restricted problems to nonunion and noncontroversial ones, but then they reversed that rule and let participants bring in any personnel problem. This was done because one aspect of the training in Step 3 involves the supervisor questioning whether or not it was the supervisor's role to handle these kinds of problems. Is it the supervisor's responsibility and does he or she have the authority? The JR 4-Step Method, therefore, filters out problems the supervisors should not be dealing with. After extensive testing, TWI discovered that this check was sufficient to keep any improper problems out of the sessions.

In the initial JR versions, participants did all the training using case studies brought in by the trainer. The main objective was to have the participants determine what the people in the case studies actually meant by what they said. The main focus was that one had to listen very carefully, ask questions and think about what someone said in order to be successful in personal relations. The trainer did this in a group conversation using an interviewing technique. In addition to being time-consuming, the participants wanted to discuss their own problems. Over time, the number of case studies decreased and the JR 4-Step Method was further refined. TWI then confined the interviewing technique to the first step "Get the facts." As a result, TWI added "Tips for listening" to the program and then replaced it with "How to get opinions and feelings." These tips (discussed more in Chapter 11) are skills that are easy to learn but hard to do. "Don't interrupt" may be the easiest of all to understand, but that alone is a habit many find hard to break.

It cannot be overemphasized that *these programs are skill-based and the 10 hours of instruction and practice are only the initial phase of skill development.* Participants require much practice once they complete the five

Exhibit 6-1. JR 4-Step Method Training Card[14]

JOB RELATIONS	How to Handle
A Supervisor Gets Results through People	**A Job Relations Problem**
	DETERMINE OBJECTIVE
FOUNDATION FOR GOOD RELATIONS	1. GET THE FACTS
	Review the record.
Let each worker know how he is getting along.	Find out what rules and plant customs apply.
Figure out what you can expect from him.	Talk with individuals concerned.
Point out ways to improve.	Get opinions and feelings.
	Be sure you have the whole story.
Give credit where credit is due	2. WEIGH AND DECIDE
Look for extra or unusual performance.	Fit the facts together.
Tell him while "it's hot."	Consider their bearing on each other.
	What possible actions are there?
Tell people in advance about changes that will affect them.	Check practices and policies.
Tell them WHY it is possible.	Consider objective and affect on individual, group and production.
Get them to accept the change.	*Don't jump to conclusions.*
Make the best use of each person's ability.	3. TAKE ACTION
Look for ability not now being used.	Are you going to handle this yourself?
Never stand in a man's way.	Do you need help in handling?
	Should you refer this to your supervisor?
People Must Be Treated As Individuals	Watch the timing of your actions.
	Don't pass the buck.
	4. CHECK RESULTS
JOB RELATIONS TRAINING	How soon will you follow up?
Training Within Industry Service	How often will you need to check?
BUREAU OF TRAINING	Watch for changes in output, attitudes and relationships.
War Manpower Commission	*Did your actions help production?*

sessions. In addition, some present day trainers believe that you should precede the JR program with a 2–4 hour session on communication skills because good communication is such an important aspect of job relations. This is often a reasonable thing to do, but the caution is that you should *add* it to the program and not use it as a substitute for any part of the program. As a result, the training program would take longer than the prescribed 10 hours.

Early versions of JR also included paired problems to show the participant how they *should* and *should not* handle a particular situation. When TWI required that participants each bring in his or her own problem to discuss, it was apparent that there was not enough time for both sets of trainer's problems. As a result, from a learning standpoint, the JR developers decided to keep as a teaching tool the possible "poor handling" of a problem and discard the "good handling" of a problem from the curriculum.

Session 4, on the fourth day of training, emphasizes Step 3, "Take action"; and Step 4, "Check results," of the JR 4-Step Method and focuses on the effects of change in the workplace. The original problem TWI presented to the participants was how to introduce the first African-American mechanic into a department. TWI had successfully used this case study in many plants during the development stage of the program in the 1940s. TWI even used it successfully in places where race relations were tenuous and kept it for quite a while because it best demonstrated to trainers how JR could effectively diffuse potentially inflammatory situations. Over time, however, participants questioned its use and consequently, TWI switched to problems associated with introducing a woman supervisor into a department. Although introducing a female supervisor was considered a problem that needed discussion back in 1945, women are part of the modern workforce and generally this would not require much attention now. Therefore, session 4 has been updated so that it deals with changing the organizational structure. The scenario involves an organizational change where team leaders are given some of the same authority and responsibility as supervisors or managers.

Applying Job Relations to a Union Environment and Other Groups

Early on, trainers successfully delivered Job Instruction programs to hospitals by simply changing some terminology. For example, TWI changed the word "bench" to "table." TWI believed that it could apply the same technique to use its programs successfully in a union environment. Some suggestions for delivering JR to union stewards were put on a leaflet for those occasions. The change in this case, however, was actually more radical than merely changing some terminology. The "steward" replaces the "supervisor" and the "union" replaces the "company" in the training manual. This meant that the foundation statement "Let each worker know how he is getting along" is replaced with "Let each member know his rights and responsibilities." Under Step 1—Get the facts, "Find out what rules and customs apply" was replaced with "Find out what union and plant rules and customs apply." Since unions are independent organizations, neither the government nor their companies funded them. TWI developed the program to a point, but funding did sometimes become a problem for expansion of the program since the unions were responsible for the cost of training. Although TWI awarded only 8,856 certificates to union stewards, the TWI program "Union Job Relations" (Union JR) was considered very successful and very well received where it was used. One union made TWI a prerequisite for anyone running for office.

Other groups, who, like the unions, were not eligible for government support, saw the advantages of JR and thus funded their own training. They would send individuals for training and then have them transfer that training to their employees. "The spirit of the Job Relations program has been followed faithfully and the only changes are such perfectly realistic ones as transposing Tom, the industry worker who sticks his hand into a machine, to Tom, the bank messenger who is careless in driving a pick-up car."[15]

In the next chapter we will look at the seven versions of the Job Methods program and at how TWI focused on creating a practical plan to produce greater quantities of quality products, in less time, by only using the organization's "available" employees, machines, and materials.

---

1. Robinson, Alan G., and Schroeder, Dean M., *Training, Continuous Improvement, and Human Relations: The U.S. TWI Programs and the Japanese Management Style*, California Management Review, The Regents of the University of California, CMR, Volume 335, Number 2, Winter 1993, p. 54.
2. In June 1943, TWI issued a bulletin entitled "How to Select Supervisors—A 6-Step Program" (Bulletin 17) that addresses the problem listed as 1-Selection of Supervisors.
3. *TWI Report*, p. 204.
4. *TWI Report*, p. 206.
5. *TWI Report*, pp. 205, 211–216.
6. *TWI Report*, p. 213.
7. *TWI Report*, p. 210.
8. *TWI Report*, p. 211.
9. *TWI Report*, p. 212.
10. *TWI Report*, p. 214. Additional information is not included in the TWI Report, so it is not possible to determine if there was a driving force that led to this decision. It is interesting to note that one of the strengths of the TWI programs is that they do not rely on standard rules, because the applicability of rules can change with time and with the environment. Knowing and thinking through a universal method is the basic strength of TWI.
11. *TWI Report*, p. 214.

12. *TWI Report*, p. 215.
13. *TWI Report*, p. 216.
14. Dietz, Walter, *Learn by Doing: The Story of Training Within Industry, 1940–1970*, Walter Dietz, Summit, NJ, p. 22.
15 *TWI Report*, p. 221.

CHAPTER 7

How TWI Developed the Job Methods Program

"The improvement demonstrated by the JM trainer resulted in better use of machine time, increased production, and decreased scrap. This improvement was not accomplished through a speed-up, but through elimination of unnecessary details."[1]

When the New Jersey group met in August 1941 to discuss the results of their Job Instruction Program, its success led TWI to the next logical step, creating another "J" program that would conserve "manpower, machine capacity, equipment, and material" and directly address improving the methods workers used every day. Glenn Gardiner set forth some guidelines for the possible program:

1. A way to comb a plant quickly in order to discover all jobs with possibilities for methods improvements.
2. A method that could be put over to supervisors and which would have practical everyday use.
3. A streamlined program for a group of 10 supervisors in 10 hours.
4. Based on sound methods engineering principles but in simplified form.
5. In accordance with the Job Instruction pattern.[2]

The resulting program had an appearance similar to Job Instruction: 10 hours of training for ten participants over the course of 5 days. Furthermore, it was based on industrial engineering concepts and written for the nonengineer. The resulting program is so practical that it can be used for improving almost any procedure, so one would not have to have any criterion for using it.

Empower the Production Supervisor to Make Changes

In the fall of 1941, Clifton Cox, an industrial engineer who had recently joined the New Jersey staff, was asked to develop a Job Methods program. He had already been "working on a 10-hour methods program for employees of Johnson & Johnson and was also currently introducing a 30-hour methods engineering course at Rutgers Extension University."[3] TWI decided that the course should follow the pattern of Job Instruction: demonstration and practice, 10 men for five 2-hour sessions, using a 4-Step Method.

TWI, however, had to address some basic differences between Job Methods and Job Instruction. Since the early part of the twentieth century, organizations had systematically used "general methods work," developed from Frederick Taylor's "scientific management" approach. However, this approach depended on using professional industrial engineers to study the work processes and implement the required changes for improvement. Only then, were the operators instructed in the new way to get work done. Taylor's approach allowed for operator suggestion programs, but these depended on the industrial engineers reviewing the suggestions and then developing and then implementing the changes—without worker participation.

The Job Methods program (JM) as envisioned by TWI could be very controversial because it would change the dynamics of engineers', operators', and supervisors' roles. The industrial engineers might think that someone is taking their jobs; the operators might think that the supervisors merely want them to work faster; and the supervisors might think that they should receive additional compensation for doing the work of the industrial engineers. To address these concerns, TWI would continue to stress that the program would recognize both operators and industrial engineers, but that it was specifically aimed at supervisors.[4] Furthermore, TWI stressed three concepts whenever discussing JM.

1. *Special training not required.* TWI created the JM program on a nonprofessional level, which would not require doing anything that a typical supervisor would not ordinarily do. This meant that no special training was required and thus the industrial engineers' jobs would not be in jeopardy.

2. *Improvements to increase speed are process oriented.* The JM program emphasized that the "improvement was not accomplished through a speed-up, but through elimination of unnecessary details."[5] Eliminating non-value-adding activities (waste) also runs through the concept of Lean Thinking. Thus, operators need not fear that improvements were about forcing them to work beyond a reasonable pace. In fact, the JM method points out that working faster (speeding up) causes mistakes and is to be avoided.

3. *Supervisors are responsible for departmental improvements.* TWI believed that a good supervisor was responsible for the productivity in

his or her department and therefore should do whatever was necessary to increase its productivity. However, these departmental improvements did not have to depend upon the engineering staff. The supervisor could achieve many of these improvements by him or herself, working with the other employees in that department.

Launch of the Job Methods Program—January 1942

TWI named the program Job Methods in January 1942 and developed it during the spring of that year. By May, the JM program was completed and presented to a panel of TWI district directors at a conference in Washington. TWI wrote specific procedures to launch the program.

1. A *headquarters representative* and the *district representative* fully discussed with management and labor advisors in each district where to hold a JM Institute (train the trainers).
2. A demonstration, requiring 1½ to 2 hours, was held for the panel of TWI directors. TWI invited both management advisors and labor advisors as well as a few select union officials that the labor advisors wished to include.
3. A similar demonstration was held especially for union leaders, selected by the district labor advisors, if they felt such a meeting would be helpful.

In addition, executives of unionized plants were asked whether it would be helpful to discuss the program with union leaders, and TWI staff members offered to assist.[6] As with the other two programs, TWI distributed a JM training card with the 4-Step Method to the participants stating critical program information. The first name suggested for the training card was "How to Improve War Production Methods," but soon this was changed to "How to Improve Job Methods."[7] Exhibit 7-1 shows the two-sided JM training card. Chapter 11 discussed the training card (reminder card) in detail.

The first revision to the JM manual (Version II) occurred in August 1942 and included putting the job breakdown in a two-column style. In addition, "supplements on safety and housekeeping" were eliminated.[8] Although the TWI Report does not give a reason why the developers eliminated these supplements, one could surmise from many of their actions that keeping the program to a 10-hour limit was a factor.

TWI held the first Job Methods Institute in September 1942, followed by the trainers going through two weeks of instruction under observation. You could consider this the official launch of the JM program with Version I, although TWI held experimental sessions in the winter of 1942. The first

Exhibit 7-1. The JM 4-Step Method Training Card

How to Improve Job Methods

A practical plan to help you produce GREATER QUANTITIES of QUALITY PRODUCTS in LESS TIME by making the best use of Manpower, Machines, and Materials, now available.

STEP I—BREAK DOWN the job.

1. List all the details of the job exactly as done by the Present Method.

2. Be sure details include all:
   • Material Handling
   • Machine Work
   • Hand work

STEP II—QUESTION every detail.

1. Use these types of questions:
   WHY is it necessary?
   WHAT is the purpose?
   WHERE should it be done?
   WHEN should it be done?
   WHO is best qualified to do it?
   HOW is the 'best way' to do it?

2. Also question the:
   Materials, Machines, Equipment, Tools, Product Design, Layout, Workplace, Safety, Housekeeping

STEP III—DEVELOP the new method

1. ELIMINATE unnecessary details
2. COMBINE details when practical
3. REARRANGE for better sequence
4. SIMPLIFY all necessary details -
   • Make the work easier and safer
   • Pre-position materials, tools and equipment at the best places in the proper work area
   • Use gravity feed hoppers and drop delivery chutes
   • Let both hands do useful work
   • Use jogs and fixtures instead of hands for holding work
5. Work out your ideas with others
6. Write up your proposed new method.

STEP IV—APPLY the new method

1. Sell your proposal to the boss.
2. Sell the new method to the operators.
3. Get final approval of all concerned on Safety, Quality, Quantity, Cost.
4. Put the new method to work. Use it until a better way is developed.
5. Give credit where credit is due.

JOB METHODS TRAINING PROGRAM
Training Within Industry Service
Bureau of Training
War Manpower Commission

Source: Dietz, *Learn by Doing*, p. 18.

group of employees participating in the experimental sessions was from the American Steel Castings Company, the same company that TWI used for the Job Instruction trials. Several important changes came out of these trials, which created Version II.

First, since an industrial engineer (Clifton Cox) had designed Job Methods, it included process maps and flow charts. Although these were in common use, it was felt that they were "too professional for first-line supervisors,"[9] and not necessary for what JM was trying to accomplish. Process maps and flow charts are useful tools, but TWI decided they were not required for a typical Job Methods project. "The program at this time was designed to develop in supervisors a constructively critical attitude toward their work."[10]

It was also apparent that participants should spend more time learning the JM 4-Step Method, which included "selling" the improvement to everyone involved. Part of the problem in learning the 4-Step Method was that supervisors would get "sidetracked" at Step 2 (Question every detail). Step 2 is an information-collecting step that asked (in this earlier version) "How is the 'best way to do it?" Therefore, supervisors were trying to develop their improvements here instead of just collecting information. In Version III, the JM developers removed this question from Step 2 so to shift the emphasis from creating a solution to gathering facts.

Version Three December 1942—Improve Production With Available Resources

In the third revision of the program in December 1942, TWI realized it needed to add the words "now available" to the objective of the Job Method. It now read: "A practical plan to help you produce GREATER QUANTITIES of QUALITY PRODUCTS in LESS TIME by making the best use of Manpower, Machines, and Materials *now available*." This emphasized to supervisors the importance of finding better ways of doing things with existing resources and that buying additional equipment or hiring additional personnel was not always necessary. Naturally, in a wartime environment, scarcity of resources was an obvious issue. Today the phrase "creativity before capital" is sometimes used.

What TWI may not have realized is that wartime is not the only time when scarcity might be an issue and that training people to deal with scarcity is valuable no matter what the conditions are. Using existing resources actually does several things. First, it means organizations do not require industrial engineering for all improvements and thus you can use these engineers for other projects that perhaps more fully use their skills and knowledge. This type of approach also mirrors the theme in Job Relations of making the best use of each employee's ability. Simply put, if a supervisor has the skills to make an improvement, then do not "waste" this skill—have the supervisor make the improvement, not the engineer. Second, this approach holds down cost adding to (or at least not subtracting from) the bottom line. As any businessperson knows, organizations will implement changes more readily if they do not cost much (or anything). Finally, and most importantly, requiring supervisors to use existing resources helps workers focus on and think about each step of their process and use only those resources that are really needed, which in turn, eliminates waste and improves the process. Furthermore, because the supervisor could initiate a change using existing resources, it was more likely that new ideas would be implemented. This lays the basis for continual improvement. Whenever TWI was selling the JM program to management, it used these concepts as reasons for adopting it. In addition, they also included other benefits which management might find useful.

> "TWI . . . stressed the by-products of Job Methods—the development of thinking among supervisors, the identification of supervisors who were thinking . . ."[11]

Because of the "emergency," scarce resources were very high on everyone's priority list and thus "developing thinking among supervisors" and identifying "supervisors who were thinking" was really an afterthought. Today, I believe these concepts are extremely important, especially when many organizations are embracing Lean Thinking and the central role that a learning organization plays in being successful. A learning organization continually trains its employees to think critically about what they are doing and empowers them with simple and clear methods to implement changes. Likewise, TWI empowers the supervisor and the workers in a department to understand processes and implement improvements by thinking critically about what they are doing. In Lean terms, you can substitute 'supervisor' with 'team leader' and 'workers' with 'team members.' The point is, what is clearly visible is that TWI helps organizations make the best use of available resources to produce GREATER QUANTITIES of QUALITY PRODUCTS in LESS TIME. What is less obvious is that it does so by leading employees to critical thinking, i.e., by developing a learning organization.

Overcoming Barriers to Implementing Changes

Having to use available resources highlighted another difference between Job Instruction and Job Methods. Job Methods, by definition, required implementing changes in the use of materials, manpower, and/or machines. Some of these changes would be completely within the realm of the supervisor's authority and he or she would not have to contact anyone outside the department to implement those changes. The majority of changes, however, might possibly affect other parts of the organization. Thus, there was a real possibility that requests for implementing changes in processes or procedures could come against barriers from other departments, slowing down or stopping the improvements.[12] For example, a given improvement might only need a safety engineer to approve a revised work place set up. However, if the engineer had different objectives and were operating under a different premise than the supervisor, delays might result, slowing down or reducing enthusiasm for change. Accordingly, TWI realized that:

"Management was going to have to show supervisors that the plant was interested in the making of improvements. This would have to be done by, first, encouraging supervisors to make improvements, and then improving the handling of proposals."[13]

Thus, in order for JM to be as successful as it could be, a plant's culture (how things are really done) had to change. We find this true today with Lean production. If an organization really wants to change from a mass production system to a Lean production system, its culture must change.

From the outset, TWI recognized that for a job improvement program to be successful, the employees (supervisors or workers) must present complete, well thought out ideas for approval. If any employee presents an idea that is incomplete, unworkable and easy to dismiss, management (or any party authorized to judge the idea) will not accept it. The program will surely fail because no one will use it. A key requirement then was to have the employee look for flaws in the suggested improvement and not present the idea until it is complete and workable.[14]

The JM program directs the supervisor to meet with all the people who are in any way affected by the change or have input to it. When the supervisor collects input from all these people, he or she usually has a firm grasp of the problem and the solution.

To train the supervisor in making suggested changes properly, the JM program required that during the first of the five two-hour training sessions, the trainer demonstrate a sample job to explain the use of the JM 4-Step Method. (This was stated as a requirement in Version I.) The job developers chose the assembly of a radio shield made out of one copper and one brass sheet for this job demonstration. (Chapter 11 discusses this demonstration). TWI chose this job because it was simple and could easily be reproduced and transported. TWI replaced the metal sheets with cardboard sheets in the demonstration because of cost and accessibility; and they replaced the riveters used to join the sheets with a stapler. In addition, this job fully demonstrated all of the ways one could develop a new method and thus all the points made by the instructor could be referred to in the demonstration.

TWI also had to make a differentiation between the Job Instruction and Job Method breakdown sheets (Chapters 9 and 11 discuss job breakdown sheets). Job Instruction requires that you first break down the job into its steps, using two columns to list the steps as main ideas. This type of job breakdown sheet serves as a guide to the instructor when teaching a trainee. Since the JI instructor knows how to do the job, it is not necessary to include much detail. The only requirement is that instructors demonstrate the steps in the correct order and list all key points. Initially, JM instructors also used two columns, which caused some confusion with the JI program. The Job Method breakdown sheet was later changed to three columns and then fourteen, to detail every step for analyzing the job.[15] Because you cannot question any aspect or process of a job unless you identify it, you must break down the job into its elements and include *all* details. The necessity for this is graphically demonstrated in the anecdote in Exhibit 4-2, "Follow the Manual," about the operator who has to jump into the air every time she wants to start or stop the machine.

Though it was not necessary for supervisors to seek approval for every change, they needed to always keep management aware of what they were doing, and having a detailed job breakdown further demonstrated that they thoroughly understood the job process which in turn gave management the confidence to encourage supervisors to implement any type of improvement.

First Job Methods Mimeographed Manual for Nationwide Distribution

TWI published the JM manual for version III in December 1942 and it was the first manual intended for nationwide distribution. Changes included:

- "Suggestion" was replaced by "Proposed new method."
- Emphasis was placed on giving credit to any operators who helped the supervisor.
- Emphasis was placed on the supervisor being strategically placed for making methods improvements.
- The phrase "now available" was added to the objective statement.
- It was conceded that not all jobs could be improved and so if a supervisor broke down two jobs without finding an improvement, he could still be certified.[16] The developers eliminated the idea in Version V.
- The use of large wall charts was eliminated and replaced with board work.[17]
- The "final form" of the card was developed at this time.[18] (With the changed wording of Step 2).

Versions IV thru VI—Minor but Important Improvements

In early 1943, TWI released version IV with minor changes. One change warned about *flash ideas* that trainers could expect when teaching JM. Supervisors would spontaneously have flash ideas while demonstrating project ideas that had little to do with applying the Job Method. The purpose of training supervisors in Job Methods is NOT to improve an operation, but to teach them how to ANALYZE jobs and THINK about *how* to improve an operation. For training purposes, whether or not the supervisor made a job improvement before leaving the training is far less important than if they learned the JM 4-Step Method. It is very easy for participants to digress and become so involved in improving the operation of the job that when a good improvement idea pops into their head the first instinct is to use that as part (or all) of the change. If participants implement flash ideas rather than continuing with the analysis, it may impede new ideas from coming to the surface during the analysis. Trainers can encourage participants to write down flash ideas, but they must always remind them to focus on the real purpose of the training: learning the *method* that reveals *how* to improve an operation.

In April 1943, the developers completed Version V with no significant changes in content. Compared with other versions, however, the trainer received the greatest help. This version included a description of how to set up the demonstration of the radio shield assembly (Details given in Chapter 11). In addition, a space was included on the proposal form to include the name of any operator who assisted the supervisor. Giving credit to workers was a concept that TWI strongly emphasized and they wanted to ensure this.

Version VI, written in May, also did not include significant changes, though it was important that those concerned were critically reviewing the program and offering suggestions on a continual basis. In this version, TWI developed the three points below to emphasize having the supervisor work with other people in the organization as much as possible.

1. The supervisor should find out from his boss whether the job is worth trying to improve.
2. The supervisor should consult with his peers.
3. The supervisor should work with the operator.[19]

Although the TWI Report does not state when it occurred, TWI eliminated the first point because the use of the method included justification of any changes. Step 2, "Question every detail," quickly showed the supervisor whether a change in the operation would be worth pursuing. Step 3, "Develop the new method," included writing up a proposal quantifying the reasons for the change. Step 4, "Sell the method," assured that the change was worthwhile and within the supervisors understanding of the job process.

Version VII—Finalized and First Printed Manual

By December 1943, the final version, VII, became the first printed manual (the others were mimeographed). The main changes from previous versions included incorporating reference material into the outline, and a Trainer's Guide. The Trainer's Guide gave tips to the trainer on strategies and some areas that might be troublesome.[20] The JM program has remained substantially unchanged from Version VII, except, as noted, for societal changes that are discussed in Chapter 11. It is interesting to note that, of the three "J" programs, Job Methods was the one that could be most easily quantified and yet it was the one in which the fewest people were certified. In the five years of TWI's existence, Job Instruction issued 1,005,170 certifications. One could explain the large number by the fact that it was the first program implemented and the most pressing need was to train people and get them into the workforce. TWI issued 490,022 certificates for Job Relations and 244,733 for Job Methods. Though the "J" programs ceased in the United States after 1945, we can fairly assume that the number of certifications in all three programs would have eventually been more or less equal, because using all three programs together lays the best foundation for worker and process improvement.

Standardized Answers to Questions About Jobs, Earnings, and Future Unemployment

During the development of the JM program, three questions arose during conversations with management, unions, and supervisors dealing with 1) losing one's job, 2) earnings, and 3) future unemployment. These questions became so prevalent during the training sessions that TWI provided standard answers during the final versions of the program.[21] (With issues such as outsourcing and creating a "Lean" organization, these questions are as relevant today as they were then.) In addition to the content provided in Exhibit 7-2,[22] some additional comments may be helpful. It should be emphasized that management, and not the trainer, should be answering these questions.

Question One. *What should be done if employees are eliminated as a result of a methods change?* This question also arises in Lean training because the purpose of Lean is to accomplish more with less and "less" also includes people. Like Lean, the best answer is that a company should make every attempt to transfer employees to another job rather than eliminating them. Theoretically, the employees no longer needed would be multiskilled because the operation is being simplified. Since they probably helped with the methods change, they have other valuable skills in job analysis that they could use elsewhere in the company. However, if it is necessary to eliminate some employees, these people can leverage their training to find a new job because TWI training is very transferable. When management recognizes these employees as a valuable resource, it will be less likely to remove them from the organization.

Exhibit 7-2. JM Questions (May 1942—Version I)

Questions about Job Methods

Three questions arose so frequently that standard answers were provided.

1. *What should be done if employees are eliminated as a result of a methods change?*
   This problem is solely one for the company to handle. A general reply which meets all situations is obviously not possible. However, since such an occurrence might be the outgrowth of the Job Methods program, Training Within Industry is interested in it. In considering this question, the following points are suggested: (a) Occasional changes in and elimination of jobs has been going on for years. Therefore, the problem is not new, nor especially related to Job Methods Training. Where such a problem arises, it should be handled according to established practice in the company. Factors of far greater importance than this training program affect the tenure of employees' jobs. (b) In dealing with a specific instance during this war period, it is recommended: that no one ever be laid off as the result of a methods change but that an employee thus affected be transferred....

2. *What happens to an employee's earnings in case of a methods change?*
   This whole question is one that is solely a problem of local management. Usually, if earnings are increased, there is little or no difficulty. However, Training Within Industry is interested in the problem because sometimes a methods change may raise the question of earnings. For company consideration, it is suggested that, from the standpoint of the individual worker, a sound and fair policy seems to be to never reduce the employee's net "take-home" as the result of a methods change.

3. *Suppose this "methods improvement" idea becomes nationwide—what effect will this have on the possibility for unemployment in the post-war period?*
   Again, this question is beyond the province of a training program, but the following points of view are suggested: (a) No one knows what will happen in the post-war economy, or post-war period. In fact, the only thing that is definitely known about the post-war period is that certain catastrophe will be the result if the United States loses the war. (b) It might be that the improvements developed during the war period would help American industry in post-war competition for world markets. It should be remembered that the industries of each country will be searching desperately for means to continue their economic existence. In the competition for the world markets, those having the best production methods may be in the most favorable situation. (c) Again, the only sure thing that is known is that the United States must win the war. No one can guess what will happen after the war.

Question Two. *What happens to an employee's earnings in case of a methods change?* If employees lose their jobs because they came up with a more cost-effective and easier way to do them, it is unlikely the remaining employees will make job improvement suggestions in the future. Similarly, if organizations downgrade employees for the same reason, employees will be less likely to suggest future improvements. If management is interested in increasing productivity and sustaining continuous improvement, it must be constantly looking ahead to see further opportunities for using surplus resources resulting from improvements. (Lean thinking also takes a similar approach. Lean is never about focusing on reducing 'head count'—it is about maximizing the skills and roles of employees around value-added processes.)

An adjunct to this question is how the organization determines rewards for employee suggestions. It is well documented that rewards are not a motivator for change or productivity. They not only decrease creativity and productivity, but they also can be counter-productive. A reward is defined as an agreement that states, "If you do this, I will give you that." Rewards and punishment are two sides of the same coin, and are methods where one person attempts to control another. Research shows that the person being "motivated" does only what is expected (if that) and no more. Because the person knows exactly what has to be done, there is no creativity and because the goal is definitive, the person does not exceed it. Rewards are classified as *extrinsic* devices because the incentive comes from outside the person who is doing the action.[23]

You can classify Job Methods as an *intrinsic* device because the person making the improvement is doing it to make his or her job easier. That is, the motivation for improvement comes from within. Because it is not reward-based, creativity is nourished and there is no defining boundary. This allows for continual improvement. Recognition is different from a reward in three ways. First, recognition is not set up before the job is started, but rather is given unexpectedly after the fact. Second, because it is unexpected, it does not happen after each accomplishment. Third, the value of the recognition does not match the value of the accomplishment. Recognition should neither help nor hurt the person's next effort. Some companies reward their employees with gifts of $1, $5, or $10 depending on the size of their improvement, but these are actually a form of recognition so that other employees can see the effect of what was done. An organization's culture determines what kind of rewards (if any) should accompany employee suggestions and process improvements. In a culture where friendly competition is encouraged and healthy, the organization can use nominal rewards symbolic of achievement. However, when rewards become significant, the employee emphasis changes from helping the organization and the team, to helping oneself. The latter is an antithesis to teamwork and sends mixed messages to employees. The organization should emphasize that improvements are everyone's responsibility and part of everyone's job.

Question Three. *Suppose this "method improvement" idea becomes nation-wide—what effect will this have on the possibility for unemployment in the postwar period?* Although labor costs and technology have an impact on employment, it is still true today that "In the competition for the world's markets, those having the best production methods may be in the most favorable situation."[24]

It appears the Job Methods did spread nationwide, except it was exported overseas—and especially adopted in Japan. It also appears that Toyota, in particular, took to heart the quote in question three, as well as all three questions when developing the principles of the Toyota Production System. In the next chapter, we will leave behind programs geared to specific common objectives (instructing, methods, and personnel) and focus on creating solutions to problems that are unique to a specific organization.

---

1. *Training Within Industry Service, The Training Within Industry Report: 1940–1945*, (Washington D.C.: War Manpower Commission Bureau of Training, 1945), p. 224.
2. *TWI Report*, p. 223.
3. *TWI Report*, 224.
4. TWI recognized that operators also should be trained in JM, but they aimed it specifically at supervisors because they thought supervisors were responsible for production. Note that when funds became scarce resulting in limited training, restrictions on who should receive instruction were put on JI, JR, and PD, but any designated employee could take JM. (*TWI Report,* p. 121).
5. *TWI Report*, p. 224.
6. *TWI Report*, p. 230.
7. *TWI Report*, p. 229.
8. *TWI Report*, p. 232.
9. *TWI Report*, p. 230.
10. *TWI Report*, p. 230.
11. *TWI Report*, p. 39.
12. This is an important point that makes JM different from the other programs. JI & JR can really be done independently. One person can train another and management does not have to be involved in how it is done. JM usually involves other people and other departments so it's important that management agrees and supports the JM program.
13. *TWI Report*, p. 39.
14 . *TWI Report*, p. 229.
15. The (14) column job breakdown form is contemporary, distributed by the Syracuse, NY MEP Center, Central New York Technology Development Organization.

16. It is my belief that all jobs can be improved, although all improvements might not be cost effective at this time. In an actual situation, one should first make changes that produce the greatest impact. Prioritize possible changes and work down the list. It may be possible to make a profitable change next year that was considered only marginally effective this year. That is the concept of continual improvement.

17. Note that this is a preference decision.

18. *TWI Report*, p. 232.

19. *TWI Report*, p. 233.

20. For example, when introducing the demonstration job of the radio shields, the participants must be able to see how this job related to what they do at work. After giving some hints on how to do this, it is emphasized that "THIS IS REALLY AN IMPORTANT PART OF THE PROGRAM. UNLESS YOU GET IT OVER CORRECTLY YOU MAY FIND THE GOING ROUGH. Job Methods Manual; Training Guide p. 4.

21. These questions and answers were included when Version I was presented to TWI District Directors in Washington, May 1942. *TWI Report*, p. 230.

22. *TWI Report*, p. 231.

23. Kohn, Alfie, *Punished By Rewards*, Houghton Mifflin, Boston, 1993

24. *TWI Report*, p. 231.

CHAPTER 8

How TWI Developed Program Development

"The developing of training plans to meet the plant's own specific needs is an in-plant job—no outsider can know the underlying causes of production problems."[1]

As we mentioned earlier, the founders divided TWI into 22 districts across the country, and each of them contributed to the development of the programs. As we saw above, in early 1941 the New Jersey District saw a need and developed a solution that became the basis of the Job Instruction Program. At about the same time, the Detroit District began to put on conferences for defense contractors with the help of the General Motors Institute (G.M.I.) of Flint, Michigan, with the express purpose of discussing general training needs and solutions. These conferences were the beginning of the Program Development plan. Each conference consisted of a series of three meetings that included information on the following topics:

- TWI organization and assistance.
- General analysis of training problems in national defense industries.
- Consideration of the contractors' own training problems.
- Induction of new workers.
- Training of trainers.
- Developing supervision.
- Trade apprenticeship.[2]

Nine of these conferences took place throughout Michigan from April 1941 to January 1942. The main prerequisite for attending this conference was that each participant must have major responsibility in the training field because they would not just be listening to a lecture, they would be working as a group to solve problems and preparing to apply what were to become the Program Development concepts to his or her plant.

"The method used in the conference grows out of the basic assumption that each member of the group knows his plant problems better than anyone else involved and that it is *his* job to develop a plan to meet his plant's needs."[3]

Preparing Program Development to Go Nationwide

The need for this type of information was apparent because TWI Headquarters received many requests to put on similar conferences. As a result, TWI asked Albert Sobey of G.M.I. to help put together a similar program to be used nationwide. The first conference was held in Flint, Michigan, February 17–22, 1942 and covered the following topics:

1. The Training Job in a Rapidly Expanding Organization.
2. Identifying Training Needs.
3. Methods of Induction.
4. Job Instruction Training or Train the Trainer.
5. Job Relations Training.
6. Organization of a Training Program.
7. Plant Trip to Observe Training Methods.
8. Apprenticeship.
9. [Display of] Group Training Methods.
10. Training Supervisors.
11. Training Conference Leaders.
12. Increasing the Effectiveness of Training.

"The members spent one day on preparation of individual training plans and then on the last day each one presented the plan he had made."[4] Each of the above subjects was handled in the same way.

1. The conference leader analyzed training problems in that subject and gave illustrations and solutions that have proved effective.
2. Each plant representative, working alone, applied the suggestions to his plant problems.
3. Each member reported his findings to the group for suggestions and comments.

This conference took a full week and afterwards, TWI decided that it might be more effective to announce various topics and have plant representatives choose which ones they thought would be most beneficial to their situations. With input from G.M.I., TWI put together its own material and developed a list of subjects similar to the one used for the Flint conference.

The only changes they made were 1) drop the plant trips because it was diffi-cult to get clearances for entry into many plants, and 2) eliminate the Group Training Methods, which was a display of participants' training methods, and add Job Methods Training instead.

The intent was to invite company executives and training personnel to a meeting, which would describe all the topics. A schedule would be available and selections could be made at that time. The method for doing each of these training modules would be the same. The Conference Leaders would explain the techniques to the participants, and then they would identify a need in their organization and come up with a training plan to address that need, which they would then implement. TWI recognized that once the participants created the training plan that it might not be documented in a way that would be accept-able to management. To address this, it was thought that after the participants made the plans, the entire group should reconvene to put the plans into a final form by reviewing the plan points in the bulletin "The Organization of a Train-ing Program."[5]

During 1942, TWI districts conducted these programs, but one difficulty, in particular, occurred: When TWI asked participants to give their suggestions on how they personally handled training needs, there was the possibility that the group might agree on ideas that TWI knew were not workable. TWI believed it should be a clearinghouse of information delivering only information that it believed *valid* and *reliable*. As a result, TWI began to change the conferences from those that exchanged information to more specific programs of instruction.[6]

Standardizing Program Development

It became clear early on that there was a great interest among participants in developing in-plant programs and that many approaches being used at the time around the country seemed acceptable. TWI decided to standardize these var-ious programs and approaches by taking several actions.

- [April 1943] TWI decided that the objective was to train "those persons in the plant who had the responsibility in the training field of originat-ing (identifying) needs, organizing, selling, and administering in-plant training programs."[7] This would eliminate those who only delivered training (instructors).
- [Jan. 1943] Since they realized that everyone in a position to meet these objectives might not have the title "training director" or might even have other duties in addition to training duties, TWI decided that the word "training" should not be used in the title. Therefore, the name "Program Development" was adopted after much discussion.[8]

- [April 1943] The training would be handled on an "Institute" level with an institute conductor heading the training. Unlike the "J" programs that divided ten hours of training into five 2-hour sessions, Program Development would take over 30 hours. The final breakdown of time in the fall of 1944 was 3 full days of training followed by a week at the home organization developing the training plan. The group would reconvene for 2 days to present and discuss their plans.

Exhibit 8-1. PD 4-Step Method Training Card

WAR MANPOWER COMMISSION
Bureau of Training
TRAINING WITHIN
INDUSTRY SERVICE

PROGRAM DEVELOPMENT
How to Meet a Production
Problem Through Training

---

1. SPOT A PRODUCTION
PROBLEM
Get supervisors and workers to tell
about current problems.
Uncover problems by reviewing
records—performance, cost,
turnover, rejects, accidents.
Anticipate problems resulting from
changes—organization, production
or policies
Analyze this evidence.
Identify training needed.
Tackle One Specific Need at a Time.

2. DEVELOP A SPECIFIC PLAN
Who will be the trainer?
What content? Who can help
determine?
How can it be done best?
Who should do the training?
Where should it be done—how long
will it take?
Where should it be done?
Watch for relation of this plan to
other current training plans and
programs.

3. GET PLAN INTO ACTION
Stress to management evidence of
need—use facts and figures.
Present expected results.
Discuss plan—content and methods
Submit timetable for plan.
Train those who will do the training.
Secure understanding and
acceptance by those affected.
Fix responsibility for continuing use.
Be Sure Management Participates.

4. CHECK RESULTS
How can results be checked?
Against what evidence?
What results will be looked for? Is
management being informed?—
How?
Is the plan being followed?
How is it being kept in use?
Are any changes necessary?
Is the plan helping production?

Responsibility for Training Results
The LINE organization has the
responsibility for making
continuing use of the knowledge
and skills acquired through
training as a regular part of the
operating job.
The STAFF provides plans and
technical "know-how" and does
some things FOR but usually
works THROUGH the line
organization.

- [Feb. 1943] The first version of a Product Development (PD) 4-Step Method and worksheets were published.

TWI revised both the 4-Step Method and the worksheets several times. The final version of the PD 4-Step Method is on the training card in Exhibit 8-1.[9] The worksheet for Step 1 of the 4-Step Method appears in Exhibit 8-2[10] and that for Step 2 appears in Exhibit 8-3.[11] Chapter 12 discusses the PD training card in detail.

Exhibit 8-2. Program Development Method Sheet 1

EVIDENCE	TRAINING ACTION NEEDED		OTHER ACTION NEEDED
	Training for Whom?	Training in What?	
One plane out of three rejected at final inspection because of leaks in hydraulic system.			
Hydraulic installers experienced			
Hydraulic installation checked— no faulty work			
Radar equipment installed after hydraulic system covered by plates	Radar installers	Location of hydraulic system	
Radar installers not protection hydraulic system—drill into it	Radar installers	Importance of hydraulic system	
		How to protect hydraulic system while installing radar	Put stop on drills?

What is the Production Problem? _____ Leaks in hydraulic system _____

"TACKLE ONE SPECIFIC NEED AT A TIME"

Exhibit 8-3. Program Development Method Sheet 2

(For use with Step 2 of PD Method—Use Card)

What is the Specific Plan? _____ Protection of Hydraulic System

Training for Whom? _____ Radar Installers _____ Training for How Many? _____ 20

What Content?	How Can It be Done Best?	Who Will Train or Help?	When? How Long?	Where?
Importance of protecting hydraulic system			1½ hr. tomorrow 20 in group	General foreman's office
Importance of hydraulic system to pilot and crew	Explanation	Test pilot		
Cost of repairing damaged hydraulic system	Analysis of cost figures	General foreman		
Location of hydraulic system	Cutaways—explanation	General foreman		
Drilling holes for radar installation Placement of holes Depth of drilling 1/8″	Demonstration—practice	Radar supervisor	½ hr. each man, schedule immediately, complete in 3 days	On job

What is the relation of this plan to other current training plans and programs?　Will take only 2 hours of each operator's time and 10 hours of radar supervisor's time—less time than to repair one damaged hydraulic system.

TWI developed various worksheets for Steps 3 and 4, but because they basically reiterated the items already listed under the steps, they decided not to use worksheets for these steps.

Further Adjustments to the PD Program After Release

After delivering many Program Development Institutes, TWI was criticized for two points:

> "The conference method was not specific and led to unsound generalizations. There was neither adequate training in the method nor time for presentation of a real plan, and consequently, the institute conductor was tempted to do a superficial remodeling of the plan in the Institute."[12]

The PD developers believed the solution to these two problems was to have the participants practice with case studies or problems brought in from their own companies sooner than they had been. Of course, this meant that the institute conductor would have to deliver the PD program completely through instruction, but this was not occurring. In the final version, the training requires each participant to use the PD 4-Step method five times: thoroughly reviewing three sample problems, making a training plan for a hypothetical problem at his or her plant, and finally, making a useable training plan for his or her plant.

As with the TWI "J" programs, when discussing any given problem there was a strong emphasis on learning the 4-Step Method rather than solving the problem. Consequently, the trainer devoted several hours drilling on the proper use of the worksheets, which are fundamental to the proper use of Steps 1 and 2. In addition to the participants wrongly placing more emphasis on specific problems, TWI also discovered that the training was not covering some of the PD concepts. "The philosophy of 'we will have only experienced men putting on this program—therefore, it is safe to leave a lot up to them' was definitely abandoned."[13] The PD developers added the following eight subjects to the content of the PD training manual to make sure the training was addressing all of the PD concepts. Details are discussed in Chapter 12.

1. *Induction.* TWI defined "Induction" as "Introduction of the workers to the place and to the work."[14] The training is viewed not just as providing information to the new employee, but rather as a training job. Induction is different from instruction in work, larger orientation programs, or anything done before a person reports to work. As part of the training, induction is presented to the participants as a way to solve a

production problem. The example TWI used was, "Production is down to 80%" and one of the plans to address this problem was to introduce workers to the workplace correctly."

Initially, the trainer explained the example, and the group participants contributed suggestions and comments as to how to introduce the workers to the workplace to solve the production problem. TWI discovered that the variations for induction among the various organizations were so great that it did not make sense to try to create a comprehensive plan from such a variety of approaches. Therefore, TWI gave the details of properly administering the induction directly to the participants. These details were also published in the bulletin "Introducing the New Employee to the Job." (Bulletin 18)

2. *Selection of Supervisors.* As noted under Job Relations in Chapter 6, as early as 1941, the National Research Council's Committee on Work in Industry had stated that proper selection of supervisors was one of three main problems that most companies had. Later, TWI received many comments from companies saying that training was not working because of the poor quality of the supervisors being trained.[15] So TWI asked R.S. Uhrbrock, head of Industrial Relations Research at Proctor and Gamble, to devise a supervisory selection procedure. Based on his experience with many companies, he created the supervisor selection process that is incorporated in the Program Development training and appears in the bulletin entitled "How to Select New Supervisors—A 6-Step Program." (See Bulletin 17.)

3. *Conducting meetings.* To further address the need for adequate training in the 4-Step Method, TWI turned to the use of meetings. Because a meeting can be a useful tool for training, TWI decided to include an approximately 30-minute segment that provided information about how to conduct the meeting effectively. The 30 minutes covers three main points:

a) Is there a need for a meeting?

b) What's wrong with our present meetings?

c) How can we help supervisors run better meetings?[16]

4. *Methods and aids for training.* Training included methods and aids to make sure that the participants were aware of the various audio-visual aids available.

5. *Getting a plan into action.* The fact that a dialogue about "Getting a Plan Into Action" had to be added to the Training Manual points out that TWI abandoned their philosophy of giving the institute conductors latitude in material delivered.

6. *Checking results*. Similarly, the fact that a dialogue about "Checking Results" had to be added to the Training Manual points out that TWI abandoned their philosophy of giving the institute conductors latitude in material delivered.

7. *Line and staff responsibility for training*. Note the "Responsibility of Training Results" added after the PD 4-Step Methods (Exhibit 8-1). Underneath is the "line" and "staff" responsibility. Since most of the people attending this Institute would be staff members, it discusses their role in solving production problems through training. Many of these people may not actually be doing much training, so it is important for them to make sure they know their responsibilities.

8. *Organization of training plans into an overall training program.*[17] Though the PD training card did not reference this module of training, TWI found that "Organization of Training Plans into an Overall Training Program" was necessary because some people in charge of training would have a tendency to attempt too much training at one time. The caution note for Step 1 reads "Tackle One Specific Need at a Time," but even that could lead to confusion. For example, if one started to work on training operators (objective 1), that would mean that supervisors would have to be trained in how to instruct (objective 2). Therefore, someone would have to be a Job Instruction trainer (objective 3) and a coach would have to be assigned (objective 4). This actually represents four training plans that constituted a training program. TWI had to make it clear that all of these activities constitute a training program and that the training plan needed to be conducted over a period of time so people had an opportunity to absorb and learn the material. If this did not happen, the training would be delivered but not successful.

Further Refinements in 1943—Solving Problems Through Training

The summer of 1943 saw further refinements of the PD program. In addition to revising the PD 4-Step Method, TWI added specific material about production. Program Development began with the approach of correcting *training* problems, but TWI soon discovered that its real objective was to solve *production* problems *through* training. The worksheet that is used for Step 1 originally stated; "What is the Training Problem?" TWI changed this to; "What is the Production Problem?" Although the title on the PD training card was, "How to Meet a Production Problem Through Training," the Institutes centered much of the discussion on solving training problems.

Making the distinction between "solving production problems through training" and "solving training problems" is extremely important. Training is merely a tool used to enable increased production. Although training problems may exist and may be the responsibility of the participants, training per se is not the focus of the program or the objective of the plant. If the participants analyze how to solve training problems, they may improve the quality of their training programs, but they may not necessary improve their plant's production.

Furthermore, if the participants analyze production problems correctly, they may conclude that training is not a solution or is only a partial solution to a problem. Because of this, TWI wanted to avoid having training directors solving every problem with training. The adage comes to mind: "If all you have is a hammer, everything looks like a nail." Furthermore, if someone misdiagnosed the problem and offered a training solution but another solution was more applicable, you've wasted both time and money. Seeing that participants were not making this distinction consistently, TWI made a decision to add 30 minutes of instruction on the definitions of production and training (see Exhibit 8-4).[18]

Most of the participants found that viewing training as a solution to production problems was quite helpful. It made what they did more appealing to management because the benefit to the bottom line was more evident. Later, for further emphasis, the PD developers changed the first step from "Spot a Specific Need" to "Spot a Production Problem." In addition, the developers added a fourth column to the Worksheet for Step 1 titled, "Other Action Needed." This encouraged one to keep an open mind that other solutions besides training were possible.[19]

TWI made the Program Development institute available on a nationwide basis in the fall of 1944, and after some important revisions, published a final version in June 1945. One improvement was to separate how to use worksheets and problem solving. The PD developers realized that the sample problems used as a "drill" to help teach participants how to use the worksheets were misconstrued as "problem-solving" problems. This resulted in participants having a poor understanding of the analysis concepts behind the use of worksheets. In the spring of 1945, TWI eliminated many of these problems when they placed special emphasis on making sure participants understood the concepts behind the worksheets. The "drill" sped up their understanding of the worksheets and enabled them to be better equipped to understand their assigned sample problem that they had to complete for homework overnight. TWI also improved the standard plan for reviewing the participants' PD 4-step plans.

Exhibit 8-4. Seven Definitions of Program Development

Program Development Training Definitions	
What is production?	End result—product or service—of an organization, plant, department, or unit.
What is a Production Problem?	Anything which interferes with production (We uncover some production problems and try to correct or improve them; others can be *anticipated* and may be prevented.)
What is Training?	A way to solve production problems. (There are many ways to deal with the material side; training deals with the personnel side.)
What is a Training Plan?	An organized method of solving a specific part of a production problem.
What is a Training Program?	A combination of training plans coordinated to meet the training needs caused by a specific production problem.
What is a Training Director?	A person who has the responsibility for developing and coordinating training plans and programs in order to help management solve its production problems through people.
What is Management?	Those persons responsible for accomplishing the end results in terms of product or service.

People or Material Causes Production Problems

The logic behind all of the TWI programs is that production problems are caused either by people or by material. "Material" is a broad term that includes raw materials and equipment. You handle production problems caused by material in various ways, from evaluating and changing raw materials, to repairing, replacing, acquiring, or discarding equipment. Production problems caused by people are solved through training because you can attribute many of the "people" production problems to poor instruction, methods, or interpersonal relations. The three "J" programs, of course, address these problems, which occur throughout all organizations.

Solutions to other production problems, however, are very dependent on and unique to the organization in which they occur. As a result, individuals in organizations with unique problems must develop unique solutions to solve those problems. As TWI formulated the PD training, specific ideas of what an organization should do to develop its own programs solidified and eventually became "The Five Needs of a Supervisor" (Exhibit 4-4). The Five Needs help to differentiate between the training TWI was going to do from the training that companies would be responsible for developing. The Five Needs also helped to clarify when a company needed special training or standard training.

TWI's overall intent with all these programs was to help people develop the skills to think about what they were doing, and how they were doing it, and then make the appropriate decisions to improve performance. TWI believed that developing the confidence and resourcefulness in how to proceed was more important than imparting standardized solutions or rules. For example, when TWI was asked when it would create training specific to quality control or costs, "The answer invariably was that the skilled supervisor is resourceful and can apply his skills to these problems as he faces them."[20] Similarly, once the Program Development training became better known, supervisors began using it to solve problems other than those directly related to training. As a result, TWI was asked to help in this area by developing training for specifically solving other types of plant problems. TWI's reply was that "The answer lies in the use of the PD method by the PD-trained man,"[21] believing that the Program Development program offered all the skills necessary to solve a problem and that additional input must come from the people themselves.

This concludes Part 2 and our look at evolution and various versions of the four TWI programs. In Part 3 we will now look in greater detail at the techniques, tools, and approaches in delivering the four training programs.

---

1. C.R. Dooley, Director TWI Service in a letter to trainers at the beginning of the Program Development Manual.
2. *TWI Report*, pp. 236–237.
3. *TWI Report*, p. 237.
4. *TWI Report*, p. 238.
5. *TWI Report*, p. 240; Note that the publication "The Organization of a Training Program" is not included in either The *TWI Report* or the Training Within Industry Materials. It is very likely that it was replaced by the two bulletins: "How to Get a Plant Training Plan Into Action," and "How to Get Continuing Results From Plant Training Programs."
6. *TWI Report*, p. 242.
7. *TWI Report*, p. 244.
8. *TWI Report*, p. 242.
9. Walter Dietz—*Learn by Doing*, p. 26.
10. *Program Development Manual*, p. 27.
11. *Program Development Manual*, p. 31.

12. *TWI Report*, p. 245.
13. *TWI Report*, p. 248.
14. *TWI Report*, p. 250.
15. *TWI Report*, p. 242.
16. *Program Development Manual*, pp. 59–60.
17. *TWI Report*, p. 248.
18. *TWI Report*, pp. 246–247.
19. Many people today support training because it is a "good" thing to do. However, it has been estimated that as much as 80 percent of contemporary training is wasted since it has no impact on the workplace. Brinkerhoff, Robert O. and Gill, Stephen J., *The Learning Alliance: Systems Thinking in Human Resource Development*. San Francisco: Jossey Bass, 1994, p. xii.

    Using PD techniques would significantly reduce this percentage.
20. *TWI Report*, p. 266.
21. *TWI Report*, p. 265.

PART 3

Delivering the Method for Each Program

CHAPTER 9

Delivering Job Instruction

"If the worker hasn't learned, the instructor hasn't taught.[1]

Having discussed the evolution of the four TWI programs, Chapters 9 thru 12 will delve deeper into the process for delivering each training program. The goal in these chapters is to provide an idea of what TWI trainers and participants can expect when participating in a TWI program. Before discussing Job Instruction, it is important to revisit some of the common characteristics among the four programs discussed in Chapter 4.

Building a Common Delivery Method

As Job Instruction became successful, it naturally became a model for designing the other programs. As discussed in the previous chapters, all four TWI programs have common characteristics that allow for a similar delivery method because, "In all of them, fact-finding and an analysis of the facts are basic."[2] Each uses a variation of the 4-Step Method based on the broader scientific method: 1) define a problem, 2) get the facts, 3) analyze those facts, 4) make a decision, 5) take action, and 6) follow up. In Job Instruction, participants break down a job and make a training timetable. In Job Methods, the participants break down a job, but rely more on questioning the process. In Job Relations, you obtain facts and feelings from the participants and then weigh them. Each program will take some sort of action and then follow up by checking the results. All the programs emphasize teaching the participants to be critical and to learn problem-solving skills. In Lean Thinking, companies use a similar scientific approach to sustaining continuous improvement: the Deming Cycle of Plan-Do-Check-Act (PDCA). As a problem-solving process, "a learning enterprise is continually using PDCA at all levels of the company, from the project, to the group, to the company, and ultimately across companies."[3] However, unlike the more general application of PDCA, and where people often have difficulty learning to use it, the TWI developers designed the 4-Step Method as a cornerstone for delivering training that people could easily learn and apply.

Common Approach for Delivering Session I

It was also reasonable for TWI to leverage the success of JI so it could provide the trainer with the same techniques and approach in delivering the different content for each "J" program. (As discussed in Chapter 8, because the
Program Development had a different purpose—instructing plant representatives to identify plant problems and develop appropriate training—TWI structured and conducted it around a 35-hour, one-week program.) All the "J"
programs use the following format for the first two-hour session, referred to as
the "famous firsts":[4]

- *Introduction by a plant executive.* The purpose of this brief introduction is to demonstrate that management fully supports the program.
  TWI offered suggested dialogues to ensure that the manager made the
  correct points.
- *Introduction by the trainer.* The TWI trainer gives the participants some
  information about him or herself and asks for similar information from
  the participants. When trainers know the participants better, they are
  able to provide better training. Instructions on how to "put people at
  ease" are included in a reference section of the training manual. Secondly, the trainer will take this time to outline the course and set the pattern for the week.
- *Sell the program to the participants.* This discussion always begins with
  "The Five Needs of a Supervisor," 1) knowledge of the work, 2) knowledge of responsibilities, 3) skill in instructing, 4) skill in improving
  methods, and 5) skill in leading (see Exhibit 4-4 for details). Program
  Development would handle the two knowledge needs (knowledge of
  work and knowledge of responsibility), although the manual never
  states it specifically. Because of the unique way each organization sat-
  isfies these two needs and the problems it may be dealing with, it is necessary to develop a PD training program specific for each organization.
  This is why it is necessary to have at least one individual from an organization capable of identifying a problem and designing a training plan
  to correct it. This is the intent of the Program Development Institute.

    The other three needs, skill in instruction, improving methods, and
  leading, are addressed by having people (specifically supervisors)
  develop skills. The trainer discusses each skill briefly and the last skill
  discussed becomes the topic of the training session. The trainer covers
  this skill in more detail, including how it will help make the supervisor
  successful. By this point, the participants, at a minimum, should be in a
  frame of mind for considering the new plan.

- *Give a demonstration of a situation without the benefit of the "J" program.* In the case of JI, the trainer tries to teach someone how to tie a knot using usual instruction techniques. In JM, a sample job is performed. JR uses a case where a supervisor reacts to an employee situation in what could be considered a typical fashion.
- *Repeat the same scenario using the "J" plan.* In JI, the instructor teaches someone to tie the knot using the Job Instruction plan. In JM, the procedure is done three times faster with no extra effort after the Job Methods plan has been used for the job.
- *Present and apply the 4-Step Method.* The trainer applies the 4-Step Method to the scenario to demonstrate how it is used as well as to show its benefits. In JR, the method is presented by reviewing the original scenario, so this step and the one above are combined.
- *Discuss results.* The intent is to get all the participants to be enthused enough about the advantages of the plan to have a strong desire to learn and use it.
- *Select volunteers to demonstrate use of the plan.* The volunteers' demonstrations take place in following sessions.

Commonality in the TWI Program Manuals

During the 5 years of its existence, the TWI Service was refining and making the "J" program manuals similar. Although all the TWI manuals arrive at the same points using the same methods, the final published copies were written by different people and have some differences. These differences point to the fact that there is no single best way to do a job. You can choose a "best way" to standardize, but this in no way demeans or discounts using other possibilities.

For example, the JI manual spends five pages discussing the "Five Needs" while the JM manual uses one line to discuss the Five Needs and refers the trainer to the reference material in the manual. Each TWI program manual includes reference material that expands on various issues that are not or should not be covered in the manual proper. For example, someone might ask how to instruct in a noisy environment. This is covered in the reference material with two other "special training problems" but is included during the session only if there is enough time. JI also has a special section for Trainer Techniques, while JM includes those techniques in its reference material. Because of its nature, JR includes eleven pages of "A Way of Looking at the Supervisory Job," which is much like a Psychology 101 for supervisors (See Appendix B). In addition, JR gives a detailed strategy for each session at the beginning of the manual, while the other two manuals are subtler about overall training strategy.

Delivering the Contents of the Program Manual Like an Actor

Regardless of which manual a trainer is using, the trainer is required to know the manual thoroughly. Merely reading it aloud is never sufficient. The trainer also needs to know if participants properly understand the content. As mentioned earlier in the book, a trainer must know the manual's content like a stage director knows the dialogue, cues, action, and intent of a script, and then be able to deliver the lines like an actor. And like a good actor, a trainer makes participants believe what he or she is saying and doing. To deliver an excellent TWI session, the trainer needs hours of rehearsal to learn the content, props, and appropriate movements, and must have a deep understanding of the TWI strategy. In order to monitor the success of the sessions, each of the original manuals encourage the trainer to review each session to see what was done correctly or incorrectly, and what could be improved. For the guidance and information of the Job Relations Trainer, the Job Relations Reference 1 section included the following policies and procedures, which are concerned chiefly with quality control of Job Relations.

1. Job Relations is to be put on *exactly* as outlined in the manual.
2. During the first 10-hour program that a Job Relations Trainer performs, he will be visited by an Institute Conductor or a Quality Control man for at least one session and preferably two.
3. Thereafter, each Job Relations Trainer may be visited in sessions once a month.
4. No Job Relations Trainer shall remain on the active list unless he conducts at least one 10-hour program every 90 days.
5. All Job Relations Trainers are expected to attend coaching sessions at the request of the TWI District Office.[5]

The point is best made in the introduction to the Reference Material for the original Job Methods manual.

"In presenting the Job Methods program, an otherwise convincing demonstration is often spoiled by a point that was improperly made because it appeared to be of minor importance. You will avoid this if you study the pages that follow. Practice the demonstration until you have mastered each step and successfully timed your explanation with each move you make.

"... A clear understanding of the points to be made is absolutely necessary to a successful demonstration. These points are covered in detail on the pages that follow.

"Illustrations, stories and examples of your own that show the practical application of the items presented are very desirable and should be used whenever appropriate. However, no item in the Sessions Outline is to be omitted or changed.

"This does not mean that the paragraphs in quotation marks are always to be given to the group *exactly* word for word as given in the Sessions Outline. The trainer may use his own words so long as the *exact meaning* is preserved at all times."[6]

As discussed in Chapter 4, the original Job Instruction Manual did not mention speaking verbatim, but because of the confusion among TWI trainers about memorizing versus reading versus telling the exact meaning, the JI manual had, at the bottom of each page, "WORK FROM THIS OUTLINE— DON'T TRUST TO MEMORY." When TWI released the second program, Job Methods, it included the phrase in the reference material and at the beginning of the session outline:

"Paragraphs in quotation marks are to be presented either by using the exact words of the text or expressing the exact meaning in the trainer's own words. In the case of the latter, special care should be taken to convey the exact meaning *every time*."[7]

This approach continued to evolve and Job Relations, the last program released, provided a Code for reading the Sessions Outline. It included a * in front of a line that the trainer should read verbatim. Reference 2 of the Job Relations Manual states: "'Following the manual' does not mean sitting down and reading it. *Learn it*—Then check yourself repeatedly."[8] Though contemporary manuals are more uniform about what trainers should state verbatim, the intent should still be for the trainer to read the manual like a good actor or newscaster, because stating the exact meaning in the trainer's own words can be time consuming and inconsistent.

One final commonality among all the manuals is that they listed the timeline on the left of each page in the Sessions Outline. The timeline gives the TWI trainer a running schedule of how many minutes he or she should use for each section and how many minutes should have expired at certain points in the session. When practicing, novice trainers find that it is not as easy as it looks to present all the information in the time allotted. This is where "knowing the manual" is so beneficial and ultimately appreciated. A TWI program is a timed event and the only way for trainers to deliver the material successfully is to know it inside and out.

Uniformity in Contemporary Version of TWI Program Manuals

Patrick Graupp, for the Central New York Technology Development Organization, Inc. (NIST MEP Center in Syracuse, NY),[9] has assembled contemporary versions of these manuals, taking steps to bring uniformity to the training. In addition to being easier to follow, the trainer tips are included in the manual proper where the trainer can locate them when needed; and like the original manuals, the contemporary versions also include supplementary material in the reference section.

One important area of improvement was the development of participant guides to be used in conjunction with the other materials during training, such as the "pocket card." The TWI Service was very clear that it did not want the training to be encumbered with paperwork. At the time, TWI was hampered by limited resources, including paper, which was scarce, and printing capabilities, which were more primitive than today. Today's organizations tend to have a better-educated workforce, and employees expect more from their training. For instance, many participants like to take notes during training and want materials to take with them at the completion of the course.

So Patrick Graupp developed a series of Participant's Guides for the three "J" courses that serve two functions. First, the guides include areas for participants to take notes and the participants have room to highlight the main concepts like "The Five Needs" and program objectives. Second, the guides now include what used to be TWI handouts, a bound copy of all the training material. Patrick Graupp has also developed additional forms that are distributed during the course. This is another example of how the program can be adapted to meet a changing society while retaining the content.

Having discussed some of the commonalities of the TWI programs, we will now, in the remainder of this Chapter and Chapters 10, 11, and 12, look in more detail at delivering each of the four programs. We will also start each section with a brief outline of each of the course contents, to give the reader a sense of each of the programs (see Exhibit 9-1).[10] For the remainder of this chapter we will use the pronoun "he" for "trainer" or "instructor" and the pronoun "she" for "participant," "learner," "volunteer," or "worker." Note: the trainer is the TWI trainer and the instructor is the participant that will train a worker at the workplace. Table 5-1 further defines roles in TWI training.

Job Instruction Session I—How to Instruct

Returning to the objective of the first two-hour training session, the goal of the TWI trainer is to get the participants to both learn the method and want to use it. The JI manual explains it this way:

Exhibit 9-1. JI Course Contents

Course Contents of the 10-Hour Job Instruction Plan

FIRST SESSION—2 hours
  Introduction
  Importance of training to production
  Instructing ability as a personal asset (Five Needs of a Supervisor)
  Demonstration of faulty instruction
  Demonstration of correct instruction
  The FOUR BASIC STEPS
  Distribution of "How to Instruct" cards
  (Selection of two volunteers for the next session).

SECOND SESSION—2 hours
  Volunteer "instructing" demonstration, to bring out the NEED for the four
    things an instructor must do to "get ready."
  Practice in making job breakdowns of:
    a. The fire underwriters' knot
    b. Breakdown of another sample job
  Summary: The four things an instructor does to "get ready."

THIRD SESSION—2 hours
  Drill on training timetables
  Practice instruction demonstrations (by volunteers) with coaching on Job
    Breakdowns.

FOURTH SESSION—2 hours
  Review of all material
  Four practice instruction demonstrations (by volunteers) with coaching on
    Job Breakdowns.

FIFTH SESSION—2 hours
  Remaining practice instruction demonstrations (by volunteers) with coach-
    ing on Job Breakdowns.
  Conclusion and Summary
    a. Questions
    b. Importance of good Job Instruction to production
    c. Necessity of using the Job Instruction Plan.

ADHERE STRICTLY TO THIS PLAN—
DO NOT DEPART FROM IT OR CHANGE IT

"First—a realization of the acute need for training of the job.

"Second—the importance of good instruction to a supervisor.

"Third—some of the weaknesses we fall into in breaking in workers (tell–show alone).

"Fourth—the instructing process which is dependable and easier to use than the others."[11]

After the introductions and the discussion of "The Five Needs of Supervisors," the trainer shows the relevance of instruction by discussing the kinds of problems the participants can solve using correct instruction. Initially, the trainer distributed a list to the group of typical problems caused by poor or nonexistent instruction (see Exhibit 9-2).[12] It has since been found to be more effective to have the group create its own list because they then consider the list to be theirs. Once the group compiles the list of typical problems, the trainer can select which problems they can solve by correct instruction. Often, there are few, if any, problems mentioned that are not affected by instruction. Therefore, this list is kept and referred to again in Session V (the last day) to emphasize the point that good job instruction is a production tool that can be used to help the participants.

Using the Fire Underwriters Knot to Demonstrate Proper Instruction

The activity TWI chose to demonstrate proper instruction was the tying of the fire underwriter's knot. They chose it because "... [it] ... (... had successfully been used by the New Jersey Vocational Education Staff for many years) [and it] was both the most dramatic and the most practical."[13] Although they knew it was successful, I do not know if the TWI developers understood what a perfect activity this is for demonstrating instruction. Knot tying is something that most everyone does. Knots are devices we use everyday on our shoes, neckties, clothing, and packages, which usually involve the simple concept of passing string, twine or rope over and under itself. Yet learning how to tie a knot is usually not easy. More often than not, when we learn how to tie a knot, someone may show us but we do it by ourselves through trial and error. That is, the trainer gives only an overview or some guidelines and then the participant learns to tie the knots herself. This approach lies at the heart of how instruction is usually conducted, and thus, it is an excellent example of demonstrating the advantages of proper instruction.

The trainer should choose a knot demonstration that most people do not know how to do. The fire underwriters knot is a good knot selection because only electricians would probably know this knot, and it is used much less today than 60 years ago. The knot was used in all appliance plugs and ceiling fixtures

Exhibit 9-2. Typical Problems Caused by Poor or Nonexistent Instruction

---

HERE ARE SOME PROBLEMS THAT
JOB INSTRUCTION TRAINING *HAS HELPED* SOLVE
IN WAR PRODUCTION PLANTS
Do you have any similar problems on your job?

Production Problems
Deliveries delayed because of errors and mistakes by workers making the parts.
Workers don't know their jobs.
Mix-ups in trucking service.
Parts returned by other departments because they were not made right.
Operators have special problems because of engineering changes.
Poor planning.
Workers have difficulty in getting up to production on new type equipment.
Aisles too congested.
Excessive wear and tear on equipment.

Safety Problems
Safety equipment not properly used.
Material not piled properly.
Poor shop housekeeping.
Don't know safety rules.
Workers don't know hazards of their jobs.
Workers get careless.
Minor injuries not reported.

Quality Problems
Meeting inspection standards.
Too much scrap or rework.
Jigs and gauges not properly used.
Not following specifications.
Too much left to operator's judgment.

Personnel Problems
Workers leave to go to other plants—couldn't "get the hang" of the job.
New men and women lack experience in mechanical things.
Lack interest in the work.
Workers want transfers—think they can "make out" better on other jobs.
Claim to have good experience but don't "come through."
Too much time to get up to production.
Instructed wrong way.
Can't get experienced workers any more.
Get discouraged learning the job.

Most supervisors say that somewhere around 80 percent of these problems
could be solved—or at least helped—if they had a better trained workforce.

How about yours?

---

but has now been replaced by quick assembly plugs and fixtures, encapsulated plugs, and tug-resistant fittings.

First, the trainer discusses how someone typically instructs you. One way is simply by telling someone how to do something. The trainer then selects a volunteer and then *tells* her or him how to tie the knot. Naturally, even something very simple can quickly become complicated when you try to describe it. In the reference section of the Job Instruction Manual are the 13 steps required to tie the fire underwriters knot (see Exhibit 9-3).[14]

Exhibit 9-3. Thirteen Steps Required to Tie the Fire Underwriters Knot

---

"Telling" How To Tie the Knot

1. Take a piece of ordinary twisted electrical cord.
2. Hold it vertically in your left hand, between the thumb and first finger, 6 inches from the end.
3. Untwist the loose ends, forming a "V."
4. Straighten the loose ends between the thumb and first finger of the right hand.
5. Hold the wire at the beginning of the "V."
6. Take the right-hand loose end with the right hand, making a clockwise loop, bringing the loose end across in front of the main strand.
7. See that this loop is about 1 inch in diameter and that the stub protrudes to the left of the main strand about 1-1/2 inches. Hold the wire at the junction between the loop and the main strand.
8. Take the loose end with your right hand.
9. Make a clockwise loop. To make this loop, pull the loose end toward you, pass it underneath the stub, behind the main strand.
10. Pass the loose end through the right hand loop, from back to front.
11. Hold the ends evenly between the thumb and first finger of the right hand.
12. Pull the knot taut.
13. Shape the knot between the thumb and first finger of the left hand as it is pulled.

The trainer is instructed not to use any hand motions (because the trainer is only *telling*, not *showing*) and in fact should keep his hands in his pockets or by his sides. In addition, the trainer must recite the procedure 'word perfect' in order not to give the volunteer any reason to find fault with the instruction. Usually, the volunteer realizes she has no idea what to do by the halfway point in the instruction. This elicits some form of sympathy from the group as they recall being given poor instructions at one time or another. Once the trainer has completed telling the volunteer how to tie the knot, he gives the volunteer a piece of wire and the volunteer attempts to tie it.

It usually does not take too long before the volunteer gives up. The trainer should only take the wire from the volunteer when she is no longer proceeding correctly. The trainer must emphasize here that the volunteer failed because of the instruction not because of an inability to learn. This is so 1) the volunteer doesn't feel foolish by not being able to perform a simple task, and more importantly, 2) the point can be made that this is a critical concept in understanding the purpose and goal of the program. *Failure of the instruction is the responsibility of the instructor and not the person being instructed.* In 1941, TWI adopted a slogan used in the sessions and written at the bottom of the JI training card (see Exhibit 9-4) "IF THE WORKER HASN'T LEARNED, THE INSTRUCTOR HASN'T TAUGHT."[15] This slogan emphasized that the responsibility for getting people trained properly falls on the supervisor. However, the learner is responsible for trying, being attentive, cooperative, and responsive.

Some trainers object to the slogan because they, correctly, say that they cannot make someone learn if that person does not want to. However, understood within the proper context, the statement is correct. The instructor is training a worker to perform a job at a company for pay, and if the worker does not learn the job, he or she cannot do the job. If the worker wants the job, then it is reasonable to assume that he wants to know how to perform it properly since people generally do not like to perform poorly if they can help it. Furthermore, the better the training, the better the worker will perform, which should provide sufficient motivation for further learning. Aside from the extrinsic motivators of "getting a paycheck," most people want to learn and be productive and thus are driven to succeed at learning a task. The trainer, on the other hand, usually has many other duties to perform, and can easily assume it is the worker's job to learn. The TWI slogan is a constant reminder wherein the responsibility truly lies.

The trainer, after having completed the first part of the demonstration, is now in a position to show that merely *telling* a person what to do does not usually work. He briefly discusses this concept with examples. The following points are made:

- Many people are not auditory learners.
- Many operations are difficult to describe.
- Few of us use accurate and precise words when describing something.
- It's difficult to tell how much information is 'just enough' for the learner to understand what is to be done and how to do it.

The trainer now discusses another method of instructing: *showing*. The trainer then selects another volunteer, faces that volunteer, and proceeds slowly and carefully to tie the knot. This time, the trainer doesn't use any verbal explanation. The only instruction the volunteer receives is watching what the trainer does. The trainer then gives a piece of wire to the volunteer and asks her to tie the knot. The volunteer is usually unsuccessful. The manual does allow for the possibility that someone will be able to tie the knot, but it is highly unlikely. If that does occur, the trainer selects another volunteer. (Note: If a person ties the knot backwards because he or she is facing the trainer, it is considered a failure.) Since it is unlikely the volunteer will tie the knot, even backwards, the trainer usually begins a discussion of why only showing is not a good instruction technique. Examples and the following reasons are used:

- Many people are not visual learners—we can't always translate what we *see* into what we should *do*.
- In this case, the volunteer would have had to remember what was done **and** mentally flip the images since the two people were facing one other.
- Even if we copy the motions perfectly, we may still not understand the job and omit something that is important.
- Some motions are hard to copy.
- We don't know what to look for.
- We might miss "tricky points."

At this point the trainer has broken the concept of instruction into two of its elements: *only telling* someone what to do and *only showing* someone what to do. These two methods have been separated to make it clear how these instruction tools are misused. Some skeptics might counter that they always combine these two methods and thus they would get better results. The JI method does, in fact, combine showing and telling, but it includes much more. First, it is important *how* you show and tell someone what to do. Second, TWI incorporates several other ideas into the training program to make it successful. These ideas are summarized on the JI reminder card or training card, which we will be discussing shortly. All of the ideas in the 4-Step Method are necessary for proper training as well as Items 2–4 on the reverse side of the card.[16]

The intent is to demonstrate how just showing or just telling can be ineffective—it is not for educating the group about the development of the JI method. In the next demonstration of tying the knot, the trainer will use the JI 4-Step Method. Obviously, everyone in the group has, at some time, learned a job using some other training method. And thus, in this situation, if the trainer had continued repeating the process (showing or telling) with either volunteer, that person would have learned to tie the knot sooner or later. The point of JI, however, is that it is a reliable and dependable method, and if properly followed, the procedure will teach a person a job quickly every time. And like the factors that underline Lean Thinking, TWI also emphasizes that when employees learn the job correctly and safely, it reduces scrap, broken tools, and equipment, and increases available production time.

Now it is time for the trainer to select a third volunteer and teach that person to tie the knot using the JI 4-Step Method. When the volunteer succeeds in tying the knot she is usually the most surprised of all in the group. Because the volunteer is concentrating on learning to tie the knot, she doesn't get the same visibility of the method as do others in the group. That is, something that seemed to be complicated was actually fairly easy to learn. This is the first time the JI 4-Step Method has been shown, and at this point an appreciation for its value is beginning to build among the participants. An important point for the trainer here is that the knot tying demonstration must be done perfectly since all the points made in this and later sessions will refer back to this particular demonstration.

Distributing JI 4-Step Method Training Cards—"How to Instruct"

At this point in the training, the trainer distributes JI training cards as a reminder to participants of "How to Get Ready to Instruct" and "How to Instruct" (see Exhibit 9-4, which is the same as 5-3). The training card has two sides. The trainer discusses the "How to Get Ready to Instruct" side of the card later in Session II after the trainee learns "How to Instruct." As discussed elsewhere, these training cards are very effective for keeping the participants focused on the essential steps in the program and helping the trainer deliver the steps according to a timetable in Exhibit 9-1.

The trainer distributes the JI training cards and goes over the JI 4-Step Method using comments relating to the instruction of the last volunteer. This section takes only about fifteen minutes—each of the steps is read, followed by some discussion about the items under each step. As the trainees go over the four points on the card, the following are some important points they must keep in mind regarding what is required to be a good instructor.

Step 1: Prepare the Worker

It is human nature to be at least slightly anxious when we are learning something new. In most cases, many other activities in the organization are occurring at the same time and in the same place as the training. At the workplace, the instructor must put the worker at ease and have her focus on the training; otherwise she will be less effective at learning the task at hand. Put the worker at ease with some introductory "small talk" until you have the worker's attention. Tell her what the job is. If there is a product involved, show the finished

Exhibit 9-4. JI 4-Step Method Training Card*

How to Get Ready to Instruct	How to Instruct

How to Get Ready to Instruct
 	
Have a timetable—
  How much skill you expect to
  have, by what date
 	
Break down the job—
  List important steps
  Pick out key points (Safety is
  always a key point)
 	
Have everything ready—
  The right equipment, material,
  and supplies
 	
Have the workplace properly
arranged—
  Just as the worker will be
  expected to keep it
 	
--- 	
 	
Job Instruction Training
TRAINING WITHIN INDUSTRY
Bureau of Training
War Manpower Commission
 	
--- 	
 	
KEEP THIS CARD HANDY
	How to Instruct
	Step 1—Prepare the worker
	• Put him at ease.
	• State the job and find out what
	  he already knows about it.
	• Get him interested in learning
	  the job.
	• Place in a correct position.
	Step 2—Present the operation
	• Tell, show, and illustrate one
	  IMPORTANT STEP at a time.
	• Stress each KEY POINT
	• Instruct clearly, completely, and
	  patiently, but no more than he
	  can muster.
	Step 3—Try out performance
	• Have him do the job—correct
	  errors
	• Have him explain each KEY
	  POINT to you as he does the
	  job again.
	• Make sure he understands.
	• Continue until YOU know HE
	  knows.
	Step 4—Follow up
	• Put him on his own. Designate to
	  whom he goes for help.
	• Check frequently. Encourage
	  questions.
	• Taper off extra coaching and
	  close follow up.
	
	--- 	
	
	If the worker hasn't learned, the
	instructor hasn't taught.

*Dietz, *Learn by Doing*, p. 16.

product. Tell her as much about it as is necessary to give her an idea of where this operation fits into the entire operation. Find something about the job to make the worker interested in learning and doing it. Pose these questions. What happens if this job is not done or is done incorrectly? What are the possible consequences to other employees, the organization, and to customers?[17]

Once the worker is more relaxed, find out what she already knows about this particular job and any skills that are required to complete it. Any existing knowledge or skills will give her confidence in learning the job and will hasten the learning process. Knowing what the worker already knows will help the instructor determine how much detail to use when describing the job without boring her.

If the worker is going to be watching you do something, make sure she is in the correct position to see the job as you are seeing it. In the knot tying demonstration, the participants faced the trainer so that all images had to be turned around in their minds. Have the worker look over your left shoulder if you are right handed so she has the best visibility. Do whatever is necessary from a practical standpoint to make sure the worker can see what you are doing. Finally, tell the worker to ask questions at any time during the training. The only stupid question is the one not asked! Asking questions will not only help workers but will give the instructor more information about what the worker knows. However, the instructor must be *sincere* when he says that no question is stupid. People can easily spot insincerity, which will inhibit questions and reduce the effectiveness of the instruction.

Step 2: Present the Operation

An important factor in instructing is to give a person only as much information as she can absorb at one time. Repeat the operation several times with additional information being added for each repetition so the worker will not be overwhelmed with information. (For a procedure like tying a knot, two or three times is usually sufficient.) First, the instructor tells the worker how many steps are involved in the job. (In the knot case, there are five.) The worker now has something concrete on which to build an understanding of the method. As the instructor performs each step, he clearly identifies the step and what he is doing, as shown in Exhibit 9-5.[18]

Using the example in Exhibit 9-5, the instructor might say, "Step 1 is to untwist and straighten the ends of the wire" as he is untwisting and straightening the wire. After the instructor finishes with one product, he repeats the procedure, but this time he states each step he is doing *and* any "Key Point" connected to that step. (Key Points will be discussed shortly.) The dialogue here should go something like this:

"The first step is to untwist and straighten the wires. This step has a Key Point. The Key Point is that the wire should be untwisted about 6 inches from the end."

Exhibit 9-5. TDO Form and Steps for Presenting a Job © 2002

Job Breakdown Sheet

Operation: _____ Tying the Fire Underwriter's Knot _____

Parts: _____ Twisted Lamp Cord _____

Tools & Materials: _____ None _____

IMPORTANT STEPS	KEY POINTS	REASONS
A logical segment of the operation when something happens to advancethe work.	Anything in a step that might— 1. Make or break the job 2. Injure the worker 3. Make the work easier to do, i.e., "knack," "trick," special timing, bit of special information	Reasons for the key points
1. Untwist & straighten	6 inches	Leave enough length for the next operation
2. Make a right loop	In front of the main strand	The knot will not tie correctly
3. Make a left loop	1. Pulling end toward you 2. Under the stub 3. Behind the main strand	1. It's easier to do the next motion 2. The knot will not tie correctly 3. The knot will not tie correctly
4. Put end through loop		
5. Pull taut	1. Ends even 2. Sliding loops down 3. Firmly	1. The knot will tie evenly 2. So the knot ties in the correct position 3. So it won't come apart

Another knot is now tied. This time any reasons for the Key Points are added to the dialogue:

"The first step is to untwist and straighten the wires. The Key Point is that the wire should be untwisted about 6 inches from the end. The reason for the Key Point is that enough wire must be available for the next operation, and too much wire is wasteful and may interfere with the next operation."

The instructor has now performed the job three times, and the worker should now know and remember that there are five steps and eight Key Points. The instructor must now pay attention to and assess the worker's comments, body language, and any other cues to determine whether the worker is ready to try the job. In the case of the knot tying, three explanations are usually sufficient for the participants. For a more complicated or more dangerous job at a company, the instructor may repeat the process. Once the instructor believes the worker is ready, he tells her to perform the job while he watches.

Step 3: Try-Out Performance

The first time the worker performs the job, she should do it silently to help her focus totally on the task. It is important that the instructor pay close attention and stop her immediately if she starts to do something wrong. The longer the worker performs the job incorrectly, the more difficult it will be for the instructor to train her properly. Once the worker performs the job completely without error, the instructor tells her to:

- Perform the job again while at the same time enumerating the steps.
- Repeat the job, but this time vocalizing both the steps and the Key Points.
- Repeat the job a third time, vocalizing the steps, Key Points, and reasons for the Key Points.

After repeating these instructions, the instructor must make a determination whether the worker can perform the job on her own. When that point occurs, the instructor turns over the job to the worker.

Step 4: Follow up

After the instructor turns the job over, he still monitors the worker's progress. Ideally, the organization should have work for the worker to continue performing the job. Although the worker has been trained, unless she can repeatedly perform the job to fix it in her mind, she will forget the training. Also, even though the instructor covered all the questions, and he believes the worker completely understood the job, an unforeseen situation or question may arise as soon as he leaves. If the instructor must leave the area, he should make sure the worker has someone to go to with any questions or concerns. He or a designee should check back with the worker in a short time to confirm that there are no problems. And check back again, somewhat later, tapering off the coaching until the person has complete ownership of the job.

Going over the four steps, prepare the worker, present the operation, performance tryout, and follow up, nearly completes the participant's first 2-hour session. All that is left to do is for the TWI trainer to select 2 volunteers to perform demonstrations of a job in the second session. Every participant must select a job and teach it to another person in the group. Only by instructing others in a job can a person thoroughly learn the JI 4-Step Method. Performing this demonstration will not make an expert out of the participants overnight, but it will help them internalize the method so that they can practice it enough to become an expert.

Job Instruction Session II—How to Get Ready to Instruct

The JI 4-Step Method is the working part of the JI program, but the instructor needs to *prepare for training* before he or she can teach the job to workers in the organization. There are four items discussed in "How to Get Ready to Instruct" on the reverse side of the training card (see Exhibit 9-4). So that the participants are not given too much information at one time, the TWI trainer uses nearly all of Session II to discuss preparing for training, Item 2. Item 3, "Have Everything Ready," and Item 4, "Have the Workplace Properly Arranged," are straightforward and are discussed at the end of Session II. (Item 1 is discussed in Session III.)

Briefly, "Have Everything Ready," means that the newly trained instructor should have all tools or equipment ready when they begin training other workers. If the instructor has to stop training to rummage through a drawer for a pair of scissors, this will disrupt the flow of the training and may result in time wasted during production. Being professionally prepared sets an example for the worker. After all, she is learning the job from you, so she will follow what you do. If the instructor is in a hurry and settles for a #3 Phillips screwdriver instead of a #5 Phillips screwdriver, the worker will most likely do the same thing. It is also extremely important to use the proper safety equipment. Saying, "Wear safety glasses when you do this" while not wearing safety glasses at the time, will denigrate both the instructor and the training.

"Have the Workplace Properly Arranged," means: Have the work area where the training is to take place in its *ideal* condition. The instructor should have *only* the tools and equipment present that are required for the job. The instructor is a model for the worker and the quality of the organization of the work area is part of that model. After all, he is not only teaching a specific job, but also setting an example for how the worker should perform her job.

Item 1: Training Timetable

Though the first item under "How to Get Ready to Instruct" is creating a timetable for training, it is not directly related to performing a job instruction so the JI trainer actually covers it in Session III. A *training timetable* is used for organizing the training of any organization and is merely a spreadsheet that keeps track of who is capable of doing what. It also indicates who should be trained, what that training should be, and when it should occur. It is very useful because in most organizations people are required to multitask. Anyone who directs the work of others (the TWI developer's definition of a supervisor) should know what employees are capable of doing. Furthermore, in most instances, it helps the supervisor plan to increase the capability of all the employees who are deficient in some areas since it is a lot of information to remember. More importantly, timetables can make this information public so that everyone in the organization knows what everyone does and is capable of doing. Exhibit 9-6 shows a training timetable.[19] The scheme for the matrix (boxes, dates, etc.) is only a suggestion. The instructor should use symbols that have the most meaning for the group listed in the timetable.

Exhibit 9-6. How to Get Ready for an Instruction Training Timetable

Simple Job Instruction Timetable							
	Drill	Bore	Ream	Race	Taper Turn	Burr & Burnish	Etc.	Etc.
White	✔	✔	✔	✔	✔	✔		
Nolan	✔	✔	✔	11-10	—	—		
Smith	11-1	11-20	—	✔	✔	12-1		
Jones	—	—	✔	11-15	12-1	12-8		
Etc.								

✔ means the worker can already do the job.
— means the worker doesn't need to know the job.
11-1, 11-15, etc., indicates the dates the supervisor has set to have workers TRAINED to do the jobs required.

Item 2: Breakdown the Job

It is important for the instructor to have the details of the job organized in his mind before attempting to teach it to a worker. This is the most important part of the JI program because the success of the training depends on how well the participant learns to write the job breakdown sheet. The reason the TWI developers delayed the explanation of the job breakdown sheet until the second session was that 1) participants had plenty of material to absorb in the first session, and 2) participants should clearly understand that the need for these sheets was sincere (not just busy paperwork) and hence would know the importance in creating them.

There are several good reasons why a job breakdown sheet is critical to good instruction, but telling someone is not as effective as having them identify the reasons for themselves. Therefore, the first volunteer presents her job instruction demonstration without the benefit of a job breakdown sheet. She selects someone from the group and trains that person in the job she has selected. She follows the JI 4-Step Method and prepares the worker, presents the operation, has the person try out the operation, and then follows up. More often than not, the person does learn the job, but the group can see that the first volunteer had a somewhat difficult time of it. The trainer leads a group discussion of how the volunteer conducted the instruction. Naturally, because this is the first volunteer, the four steps are usually not done expertly. The usual outcome of the first volunteer's demonstration is evidenced by one or more of the following actions:

- The steps are not outlined clearly.
- One or more steps are not explained well.
- The volunteer forgets one or more steps and inserts it out of order.
- All Key Points were not mentioned.
- Some Key Points were mentioned out of order.
- All tools are not available.
- The trainee gave information that was not necessary to learning and performing the job.

The JI trainer must emphasize at this point that the ineffective training was not the fault of the volunteer and further explain that although the volunteer followed the four steps as discussed in session one, its proper execution is not always sufficient to provide good training. Now the participants are beginning to see that proper preparation for training can be as important as the training itself.

This method of having the group learn from the first volunteer's mistakes caused by the lack of a JBS deserves some comment. During subsequent sessions, the participants will all learn from watching other demonstrations and thus the first demonstration is no different. In the second session, however, the JI trainer wants to be sure to sell the idea of a JBS. In order to best do this, the participants observe a demonstration which has been done without the benefit of a JBS. Many people do not like paperwork. However, it is vital to the success of the JI training to have all participants strongly believe that a JBS is essential. The JI trainer does not give the volunteer incomplete instruction, he helps to convince the participants that something else is required. The JI manual instructs the JI trainer to take aside the 2 volunteers after the first session, and thank them for being the first volunteers. He explains that, being the first, they are not expected to perform the training correctly the first time. Everyone is here to learn and both they and the group will benefit from any mistakes made. Normally those who volunteer first have a higher degree of self-confidence. This experience is not detrimental.

The trainer then directs the group's attention to the card "How to Get Ready to Instruct" (Exhibit 9-4) so they can discuss the four items and them tells them that they will discuss the training timetable in session III and deal with "Have Everything Ready," and "Have the Workplace Properly Arranged" shortly. He proceeds to tell them that Item 2, "Breakdown the Job" is critical to delivering good instruction. Blank breakdown sheets are distributed and the trainer proceeds to break down the fire underwriter's knot job. The completed Job Breakdown Sheet for the Fire Underwriter's Knot is shown in Exhibit 9-5.

Reasons to Use Breakdown Sheets

There are ten reasons why a Job Breakdown Sheet (JBS) is important for delivering good instruction,[20] many of which became apparent in the first volunteer's demonstration above. Using a JBS properly helps you:

1. Convey all unwritten knowledge to the trainee.
2. Confirm that you do not forget anything during the training.
3. Make sure that steps are presented in the correct order.
4. Create a checklist to confirm that the trainee has learned everything.
5. Check that too much information is not given to the trainee at one time.
6. Make sure everything (methods, tools, and equipment) is included in the training.
7. Review explanations so that they are not confusing.
8. Determine the important parts of the job. Check that easier parts of the operation are given before the harder parts.
9. Confirm that the method used is correct, standardized, and safe.
10. Accumulate data for work planning—length of time to train, skills required, and materials and tools required, etc.

The JBS properly helps to ensure good instruction, which increases production, reduces scrap and tool/equipment damage, and impresses appropriate safety measures on the worker.

In fact, this demonstration is used to show that the JBS is a critical part of the JI program and the quality of the JBS can make or break the job instruction. First, breakdown sheets serve as an exercise to prepare the instructor at his or her work-place to think through the entire job and confirm that all equipment, tools, and parts are ready and available for training. In addition, this exercise forces the instructor to analyze and plan out the job and then to break it down into important steps. (The definition of an important step will be discussed shortly.)

The JBS helps the instructor to not only remember the critical steps of the job, but also prevents the introduction of information that is not pertinent to the successful completion of the job. Reexamining and breaking down the job also confirms that the proper procedure is used, safety precautions are taken, and that the job tasks are broken down into appropriate units so the worker can learn one unit of the job at a time. The instructor uses the JBS as a guide while training and as a checklist that he can glance at to ensure nothing is forgotten in the teaching process. Therefore it must not be too detailed or "busy."

Thinking through the job in this way also gives the instructor an opportunity to create innovative ways to convey complicated ideas to the worker. This upfront preparation helps the instructor anticipate questions and avoid giving confusing explanations during the training. Sometimes, an instructor is so familiar with the job he is teaching, that he performs critical parts or steps without thinking, or an instructor may think he knows a job, but for various reasons, does not know it well enough to explain it to someone else. Writing down the important and critical steps ensures that the instructor does not omit anything and that he conveys *everything* to the worker, and in fact, ensures that he knows the job well. The worker benefits from the important steps (discussed below) because it gives her specific "chunks" of information to learn. If done correctly, the size of those chunks will be neither trivial nor over-whelming. Material is easier to learn if the amount in each chunk is about equal. Furthermore, the JBS can also serve as a checklist to confirm that the worker has been instructed in all parts of the job

As we've discussed, the JBS is used as a guide by the instructor for both the order and the content of the training, and it is critical that he perform each step of the job correctly the first time it is demonstrated to a worker. It is not acceptable to repeat a procedure that was done incorrectly the first time, since this can confuse the worker and set back the training. The process of learning is analogous to writing in that if an error is made, the erroneous words must first be erased before the correct words can be written. Writing correct words over incorrect ones only causes confusion. Therefore, if someone learns an incorrect step, that step must be "unlearned" before it can be replaced with the correct one. Since people have a tendency to remember best what they hear and see first, this usually results in adding additional time so that the correct step is firmly set in the worker's mind.

Important Steps in the Job Breakdown Sheet (JBS)

The trainer uses the JBS to list the important steps in the job and to list the Key Points for those steps and the reasons for the Key Points. Because the trainer creates the JBS for his own use, he controls which steps to include, but he should keep in mind that a worker performs many actions when completing a job, some of which will be completely new, but some of which will be routinely familiar, and those familiar actions should not be included in the JBS. In other words, the instructor should consider the worker's ability and experience when choosing the important steps. For example, computer navigation techniques have some commonality, so operating the computer and accessing programs would be second nature to the word processing software program expert. The instructor would not include these operating details in the JBS. Though any actions that move the job along are considered important steps, the instructor has to be careful to list only those steps that advance the progress of the job and the worker's training.

Exhibits 9-7a and 9-7b[21] provide an example job breakdown for milling a dovetail. A miller with machine experience would use Exhibit 9-7a. For someone with less experience, one of those steps (Step 4—Rough Cut) has its own breakdown sheet (see Exhibit 9-7b) for the Rough Cut operation that is only part of the larger milling operation.

Three Criteria for a Key Point

The term "Important Step" means a list of "What to do" steps when performing a job; the term "Key Point" means "How to do" that step; and the reasons for a Key Point is "Why" one should do the Key Point.

- Important Steps: What to do.
- Key Points: How to do it.
- Reasons for Key Points: Why do it.

The Job Breakdown Sheet form lists three criteria for a Key Point:

1. Makes or breaks the job.
2. Could cause injury to the worker.
3. Makes the job easier to do.

1. *Makes or breaks the job.* When installing a drain in a porcelain sink, the drain fitting must be put into the drain hole at the bottom of the sink and then tightened against the sink. If the drain fitting is not tightened enough, water will leak out of the sink. If the drain fitting is tightened too much, the sink will crack. Although this may not make the sink leak, it destroys its appearance.

Exhibit 9-7a. JBS for Training Person on New Job

Job Breakdown Sheet for Training Worker on New Job

Part: Slide Base 235310   Operation: Mill Dovetail

IMPORTANT STEPS IN THE OPERATION	KEY POINTS
Step: A logical segment of the operation when something happens to ADVANCE the work	Key Point: Anything in a step that might— Make or break the job Injure the worker Make the work easier to do; i.e., a "knack," "trick," special timing, bit of special information
1. Select cutter	Small—minimize chatter
2. Select holder parallels	Narrow—yet to give good hold
3. Place piece in vise	Check with tissue
4. Rough cut	Start by hand—1"—Check for finish stock and location
5. Trial finish cut	Check—make correction
6. Finish cut	Finish without stopping
7. Remove from vise	
8. File burrs	
9. Check	

An experienced worker in a machine shop made this breakdown in 7 minutes. This instructor uses this breakdown "as is" for workers who have other milling machine experience.

For "green" workers, each of these steps might constitute an "instructing unit" by itself and require a separate detail breakdown.

[Exhibit 9-7b] shows the detailed breakdown for Step 4, above, Rough cut.

Thus, the Important Step would be: Tighten drain fitting to sink. The Key Point would be: "firmly." The reason for the Key Point would be to prevent leaks and cracks. During the instruction, the instructor must convey this concept of "feel" to the worker. (The Reference Material at the end of the JI manual discusses how to convey the concept of "feel.") With the drain fitting, the instructor tightens the nut properly and then the worker feels how tight it is by loosening and tightening it a little. The worker then loosens the nut completely and tightens it to what she thinks is the proper tension. The

Exhibit 9-7b. JBS for Training Person on New Job

Job Breakdown Sheet for Training Worker on New Job	
Part: Slide Base 235310	Operation: Mill Dovetail

IMPORTANT STEPS IN THE OPERATION	KEY POINTS
Step: A logical segment of the operation when something happens to ADVANCE the work	Key Point: Anything in a step that might— Make or break the job Injure the worker Make the work easier to do; i.e., a "knack," "trick," special timing, bit of special information
1. Run up table by hand	Slow when nearing cutters
2. Feed 1″ by hand	
3. Stop machine and run back table	Never run table back when cutters are in use
4. Check cut	Location and finish
5. Set feed	
6. Start machine	
7. Finish cut	
8. Check	

worker checks the tension also by loosening and tightening and this goes on between the two until he believes the worker understands what is meant by "firmly" for this application. It would be helpful in this case to have a throw away sample so the worker could see how much force she has to apply to crack the porcelain.

2. *Could cause injury to the worker.* Safety issues are always Key Points because of the possibility of injuring the worker. For example, an Important Step might be to dilute acid to a 10 percent solution. A Key Point would be to pour the acid into the water and not vice versa. The reason for the Key Point would be that acid should be kept to a smaller quantity proportionately than the water in case of splashing. Note that in this example many of the steps probably require the use of safety equipment. Perhaps rubber gloves and safety glasses are required for the entire job. If this is the case, wearing rubber gloves and safety glasses are Key Points, but they are considered common

Key Points and should be placed at the top of the Job Breakdown Sheet. This means that they apply to the entire job.

3. *Makes the job easier.* Sometimes there are tricks that we learn through experience that make the job easier and often are what differentiate the productivity of an experienced worker from a novice. When appraising a used car, an Important Step might be to "Check body for fiberglass or lead patches." A Key Point would be "Use a magnet." The reason is that most auto bodies are steel; steel is magnetic, while fiberglass or lead patches are not magnetic. Another Key Point might be to "Use a cloth over the magnet." The Reason would be to "Prevent the car from getting scratched."

The concept of a Key Point is a discriminating factor that distinguishes the Job Instruction training program from other training programs. Effective training is accomplished when the instructor, who is experienced, transfers all of his information about a job to the worker. That information includes the routine steps that may be obvious when one is watching the job being done. But it also includes all the subtleties of the job that the experienced person has learned from others or from doing the job repeatedly over much time. Therefore, these "tricks" must be conveyed to the worker so that she can be as productive as possible, in as little time as possible. In most cases, instructors in training programs don't mind passing on this information but fail to do so because either the instructor does not recognize the Key Point or there is not an established method or procedure in which to convey the idea. The JI Program provides that method.

Note that the contemporary JBS has a separate column for 'Reasons for Key Points' (Exhibit 9-5). Though the original version included reasons, it did not include a separate column for listing them. While the Key Points will help workers do the job correctly, the Reasons for the Key Points help them remember both the Important Steps and the Key Points to ensure they do the job correctly. Also, writing down the reasons for a Key Point helps lead the instructor in writing the JBS.

Job Breakdown Sheets Versus Work Instructions

Many organizations have documents that are used for demonstrating, training, or standardizing a job. These documents vary, but they usually have the word "methods," "instructions," or "process" in their titles, such as Job Methods Sheets, Work Instructions, or Process Sheets. Once an organization has determined how a job will be done, someone documents it with words, pictures, and diagrams. When trainers give the JI program, a common remark from the participants is that their organizational Job Breakdown Sheet already exists and thus they do not have to create one. Unless an organization is practicing JI, however, Job Breakdown Sheets very likely do not exist, because there is a difference between the use and the intent of a JBS and Work Instructions (see Exhibit 9-8).

The main difference is that a JBS is intended to help the instructor *train* someone in a job, while Work Instructions only *describe* a job in detail so that anyone with a given level of knowledge can follow them and complete the job successfully. With a Job Breakdown Sheet, the smaller job "chunks" help the trainer keep everything in order, which ensures the learner will thoroughly know the job. Work Instructions include all the information necessary to complete the job.[22] Because they are so detailed, Work Instructions are not used after someone is familiar with the job because referring to them takes too much time. To see the difference between Work Instructions and a Job Breakdown Sheet, look at Exhibits 9-3 and 9-5. Exhibit 9-3 is the script that the TWI trainer uses to instruct someone to tie the knot "by telling alone." These actually are Work Instructions without pictures. The TWI trainer's manual includes the pictures so that the trainers can learn to tie the knot by themselves. Exhibit 9-5 is the JBS for tying the knot. There are 13 steps, 163 words in the verbal description (Work Instruction), 5 steps, and 36 words in the Job Breakdown Sheet. Work Instructions are important because they document and standardize a job, but JBSs are important because they help organizations train people to do what is detailed in the Work Instructions.

Sessions III-V: Using Job Demonstrations to Deliver JI Training

A quick summary of the training so far shows that the JI trainer:

1. Presents the majority of the instruction during the entire first session.
2. Observes and critiques (with the group) the first participant's JI demonstration.
3. Develops and explains the JBS during half of the second session.[23]
4. Explains the training timetable during the first 30 minutes of the third session.[24]

The remaining 90 minutes of sessions III, as well as sessions IV and V, are[25] spent on the participants practicing the Job Instruction method on each other.

During the 5-day, 10-hour course, the trainer uses a standard procedure for reviewing each demonstration. As the week progresses, the trainer uses more and more exacting comments to critique the demonstrations, making for a fairly steep learning curve. This learning curve is achieved because during

Exhibit 9-8. Breakdown Sheet Notes: JBS vs. Work Instructions

Breakdown Sheet Notes

The concept of a Job Breakdown Sheet is different than that of Work Instructions.

Work Instructions	Job Breakdown Sheet

1. Its purpose is to document all the steps and information necessary to complete a job so that someone with a given knowledge can complete that job
2. Lists what to do to accomplish the job
3. Includes specifications
4. May include pictures
5. Should be printed and legible to all
6. Not meant to be memorized
7. Intended for anyone doing the job
8. In ISO, is regulated; tied to part #, etc.
9. Is very detailed
10. Can be as long as is necessary to describe the job
	1. Its purpose is to be:
	  a) a reminder to someone who is instructing a person in a specific job
	  b) a tool to assist the instructor to list all important Steps & Key Points
	2. Lists *what* to do (Important Steps), *how* to do it (Key Points), and *why* to do it (Reasons for Key Points)
	3. Refers to other documents for detailed specifications
	4. Does not include pictures
	5. Can be printed or hand written; legibility required for only the instructor
	6. Not meant to be memorized, but include only enough detail to remind the instructor what the next Important Step, Key Point, or Reason is
	7. Intended only for the instructor
	8. In ISO, not recognized since it is considered personal notes
	9. Is not detailed and includes only words that will trigger the instructor's memory
	10. Should be short enough so that trainee can absorb in the time given and submit the steps to memory

The instructor can perform the job without looking at any notes. The knowledge that he/she uses is the knowledge that must be transferred to the trainee. Therefore, the Breakdown Sheet must be short enough for the Trainee to remember. The Breakdown Sheet is a tool the instructor uses to organize his/her thoughts

Exhibit 9-8. (*Continued*)

so that all information is included and it is in the proper order. People may perform a job perfectly when doing it by themselves, but they may forget steps when they have to tell someone else how to do it.

The Breakdown Sheet has two main purposes:

1. A tool to help the instructor list all the important Steps & Key Points. We may know a job so well that we do steps we do not even think about. We may do some steps in a way that we have learned over the years and now consider the method to be intuitive. Also, we probably do not know how many Important Steps are in a job. Telling a trainee the number of Important Steps aids in his/her ability to remember them.

   • Listing all the steps lets us know how much information we are giving the trainee at one time. We can then increase or decrease the amount as required.

2. A reminder for the instructor of all the Important Steps and Key Points. When we are instructing, we are telling and doing at the same time. This can result in forgetting steps or getting them out of order. In addition, while we are telling someone how to do a job, we may mix up Important Steps and Key Points. A Job Breakdown Sheet helps us to keep them separate.

NOTE:
If a trainee has trouble remembering all the steps, consider the following:

1. The procedure may be too long for the person to remember at one sitting. Perhaps the job can be broken down into smaller parts.

2. Refer the person to the work instructions which he/she can use as a guide for the job until he/she has it memorized.

The JI Instructor's Training Manual is his/her Job Breakdown Sheet.

each demonstration, and the critique that follows, all participants in the session gain knowledge of the method. Furthermore, the two volunteers who provide the demonstration usually gain the most. Knowing beforehand what should be done during the demonstration may enable the volunteer playing the "worker" to learn as much about the method as does the person who is playing the "instructor." When a participant is being trained during a demonstration, she gets a very good idea of what to do and what not to do. What was said during the sessions on "How to Instruct" and "Preparing to Instruct" now seems to make sense during the demonstration.

The participants give the first demonstration during Session II. As mentioned, a main point of this demonstration is to convince everyone of the need for a JBS.[26] The trainer uses a standard procedure for reviewing the demonstration, which is to go through the JI 4-Step Method point by point with the group. (See Exhibit 9-9 for the Job Instruction Procedure.[27])

Exhibit 9-9. Job Instruction Standard Procedure

Job Instruction Standard Procedure
How to Comment Constructively on Practice Instruction Demonstrations[1]

1. BEFORE the demonstration starts:
   a. Distribute breakdown sheets.
   b. Ask members to jot down what they can "catch" of the STEPS and KEY POINTS of the operation.
   c. Review as is necessary what a "KEY POINT" is; i.e., something that is the "KEY" to the right way of doing a step. Remember, however, that *every* little point or precaution is not a KEY POINT.
   d. Ask them to follow their "How to Instruct" cards and note any errors or omissions.

2. Call on a member to give his demonstration.
   a. Call for a volunteer to act as the "worker."
      Note: See that each member serves as the "worker" in one demonstration and that the "worker" does NOT know the job whenever possible.
   b. Caution "instructor" to have everything ready and in order.
   c. Ask him to state the JOB SETTING for his demonstration.
   d. Ask him for his job breakdown.
      – Explain that you just want to see if he has caught the "knack" of breaking down the job—that you will return the sheet to him.
   d. Have a supply of breakdown sheets for your own use.
      – As the instruction proceeds, jot down both important STEPS and KEY POINTS as you catch them from the demonstration. DON'T COPY the member's breakdown. Make your own. This will provide an interesting comparison and basis for your comments.
      – Make notes on the same breakdown sheets as to errors, omissions, and mistakes you have observed in the GET READY points and keep STEPS II and III notes in parallel columns, so you can compare notes CHECKED against points PRESENTED.

3. AFTER the demonstration, comment as follows (allow 10 minutes):
   Thank the "worker" for his cooperation and let him return to his place. Ask the "instructor" to leave his demonstration job set-up and remain at the front.
   a. STEP 1—PREPARE THE WORKER
      To Group   – Let's review this demonstration with our 4-Step Method.
                    Let's look at Step 1 on our cards.
       Select for comment from the following as appropriate:[2]
      To Group   – What is the first item?
                      (Answer: Put him at ease)
                 – Was this natural, or overdone, or poorly done?
                      (Group's answer)

Exhibit 9-9. (*Continued*)

To Any Group Member	– What is the second item?
	(Answer: State the job, etc.)
	– What was the job the worker had to learn?
	(Member's answer)
	– How much did the worker know about it?
	(Member's answer)
To Group	– The third item on the card is—"Get him interested in learning the job."
To Any Group Member	– How did the instructor get the worker interested in this case?
	(Member's answer)
To the Worker	– What is the last item under Step 1?
	(Answer: Place in correct position)
	– Were you in the best position to see the job?

b. STEP 2—PRESENT THE OPERATION

To Group	– Let's see how this job was presented.

Select for comment from the following as appropriate:

To Group	– What is the first item under Step 2?
	(Answer: Tell, show, and illustrate one IMPORTANT STEP at a time.)
	– How many important steps did you catch?
	(Answers from several members. If a difference exists, it serves your purpose excellently. In any case, say: Suppose we hold discussion on how each important step was presented until later.)
To Group	– What is the second item?
	(Answer: Stress each KEY POINT)
	– How many KEY POINTS did you catch?
	(Answers from several members. If a difference exists, it serves your purpose excellently. In any event, say: Let's discuss the KEY POINTS later when we look at the Important Steps.)
To Worker	– What is the last item under Step 2?
	(Answer: instruct clearly, completely, patiently, etc.)
	– Were the instructions clear, understandable, and complete, or is there more information you would like to have?
	(Worker's answer)

c. STEP 3—TRY OUT PERFORMANCE

To Group	– The first item on the card under Step 3 "Try Out Performance" is: "Have him do the job—correct errors."

Select for comment from the following as appropriate:

To Any Group Member	– Were any errors corrected the first time the worker performed the job?
	(Member's answer)
	– If appropriate, ask:
	What were they?
	(Member's answer)

(continued)

Exhibit 9-10. (*Continued*)

      To Group   – What is the next item under Step 3?

                        (Answer: Have him explain each KEY POINT, etc.)

                 – Was each KEY POINT explained by the worker or did he miss some?

                        (Answers from several members. If a difference exists, it serves your purpose excellently. In any event, say: Let's save the discussion on checking these KEY POINTS until later.)

      To Worker   – What's the next item under "Try Out Performance"?

                        (Answer: Make sure he understands.)

                 – Do you understand all the KEY POINTS of this job, or are you hazy about some?

                        (Worker's answer)

      To Group   – How many times did the instructor have the worker do the job and explain the KEY POINTS?

                        (Group's answer)

      To Instructor   – What is the last item in this step?

                        (Answer: Continue until YOU know HE knows)

                 – Why were you satisfied the worker knew the job in this case?

                        (Instructor's answer similar to: Worker did the job and explained it again and again until he knew it perfectly.)

d. STEP 4—FOLLOW UP

      To Group   – Let's look at Step 4 of our method—What is it?

                        (Answer: Follow up)

  Select for comment from the following as appropriate:

To Any Group Member – What's the first item?

                        (Answer: Put him on his own. Designate to whom he goes for help.)

                 – To whom does the worker go in this case?

                        (Member's answer)

      To Instructor   – The next items on the card are:

                        (Answer: Check frequently. Encourage questions.)

                 – How soon will you have to check?

                        (Instructor's answer)

                 – The last item in Step 4 is "Taper off coaching and close follow up."

                 – How would you taper off your follow-up during the next several hours, several days?

                        (Instructor's answer)

e. REVIEW THE USE OF JOB BREAKDOWN IN STEPS 2 AND 3

      To Group   – Let's review how the job breakdown was used in this case.

                 – Our card tells us under Step 2 "Present the operation to STRESS <u>each</u> KEY POINT."

                 – And under Step 3 "Try out Performance to have him EXPLAIN <u>each</u> KEY POINT."

                 – In order to find out if <u>each</u> KEY POINT was properly handled, let's slow down the job, and look at each important step one at a time.

Exhibit 9-9. (*Continued*)

To Any Group Member   – As I caught the instruction, the first important step was . . .
    – What KEY POINTS did the instructor <u>stress</u> in that important step?
      (Member's answer)
    – What KEY POINTS did the worker explain when he performed that important step?
      (Member's answer)

Note to Trainer: Continue the above questioning on each important step using different members. "Smoke out" Key Points you feel should have been brought out using the "What would happen if—, Why did you—, etc." technique with the instructor and the worker. Where Key Points were brought out in Step 3, for the first time, or not checked in Step 3, or missed in both Steps 2 and 3, always make a convincing statement about the importance of properly handling Key Points.

To Group   – The last item on the card reminds us "If the worker hasn't learned, the instructor hasn't taught."
    – Let's turn our cards over to the other side.

f. THE 'GET READY' POINTS

Select as appropriate from the following:

To Instructor   – What is the first GET READY Point?
      (Answer: Have a Time Table.)
    – How does this fit into your training plans?
      (Instructor's answer)
    – What are you going to give him next?
      (Instructor's answer)
    – Why are you going to give him that particular operation?
      (Instructor's answer)
    – When are you going to train him by it?
      (Instructor's answer)

To Group   – The next GET READY point on the card is "Breakdown the job."
    – We have just reviewed the breakdown for this job.

To Instructor   – Were there any points brought out in our discussion of the breakdown that would make the job easier for you to put over if you had to instruct the worker again?
      (Instructor's answer)
    – What, for instance?
      (Instructor's answer)

To Worker   – Did our discussion clear up any points for you?
      (Worker's answer)
    – Will you illustrate?
      (Worker's answer)

To Any Group Member   – What is the third GET READY Point?
      (Answer: Have everything ready.)
    – Were there any fumbles—did the instructor forget anything?
      (Member's answer)

(continued)

Exhibit 9-9. (*Continued*)

To Any Group Member   – What is the last GET READY Point?
                                     (Answer: Have the workplace properly arranged.)
                                  – Did the instructor have to change the workplace during the instruction or apologize?
                                     (Member's answer)

To Group   – What effect will this kind of instruction have on production, quality, safety, and on personnel problems?
                                     (Answers and reasons from several members.)

To Instructor   – Will this 4-Step Method help you in training your workforce?
                                     (Instructor's answer)
                                  – Thank instructor for bringing in the job and remind him that the comments and suggestions were not meant to be personal. They were directed at the job for the purpose of bringing out the "fine points" and "knacks" in job instruction.

Suggestions Regarding the Standard Procedure
The first demonstration in Session III will have many flaws. The trainer will have to pick out a few of the more basic ones and drive home his constructive suggestions concerning them. If he tries to correct every little detail in these early demonstrations, the timetable for the session will be adversely affected, but what's more important, neither the instructor nor the group will be able to retain all the ideas discussed. Don't try to make the first demonstrations letter perfect. Select a few of the basic faults in each of the early demonstrations and really correct them. It may even mean that the trainer will have to leave out discussing some of the items in the standard procedure in order to drive home the points selected. The trainer should be more and more exacting in a friendly way as the demonstrations progress, correcting the minor details as the members show that they have mastered the basic ideas. It is not until the demonstrations in Session V that he does not let any fault go by unnoticed. If the trainer has done a good job of driving home his suggestions a few at a time in the early demonstrations, there will be few points needing correction in Session V.

    The following are some devices that trainers have found helpful in making the discussions interesting as well as being effective in driving home points.

1. Ask the worker about points that were not made clear by the instructor. This provides a nice lead in to "If the worker hasn't learned, the instructor hasn't taught."
2. If the group has difficulty noting the Important Steps and Key Points as a demonstration is put on, remind them when a job is presented one Important Step at a time with the Key Points *really stressed* it permits everyone to catch these details.
3. Frequently when discussing the handling of a Key Point that the worker forgot, the instructor will say that he "told" the worker about it. This provides a good opportunity for the trainer to drive home the need for *stressing* Key Points and not merely mentioning them.[3]

Exhibit 9-9. (*Continued*)

---

4. Where the instructor has not been too exacting in getting back an explanation of the Key Points in a job, the trainer might refer to the card and ask the instructor how he can be sure that the worker understands. This will give the trainer a chance to sell the idea that workers should be able not only to *do* the job but *understand* "what they are doing and why."

As you gain experience in using the standard procedure you may wish to vary the actual words used from those given. This makes for interesting sessions and less stereotyped procedure. You may also find it desirable to vary the actual pattern used from demonstration to demonstration. For instance, where the standard procedure calls for asking a member what the next item on the card is, you might read the item and then ask the member the appropriate question about it. In any event, do not change the intent or strategy of the standard procedure. To be on the safe side, if there is *any* doubt in your mind about a variation in the standard procedure, follow the exact pattern given.

In using the standard procedure, where the member's or group's answer does not agree with what you have recorded on your "trainer's notes," guide a brief discussion to the correct conclusion. *Always* be constructive in your comments. We are not *testing* the instructor to see if he did or did not follow the 4-Step Method. We are trying to *help* him and the rest of the group to use the Method properly.

---

1. In this procedure, the trainer is the person conducting the JI session, the "Instructor" is the participant who is giving the demonstration, and the "Worker" is the person who is being trained by the Instructor. The Group includes all participants.
2. Note that it is NOT intended for the trainer to go through this procedure completely with each demonstration. Select the items that will be most useful to the instructor and the group within the time allotted.
3. Note that this becomes less of a problem when the worker must also recite the reasons for the Key Points. Remembering Key Points may be less of a problem today than it was with the original training because of this.

For the first demonstration in Session III, the review emphasizes Step 2, "Present the Operation," so that the participant can see the value of the JBSs. During the remaining two-hour sessions, the trainer uses his judgment on what to emphasize: The JI 4-StepMethod, Job Breakdowns, or How to Get Ready to Instruct. Ideally, each concept should be discussed during each session, but often there is not enough time. Because Job Breakdowns are a critical element of the program, the trainer should have the participants perform at least one job breakdown during each of the last three sessions.

Except for the first demonstration, during every demonstration each participant who is not involved in a demonstration has a blank JBS to fill out. All are asked to follow the JI 4-Step Method and write down comments, noting errors and omissions. Then the trainer goes through the JI 4-Step Method with the group. This is a great learning experience because if the Job Breakdown has been done well, the Important Steps and Key Points are easy to identify and the participants begin to get a better idea of how to breakdown a job by watching other jobs being performed.

During Session III, the JI trainer makes gross corrections while ignoring details. Significant gains are usually made with the demonstrations by the fourth session and the comments usually become more focused. By Session V, the JI trainer should not let any incorrect detail pass unnoticed. During this session, confidence is the greatest and the participants are at the point where most are very comfortable with the JI method. However, the trainer should caution them that they are only trained in the method and that it takes time to master it.

Reference Material: Three Special Instruction Problems

TWI included three special instruction problems in the reference material because the trainer should be versed in them in response to a question or if some extra time becomes available. The problem of conveying the concept of "feel" has already been discussed above in the porcelain sink drain-fitting example. This is under *makes or breaks the job*.

Instruction Problem One: The Long Operation

The question of how to apply the JI 4-Step Method to a job that can take 3 hours or 3 days is important because both the worker and the instructor can become confused and lost the greater amount of time the job takes to perform. The solution is to break up long operations into smaller, more easily handled ones. Recall that this is what was done with the lens-grinding job referred to in Exhibit 5-2. A long job might be broken up into say, five or six work units, the size and number depending on the learner's ability to understand and retain the information. Furthermore, some long jobs are repetitive so the learner can more easily master the work unit before moving onto the next. Other jobs are continuous so the worker must perform the entire job without stopping. In either scenario, the JI 4-Step Method would be modified as follows:

- The job would be broken up into manageable work units.
- Step 1 "Prepare the Worker" would be done as usual.
- Step 2 "Present the Operation."

- Step 3 "Try Out Performance" would be repeated for each work unit until the trainer thought that the learner was proficient.
- Step 4 "Follow Up."

In repetitive, long jobs such as assembly, the worker can stay with the first work unit until she becomes proficient. In long jobs, such as machining, which cannot be stopped, the instructor must take the worker through the entire job explaining all of the Important Steps and Key Points. Naturally, this amount of information will be too much for the worker to retain upon first learning, so while the machine is cutting the work piece, the instructor can review the Important Steps and Key Points and have the learner recite them. The instructor will repeat this process for the next work piece being machined, but by this time, the worker will be familiar with much of the information. Breaking up the job into units and breaking each unit down into its Important Steps and Key Points will help the worker learn and retain the material faster.

Step 4, "Follow Up," would occur once the instructor believed that the worker could complete the entire job without assistance.

Instruction Problem Two: Handling a Noisy Environment

Because of the inability to communicate in a noisy environment, the JI 4-Step Method must be conducted in both the actual (noisy) environment and also a quieter one. Start in the quiet environment and perform Steps 1 and 2. Since the actual equipment will not be available, some simulation will be required. Enter the workplace and repeat Step 2. In this case, the "showing" must be done with special care since it will carry the majority of the training. Depending on the situation, the instructor can return to the quiet area or proceed with Step 3. This process is repeated until the training is complete.

Instruction Problem Three: Use of Job Instruction

The JI sessions as described will train workers to use the JI method, but it is strongly suggested that they form groups at the conclusion of the training and continue practicing so that they can improve their skills. Writing Job Breakdowns and identifying Key Points are critical to Job Instruction. These are the skills that the workers must practice daily, an activity that will require approval and direction from management, especially since, initially, this activity will be time consuming. However, over time, the organization will save time and other resources, not only because JI saves time, but also because JBS's will take less time as workers become skilled in writing them.

An ideal situation for having workers form into groups is in a company that uses many temporary workers. The workers who have received the training should immediately do job breakdowns on many jobs and then instruct the temporary workers as they are hired. In organizations with a more stable workforce, you can use JI to help standardize operations. For example, a group of 2 to 4 people who have received JI training would immediately break down a job and then get together to create a final JBS. These discussions may also inform some experienced workers about Key Points that they were not aware of and by sharing information and finding agreement on a process, can improve production. Whatever the situation, however, the participants must practice and use the skills learned during the JI training if an organization wants to ensure a positive return on their training investment.

1. Slogan on the Job Instruction reminder card (training card).
2. *TWI Report*, p. 179.
3. "The Toyota Way," Jeffrey Liker, p. 264.
4. Since the 4-Step Method and the majority of the instruction was included in each of the first sessions, they came to be known as the "famous firsts" and were used as presentations of the program at business and professional meetings. (*TWI Report*, p. 42.)
5. Job Relations Manual, p. 97.
6. Job Methods Manual, p. 69.
7. Job Methods manual, p. 3.
8. Job Relations Manual, p. 103.
9. Also referred to as CNYTDO or TDO.
10. Adapted from Job Instruction Manual, p. 2.
11. Job Instruction Manual, p. 50.
12. Job Instruction Manual, p. 49.
13. *TWI Report*, p. 192.
14. Job Instruction Manual, pp. 50–51.
15. *TWI Report*, p. 193. Note that the original slogan was, "If the learner hasn't learned, the teacher hasn't taught."
16. As you read these, check to see which ones you use and which ones you don't when you're instructing someone. How many and which ones you omit will influence the effectiveness of your instructing
17. It is useful to schedule a time after the training to have the trainee see the next step in the process. An employee should know the person who is the recipient of the product she is making. This adds relevance to the job.
18. TDO Job Instruction training form; © 2002.
19. Job Instruction Manual, p. 56.
20. Reasons for creating a job breakdown sheet for Job Instruction from: TDO Pub. Guide to Job Instruction Breakdown; © March, 2003.
21. Job Instruction Manual, p. 57.

22. Note that since many Work Instructions do not include Key Points, they actually do not include all necessary information.
23. This is 1.5 hours in the contemporary training.
24. This is 1 hour in the contemporary training.
25. About 5.5 hours with the contemporary training.
26. Originally, it was recommended that two demonstrations be given on the second day. However, it was realized that the two participants did not really get the full benefit of the training since they were not using Job Breakdown sheets. It was suggested that they repeat their demonstrations on the last day if time permitted. This has since been changed to have only one person give a demonstration on the second day.
27. Taken from Job Instruction Manual, Reference section, pp. 58–65.

CHAPTER 10

Delivering Job Relations

"Make the best use of each person's ability."[1]

The creation of the Job Relations program (JR) may be the TWI Services' greatest contributor to industrial success. The other two "J" programs organized and simplified training material that others were already using in various forms. Job Relations, however, took an existing (scientific) method and applied it to human relations. At the time this was done, there was no precedent in job relations.[2] In the ensuing years, the science of human relations has advanced, but I believe that the JR program remains one of the best, easiest to use, and easiest to learn methods for successfully dealing with personnel situations. Successful and/or experienced managers will not find anything new here. JR makes its greatest contribution to people who are new at "directing the work of others." The skill in dealing with personnel problems requires a combination of analysis (left-brain activity) and emotional intelligence (right-brain activity). The JR program creates a method of *"what" to do and adds instruction of "how" to do it*. Everything a supervisor does is the result of a decision. Even taking no action is a decision. JR gives supervisors an easy method to use on a daily basis to inform their decisions and make their jobs easier.

Six Main Concepts of the Job Relations Program

The JR method consists of six main concepts, which the trainer discusses throughout the sessions and emphasizes at various points throughout the week of training.[3] We will briefly discuss each of these.

1. *Supervisory responsibility.* Most of us have had experience with personnel issues and the problems that can interfere with work. However, the supervisor actually has to manage the personnel issues. In addition to handling personnel problems, supervisors are accountable to the organization for objectives they must attain by working in collaboration with, and through, the efforts of others. Consequently, it is extremely important for supervisors to be adept in dealing with, and getting results from people. The successful supervisor gains much of

his or her experience through trial and error. Some people who are qualified in every other supervisory requirement do not become successful supervisors because, on their own, they do not know how to acquire this learned skill of working through people. People are successful with the "trial and error" approach to learning, while others are not. In this respect, JR provides an approach to issues that "levels the playing field" for all supervisors.

2. *Foundations for good relations.* In addition to learning a method to handle problems, supervisors must also understand some of the underlying motivations that help drive and make workers productive. In "Foundations for Good Relations," TWI summed up in four foundation points some of these basic motivations. These points help the supervisors anticipate problems and/or prevent them from occurring. Here are the four foundation points.

- Let each person know how he/she is doing.
  - People like to know what is expected of them and what may be obvious to the supervisor may not be obvious to them. The organization needs to make sure both the supervisor and the person know what is expected.
  - People inherently want to do a good job and they want to improve what they are doing. They cannot always determine ways to improve and so it is part of the supervisor's responsibility to positively point out ways for them to improve.
- Give credit where due.
  - No matter how detailed a job description gets, there is always room to work beyond what is normally expected. The supervisor needs to look for outstanding performance and make sure he or she sincerely expresses appreciation for it. This is not a reward but recognition. The type of recognition is less important than the fact that it happens.
  - When giving credit, do it when the situation is current. A time lag between a great performance and recognition diminishes the impact of the recognition.
- Tell people about changes that will affect them.
  - The usefulness of this approach varies with the amount of trust between the supervisor and the individual. When there is no trust, an adversarial relationship exists, and it is never a good idea to give your opponent strategic information. Besides, if there is no trust, there are deeper problems and the supervisor should take other actions. However, if the organization or

supervisor's reasons are valid, and there is a measure of trust with employees, explaining why a change will take place is valuable in maintaining good relations.

– Make efforts to inform and educate people to understand the need for change. If they are to be part of the change and its implementation, their acceptance and understanding of it are critical.

- Make the best use of each person's ability.
  – Look for abilities not being used. This perhaps was more apparent during the "emergency" of World War II, but the same concept is true today. Many people's talents are not fully utilized; and, in fact, wasted talent is cited as one of the eight great wastes corrected by Lean Thinking. In order to make use of a person's talent, one must first know what that talent is. That requires making the effort to know the person.
  – Never stand in a person's way of advancement. Letting go of a valuable employee may make a supervisor's job more difficult because replacing that employee requires extra work, usually in training. But an untrained, satisfied employee is always more valuable than a fully trained, disgruntled one.

3. *Treat people as individuals.* This may be the most important concept in the JR method. It is human nature to inherently simplify and categorize problems so that we can better understand and deal with them.[4] When we attempt to do the same with people and put them into categories or make assumptions about them, we are making a significant mistake. The harsh truth of the matter is that each person is unique. As we mentioned in Chapter 1, the discussion on day one includes a comment that machines come with service manuals, but people do not. It is necessary to obtain information about your employees: their unique backgrounds, experiences, talents, health, and philosophy of life, to name a few things. Not only are people different from each other, their circumstances are also changing daily, which can affect their work. "It is [more] important to know the kind of person who has a problem— rather than what kind of problem that person has."[5]

4. *The 4-Step Method.* This is the heart of the Job Relations program as discussed in Chapter 7. Exhibit 10-1 shows the JR 4-Step Method on the two-sided training card that the trainer hands out during Session I.

5. *Trainer's and supervisor's problems.* The trainer presents four case studies, each of which emphasizes a point of the JR 4-Step Method. The participants each bring in a problem of their own using the 4-Step

Exhibit 10-1. JR 4-Step Method Training Card

JOB RELATIONS

A Supervisor Gets Results through People

FOUNDATION FOR GOOD RELATIONS

Let each worker know how he is getting along.
Figure out what you can expect from him.
Point out ways to improve.

Give credit where credit is due
Look for extra or unusual performance.
Tell him while "it's hot."

Tell people in advance about changes that will affect them.
Tell them WHY it is possible.
Get them to accept the change.

Make the best use of each person's ability.
Look for ability not now being used.
Never stand in a man's way.

People Must Be Treated As Individuals

JOB RELATIONS TRAINING
Training Within Industry Service
BUREAU OF TRAINING
War Manpower Commission

How to Handle A Job Relations Problem

DETERMINE OBJECTIVE

1. GET THE FACTS
Review the record.
Find out what rules and plant customs apply.
Talk with individuals concerned.
Get opinions and feelings.
Be sure you have the whole story.

2. WEIGH AND DECIDE
Fit the facts together.
Consider their bearing on each other.
What possible actions are there?
Check practices and policies.
Consider objective and affect on individual, group and production.
Don't jump to conclusions.

3. TAKE ACTION
Are you going to handle this yourself?
Do you need help in handling?
Should you refer this to your supervisor?
Watch the timing of your actions.
Don't pass the buck.

4. CHECK RESULTS
How soon will you follow up?
How often will you need to check?
Watch for changes in output, attitudes and relationships.
Did your actions help production?

Method in dealing with it. The review of these four problems, in addition to dealing with one of their own, gives most people sufficient practice to be competent in using the 4-Step Method. Both the case studies and the supervisor's problems will be discussed later.

6. *Other supervisory relationships.* The focus of the JR program is on developing skills to manage relationships between a supervisor and the employees he or she directs. However, a supervisor's success depends on having good relationships with many other people, at all levels, both within and outside of the organization. Supervisors can likewise successfully use the JR program in all of these relationships.

The obvious focus of the above six concepts in the JR program is on developing skills in dealing with people. The training manual details the presentation and describes the overall strategy and emphasis on a daily basis (see Exhibits 10-2[6] and 10-3[7]).

Job Relations Session I

The training starts out with "The Five Needs of a Supervisor" (Exhibit 4-4) and then goes into how a supervisor must accomplish objectives by working *through* people. This is followed by a discussion of the six points in the "Foundations for Good Relations." The completed board work describes all the points made (see Exhibit 10-4).[8] The trainer makes it clear that the definition of "a problem" is *anything on which the supervisor has to take action that affects production.* This means that if an employee has a personal problem that does not affect production, the supervisor should not deal with it, such as an employee having a behavioral problem with her child, because this does not adversely affect the employee's work or production. On the other hand, if the employee is consistently tardy because of the child, the supervisor needs to get involved.

To be able to determine whether or not a personal problem actually affects production, the supervisor must have a good "open door" relationship with the employees. As the supervisor practices the skill in handling personnel problems, using the six concepts of the JR program, he or she will develop the skill of anticipating or reducing problems. The original list of possible situations or problems that could be successfully dealt with is included in Exhibit 10-5.[9] As discussed in Chapter 7, it is now preferred to have the group create this list so they have more ownership of it and can refer to it in the final session, Session V, for closure.

A recurring question that arises when the group discusses problems is: "How did this supervisor come upon this problem?" There are four ways a supervisor becomes aware of a problem:

1. With experience, a supervisor can anticipate a situation and "size up" a problem before it actually happens. This requires knowing both the environment and the individuals and requires being aware of what is happening in areas beyond the supervisor's authority. This is the ideal situation and that which should be the supervisor's objective. When a

Exhibit 10-2. JR's Overall Strategy and Emphasis on a Daily Basis

Summary of Purpose and Emphasis of Job Relations Sessions

1. To establish the fact that everyday job relations are one of the most important parts of the war production supervisor's job.
   To present the foundations for good relations.
   To establish a 4-Step Method for meeting job relations situations.

   A supervisor gets results through people. People must be treated as individuals. Good supervision prevents many problems, but the supervisor must know how to handle those that do arise.

2. To develop skill in Step 1, "Get the Facts."
   To give the group practice on Step 1 through emphasis on this step in a problem presented by the trainer, and to give members of the group practice in looking at the 4-Step Method in two problems brought in by supervisors.

   Complete facts must be known or obtained. Opinions and feelings must be found out and considered along with facts. It is necessary to look at people as individuals, as each person is unique.

3. To develop skill in Step 2, "Weigh and Decide."
   To give the group practice on Step 2 through emphasis on this step in a problem presented by the Trainer and to give members of the group practice in three problems brought in by supervisors.

   Decisions are made on the basis of facts properly evaluated and related.

4. To establish the importance of Steps 3 & 4, "Take Action" and "Check Results."
   To give the group practice in Steps 3 and 4 through emphasis on these steps in a problem presented by the Trainer and to give members of the group practice in looking at the 4-Step Method in three problems brought in by supervisors.

   The supervisor must know his responsibility. He must watch the timing of his action and follow up, and watch for the effects of his actions on the objective, the individual, the group, and on production.

5. To give members of the group practice in looking at the 4-Step Method in two problems brought in by supervisors.
   To review and summarize foundations, 4-Step Method, and tips for getting opinions and feelings.
   To consider the other working relationships of the supervisor—to other operating departments, to staff departments, and to his boss.

   Further develop the habit of using the complete method. Point out application of the method to the supervisor's other relationships. A supervisor gets results through people.

Exhibit 10-3. JR Course Contents

Course Contents of Job Relations

SESSION I—2 hours
Getting acquainted
The Supervisor's Five Needs
Chart on Supervisory Responsibility
Foundations for Good Relations
Chart on the Individual
The Joe Smith Problem (Introduction of the 4-Step Method)
How Problems Arise
Problem Sheets (list of typical problems)
Request for problems (for discussion in next session)

SESSION II—2 hours
The Tom Problem (importance of getting the facts and remembering that opinions and feelings must be considered the same as facts)
Applying the 4-Step Method to problems brought in by participants

SESSION III—2 hours
Comparison of a doctor's process with the JR 4-Step Method
The Shipyard Problem (importance of "weigh and decide")
Applying the 4-Step Method to problems brought in by participants

SESSION IV—2 hours
The First Woman Supervisor Problem (importance of anticipating problems and recognizing natural leaders)
Discussion of the effect of change
Applying the 4-Step Method to problems brought in by participants

SESSION V—less than or equal to 2 hours
Applying the 4-Step Method to problems brought in by participants
Review of 4-Step Method
Statements from participants about the 4-Step Method
Review Chart on Supervisory Responsibility
Conclusion

---

situation can be anticipated, it can be controlled more easily and can cause less damage. A campfire is easier to extinguish than is a forest fire. When one anticipates a problem, data is collected and analyzed and deductive reasoning is used to reach a conclusion. Since there often is no tangible proof that a problem exists, it requires a good "sales" effort to convince people to take action.

Exhibit 10-4. How to Meet Supervisory Responsibilities through People

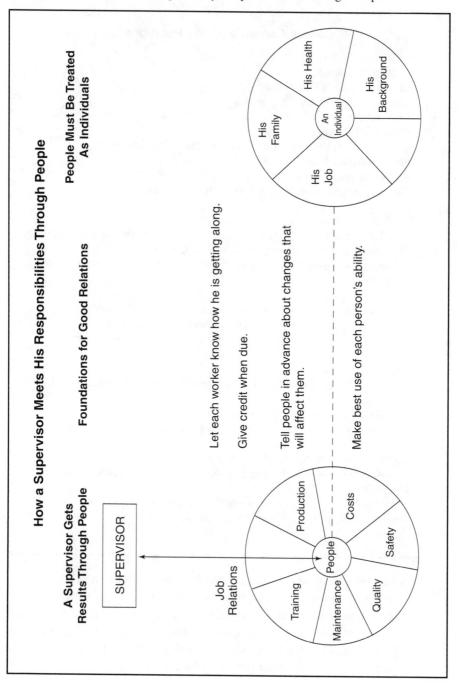

Exhibit 10-5. JR Situations and Problems

Job Relations Situations and Problems

Lack of teamwork in department
Worker doesn't understand his part in the whole job
Worker goes to your boss to complain
Worker kicks about working conditions
Prospective change in hours is apt to make trouble

Worker wants to change jobs often
Worker takes chances at work
Worker fails to come to work every day
Worker loses interest in job
Worker feels he is being pushed

Worker resents changes
Drop in individual production
Drop in overall production
Worker irritable and touchy
Worker kicks when not promoted

Plant protection regulations are going to be stiffened
Worker wants more money
Worker does something stupid
Operator refuses to do certain work
Workers are not going to get expected bonus

Careless with materials and equipment
Worker gets discouraged learning job
Time-clock rules are going to be enforced
Worker wants transfer for more money
Friction between shifts

Pay differential causes trouble
Some day-work jobs are going to be put on piece-rate
Worker loafing on job
Worker doesn't like responsibility
Plant is going to start hiring women or Negroes

The problem sheets are used to get conviction from the group that the Job Relations program is aimed at the kinds of problems that supervisors encounter every day. It also gives hints on the type of problems which the members of the group will bring in for discussion.

---

2. If a supervisor is alert to what is happening in the department, he or she will notice changes that signal developing problems. That is, the supervisor will be "tipped off" so that she or he can take action before the problem actually occurs or before it causes significant interruption in production. This is the next easiest situation to handle. The problem has already surfaced to some extent and therefore something must be dealt with, however, it is not yet large enough to require many resources. Some people may actually prefer being "tipped off" to "sizing up" because there is some evidence of the problem and it is easier to convince more people that it actually exists. When one "sizes up" a problem, there is often no direct evidence and thus it is more difficult to convince people to take action.

3. Sometimes a problem will "come to" a supervisor. The problem already exists, but it may not be extensive and someone brings it to the supervisor's attention. This "third level" often demonstrates that the supervisor is not fully experienced since someone had to notify him about the situation.

4. Supervisors can also "run into" problems by happenstance. For example, a supervisor may ask an employee to do something and the employee refuses, bringing to light a problem that existed but was not apparent. This indicates that the supervisor is inexperienced, over-extended, or just out of touch with the department. This situation takes the most amount of time to deal with because the problem is usually large and out of control. It often requires immediate attention and damage control, significant investigation and extensive corrections.

Furthermore, when supervisors are cognizant of the ways in which they uncover problems, they are in a position to develop ways to better anticipate them, reducing the number of "surprise" problems, which have more potential of disrupting production. Handling problems that you have anticipated is easier than handling surprise problems. If nothing else, the supervisor has had more time to think about possible solutions. Often, however, an anticipated problem is smaller and less serious than an unanticipated one and takes less effort to solve.

Lessons From the "Joe Smith Problem"

Also during this first session, the trainer introduces the JR 4-Step Method using the "Joe Smith Problem" (see Exhibit 10-6).[10]

"Joe Smith" is a simple problem that clearly demonstrates and develops all four points of the Job Relations method and shows the participants how a supervisor can make a poor situation worse by incorrect handling, i.e., by not

Exhibit 10-6. The Joe Smith Problem

Job Relations

The "Joe Smith Problem"
To Develop the 4-Step Method

Joe Smith was a good worker and his earnings were high. The department was busy and was on a regular 6-day schedule. Some time ago Joe had fallen into the habit of laying off every *Monday*. The rush of work was so great that his staying away held up a lot of work. The supervisor had spoken to Joe about it several times, but Joe just said that he was making more money in five days than he used to make in two weeks. The supervisor tried to appeal to Joe's patriotism, but saw that he did not get any place.

Then Joe got married and he started working six days regularly. The supervisor decided that the extra money looked good to Joe and that was why he came to work all the time. Joe kept up the good record for a few months.

Then one Monday a general increase was announced. On Tuesday Joe failed to come to work. The supervisor decided that the extra money had again brought Joe to the place where he could get along on five days' pay. He decided that he was going to teach Joe a lesson, and that the only way to get at Joe was to show him how it would feel to lose five days' pay.

When Joe came in Wednesday, the supervisor was waiting for him on his way to the locker room and called out, "Hey, Joe, don't bother changing. I'm laying you off for a week. That'll give you a chance to think over what's in your pay envelope. Maybe you'll decide it won't be so bad to get six days' pay next time."

The supervisor stops the story and discusses the supervisor's objective:
Objective: The Supervisor wanted Joe at work regularly.

Well, the supervisor laid Joe off. A few days later at lunch another supervisor came up to him and said he'd heard he was pretty tough on Joe Smith. Joe's father had been hurt in an accident last Tuesday. Joe had asked his next-door neighbor to send word to the plant that he was called out of town. The neighbor forgot. When Joe went back to the plant Wednesday, he didn't know that his supervisor hadn't heard about what had happened.

---

using the JR 4-Step Method indicated on the JR training card (refer to Exhibit 10-1).[11] To make more of an impression, the trainer tells the problem as a story with some expression rather than reading it. "Don't just read from the manual—talk informally with feeling and expression—make it live! Don't lecture or preach."[12] The problem also gives the group its first practice in analyzing a JR case study, so they can get an idea of what is to be expected of them when they describe their sample problem to the group. The trainer tells the story up to the point where the supervisor lays off Joe for a week. Then the trainer asks the group what the supervisor in the story was trying to accomplish. The objective the supervisor was trying to accomplish was to keep Joe at work because the department was busy and Joe was actually a good worker. However, what the supervisor did was completely the opposite; he got rid of Joe for a week. This result occurred for two main reasons: 1) the supervisor did not seek additional information about Joe's situation, and 2) he did not think very much about the information he did have. The supervisor assumed Joe had not changed after he had gotten married and was still irresponsible. The resulting action hurt the department.

The trainer continues with the story, which includes additional information about Joe. This leads the trainer to ask the group to look at the supervisor's action from three points of view:

1. How does the employee feel toward the supervisor?
2. How do people in the department feel about how the supervisor treated the employee?
3. What did the action do to production?

Asking these three questions are keys to checking out the reasonableness of any action that a supervisor will take. This is why the questions are repeated for each problem analyzed. The third question is of critical importance because the focus of the course is to improve production. However, it is important to ask the first two questions because the supervisor's relationship with the employee in question and with the department as a whole, can greatly affect production. As mentioned, this problem is an excellent lead-in to the group discussing the JR 4-Step Method. Everyone in the group can see that the supervisor did not handle this situation well. The question the trainer can ask now is, "What could have been done better?" and more specifically, "What should the supervisor have done first?" The answer from the group should be, "Get more information," which is Step 1, "Get the Facts."

Group Discussion of the JR 4-Step Method

Note that the trainer does not immediately discuss the items listed under the four steps because providing too much material early on can be confusing. However, the trainer does present the caution points and writes them on the board along with the four steps. The caution point for Step 1 is "Be sure to have the whole story." The trainer then leads the group through the analysis of the Joe Smith problem so that they actually come up with the 4-Step Method on their own, giving them a sense of ownership. The TWI developers believed that people are more willing to buy into and use something that they develop. Once the trainer presents the method, the group discusses it more fully.[13]

STEP 1: Get the Facts

Collecting facts may be more difficult for some people than for others because it requires an unbiased collection of information. Preconceived notions are not allowed. A supervisor must collect all data that pertains to the problem at hand, whether he or she likes it or not. Joe's supervisor knew of his previous poor record, but he ignored his more recent good record. This is what TWI referred to as "The Formula Habit," and is discussed in "A Way of Looking at the Supervisory Job" (Appendix B). When supervisors classify people into "types," they then habitually deal with each "type" in a certain way.

"Of course, these methods work a good deal of the time with many of the people with whom supervisors and instructors have to deal. Otherwise, they would not be so commonly accepted. But they become a hindrance when they are used as excuses for lumping people together in groups or types and avoiding the responsibility of trying to understand each person as an individual.

"In short, people cannot be handled like piece parts or apparatus. Each is an individual, different from each other. "Stereotyping" them, classifying them, standardizing them, or reducing them to formulas— habits of thinking that work well with inanimate things—often proves to be actual hindrances in handling people."[14]

Collecting facts from records means that supervisors must go beyond just paper or electronic records. TWI considers any fact obtained from anyone a record. That is why it is important to talk with other people to gather additional facts. Joe's supervisor neglected to do this. Also, when the supervisor is collecting information directly from the individual involved, it is important for the supervisors to not only note the "real" facts, but also to handle as "fact" what that person believes to be true, whether or not it is true. An item under this step says to "Get Opinions and Feelings." This is important because the supervisor is trying to see the problem from the point of view of the individual. This does not mean the supervisor will necessarily agree with or believe what the person in question says, but it is important to develop a broad profile of the interpretations and feelings regarding the circumstances. Additional information on how to cull opinions and feelings from people is discussed during Session II.

During the process of collecting facts, the supervisor must take into account the organization's rules and customs, and list them as facts if they are relevant. Note that in some cases, unwritten customs are stronger than written rules. In this example, it may have been acceptable for an employee to have a designee call in sick for him. Finally, the caution point at the end of the step says to get the whole story. Whether or not one really knows "the whole story" is really a judgment call by the person collecting the information. Usually, however, making the effort to collect a broad range of information is usually sufficient. When the supervisor believes he or she has enough facts to make a decision about what to do, then it is time to move to Step 2.

STEP 2: Weigh and Decide

This step works in tandem with Step 1. The supervisor collects data and then analyzes the data before making a decision. The analysis includes determining whether there is enough data. If there is not sufficient information to make a clear decision, then the supervisor goes back to Step 1 and collects more. TWI used the term "weigh" because the analysis includes piecing the facts together to see if they make sense. If the supervisor finds that they don't make sense because there are gaps or contradictions, then the supervisor should return to Step 1 to collect more information. Note that the caution point to Step 2 is "Don't Jump to Conclusions." This may take practice for some people, but if they remember to refrain from making a decision until they can piece together a reasonable scenario, chances are that the decision will be a good one.

Once the supervisor has a reasonably accurate idea of what actually happened and it all makes sense, he or she can consider possible actions to take. Most often the supervisor has a choice of actions to take, and though the supervisor might not like all the possibilities, and some of them may not be practical, all of them should be listed so that the supervisor can review them. When listing the possible alternative actions, the supervisor must keep in mind the rules and policies that govern the organization. When making a final decision on what action to take, the supervisor needs to consider the four questions stated below:

1. How will the employee feel toward the supervisor?
2. How will people in the department feel about how the supervisor treated the employee?
3. What will the action do to production?
4. How will the action impact the supervisor's objective?

It clearly depends on the situation and the organization if all four effects are weighed equally. The point is that one must think about these questions before taking action. The supervisor should consider the affect that an action has on the employee because it will impact future work. The importance of how the rest of the department thinks and feels about the action also will vary because of the situation and the organization. However, it is rare to take action regarding an individual that others in a department do not know about to some extent. Seeing how other employees are treated sets a precedent and helps create the culture. These interactions do not occur in a vacuum.

How the action affects production is always important because a supervisor is responsible for production. In this story, the supervisor was trying to increase production. His objective was to get Joe to come to work regularly, but his action had the opposite effect; keeping Joe away from work for a week hurt production. Furthermore, it probably made Joe angry which did not do a lot for his motivation. When Joe returns to work, he may act differently. When the other employees learn what happened and get the 'whole story,' they may see it as a capricious act by the supervisor and realize that something similar could happen to them. This could negatively impact *their* motivation. The caution point for Step 2 is "Don't Jump to Conclusions." Remember that managing people is a skill that you acquire through practice.

STEP 3: Take Action
This step is a list of checkpoints the supervisor uses when he or she is about to implement a decision. The caution point says, "Don't Pass the Buck." Supervisors must know their responsibilities, and make his or her best decision on how to resolve an issue. If the supervisor is not qualified or capable of taking the needed action, then it is acceptable to seek assistance. Of course, supervisors should always keep upper management informed of what they do. In some cases then, the action might be a recommendation to top management on what action is appropriate. Finally, "Timing of the Action" is important. If the supervisor knows he or she should take action immediately, but there is not enough information to make a good decision, the right action might be to tell the employee what is going on and that you will make a decision after collecting and analyzing all the facts.

STEP 4: Check Results
As in Step 3, this is a checklist for supervisors to follow. How soon and how often will you need to check on results? What results do you expect? Have you attained your objective? The supervisor is also reminded here to look for changes in output, attitudes, and relationships, because what sometimes appears as a solution to a problem actually causes another, worse problem. Watching for changes immediately after a decision is very important.

End of Job Relations Session I
The remainder of the first session includes "The Foundations for Good Relations," "How Problems Come Up," and various problems that can occur. We

already discussed the first two topics earlier. The purpose of covering various problems that might occur is to give the participants an idea of the types of problems that the JR program can address. They will be looking for and solving one of their own problems and the list of situations and problems (Exhibit 10-5) gives them an idea of what to look for.

Often participants think of larger or more complicated problems to solve, but they are not appropriate for two reasons. First, the participants are learning the 4-Step Method and so they should start with easy problems. Furthermore, many larger problems result from small problems that were handled improperly.[15] Thus, learning to deal with small problems can probably prevent larger ones from occurring. More importantly, for the purposes of the JR program, the trainer only allows each person about 30 minutes for problem review and discussion—hardly enough time to tackle larger problems.

Job Relations Session II

The trainer starts Session II with a short review of the JR 4-Step Method, and then reads another case study that emphasizes the first step, "Get the Facts" (see Exhibit 10-7).

Exhibit 10-7. The Tom Problem

Job Relations

The "Tom Problem"
To Develop Skill in Step 1: "Get the Facts"

A supervisor is out in the shop and notices a workman reaching into a machine.

Supervisor calls out: Tom, I've told you to shut off that machine when you take off the guard.

> *[Trainer comment: The supervisor is mad. He's apparently warned Tom before.]*

Tom yells back: If you want to fire me, why don't you just say so instead of nagging at me all the time?

> *[Trainer comment: Tom is mad, too.]*

Supervisor: Keep your shirt on! It's far from firing you, Tom. I just don't want you to fire yourself by getting your hand mashed. The number of times that machine has to be adjusted makes me think there must be something wrong with it.

Tom: Well, I'm not going to take anymore panning.

Exhibit 10-7. (*Continued*)

[Trainer comment: The supervisor is certainly facing a problem and here is what went through his mind very quickly before he took any action.]

Supervisor: Now, let's see. I've known Tom a long time. He's been one of the best men in the department. He says I've been nagging him. He is reckless as the devil about his machine. Yesterday I had to call him on quality. And it hasn't been so long since I had to tell him that his line wasn't keeping up with the rest. What's happened to Tom? I guess I have been on his neck a lot. But it was always something that had to be done. And I can't have him taking chances the way he does.

[Trainer comment: Do you notice how this problem came up? There had been a change in Tom, but the supervisor didn't get into the problem then. He waited until it burst in his face.]

Supervisor: Suppose we get together this afternoon and talk this over. I'll let you know when I can get someone to relieve you.

[Trainer comment: Why do you think the supervisor didn't talk to him then? Do you think it would have done any good to stay there right then and <u>argue</u> with him? He isn't going to talk in the department or while Tom is mad.]

That afternoon, Tom comes into the supervisor's office.

Supervisor: Hello, Tom. Sit down. Now, Tom, I guess you think I've been riding you. I don't want to do anything like that. A couple of times I felt I *had* to stop you because you were doing something dangerous. And there've been a couple of times lately when your work hasn't been quite up to par. I'm used to quality work and plenty of it from you.

Every time I see you taking a chance that might cause trouble, I've got to stop you. When your work isn't up to standard, why then I've got to say something about that too.

Now is there something the matter with the machine? I know you're always raising the guard and reaching into it. If there's something wrong with that machine, I want to get it fixed.

[Trainer comment: What is the supervisor doing here? The supervisor is trying the obvious thing first—to see if the trouble is connected with the machine.]

Tom: Well, if you think I'm going to run over to that switch and pull it, and hang the "don't touch" sign on it—you're just crazy. You're

(continued)

Exhibit 10-7. (*Continued*)

	yelling now about how little I get done. If I had to spend half my time turning that switch off and on, I wouldn't get anything done. And the other day you said the parts were below standard. Well, if I didn't fix that machine they'd all be below standard.
	[Trainer comment: Tom isn't going to make it easy, is he? The supervisor could have cut in there and told him it wouldn't take half the time to turn off the switch. Here again he could have argued, *but he had gotten Tom in there because he wanted to talk with him, so he wasn't going to* interrupt *him.]*
Supervisor:	Now, Tom, there's more to it than breaking a safety rule. There's a reason behind that rule. You're apt to get your hand mashed.
Tom:	And that'd cost the company money, wouldn't it?
	[Trainer comment: The supervisor might think that Tom was sore at the company about money—or would that be jumping to a conclusion?*]*
Supervisor:	Oh, sure it would cost the company money. But have we made you think that's all we're interested in?
Tom:	Well, that's all that counts to some people.
	[Trainer comment: He's bitter about something.]
Supervisor:	It'd cost us a good man. And that's a harder thing to replace than money.
Tom:	Well, not everybody feels that way.
	[Trainer comment: He seems to be thinking about the importance *of money to people. The supervisor has a clue here—will he follow it up? Tom has been pretty hard to talk to. What does the supervisor have to follow up from here?]*
	[Do not allow extended discussion. If the group does not make the point, say that Tom seems to be thinking about the importance of money to somebody.]
Supervisor:	Why are you so strong on the money angle? You're doing alright that way, aren't you? Seems to me you told me last spring you were going to build on that land of yours out on the pike. When are you getting married? When you have a wife, she won't want you to take chances.
Tom:	Oh—nobody cares if I do get a hand off.
Supervisor:	Your girl would care.

Exhibit 10-7. (*Continued*)

Tom:	I don't have a girl anymore.
Supervisor:	I'm sorry, Tom. I just wanted to get you thinking of what an injury to you might mean to somebody else.
Tom:	Well, it doesn't mean anything to anyone now. Nothing about me would hurt her. Why, she knew I was going to start to build, but she married someone else. So, all I have is a half-finished house. And that's all I've got to show for it.
	Nobody cares what happens to me anymore. And I don't need to try to make anymore money, or save it either. It changes a lot of things.
	[Trainer comment: This takes careful handling. The supervisor wants to get Tom back to normal production; he wants to stay on good terms with Tom. Now the supervisor has a chance to make a speech—he could tell Tom he was lucky to get rid of her, but he's going to listen to Tom, and <u>not do all the talking himself</u>.]
Supervisor:	A blow like that's bad, and it's no use saying it isn't. But sometimes you have to take it on the chin. Some things can be fixed up though. And I wish you'd see your way clear to helping me figure out what's wrong with the way that line is running.
	I can see why you have gotten a bit careless about taking chances. But I know you wouldn't have had to take those chances unless something else was wrong. Now, is the machine worn? Does it need overhauling? How are the tools?
	[Trainer comment: There seem to be <u>two</u> things to look at: (1) the man and (2) the machine.]
Tom:	No, it isn't the machine. The parts aren't coming through the same as they used to. There's a burr left on them, and after so many have gone through, well, I just have to clean the machine out.
	[Trainer interrupts the story to set objective, list facts, weigh facts, and list possible actions.]
Supervisor:	I can see why that would cause you trouble. Suppose we go down and take a look at those parts. Now, I'm sorry about your tough luck. But I do thank you for helping me.
	[Trainer comment: Throughout, the supervisor had listened sympathetically to Tom, he had encouraged and helped him to talk about the things that were important to him. Now that

(continued)

Exhibit 10-7. (*Continued*)

> *he had reached something specific, bad parts, he's going to check that.]*
>
> *[Later the supervisor comes back to his office and calls his own chief.]*
>
> Supervisor: Jones, can I come up a minute? I want to talk to you about the parts we're getting from the punch press department. They're not coming through clean. I have a good operator on our line, and it's interfering with his work and slowing down our output.
>
> *NOTE*: This problem has been updated slightly to appeal to contemporary society. The worker is now a woman, Tina, who was planning on buying a house with her husband. The savings for the down payment was in the stock market and its value decreased significantly (junk bonds?). The bank will not give them a loan without a down payment, and so she and her husband quarrel a lot and it's usually over money.

Lessons From the "Tom Problem"

The "Tom Problem" demonstrates why it is important to make sure supervisors have all the facts before making a decision. It also focuses on how feelings and opinions are as important to people as facts in situations that concern them. It shows how supervisors cannot take some information at face value, but sometimes must probe beneath the surface to get to the true meaning. The Tom problem also gives the trainer an opportunity to mention how supervisors should handle confidential information. Because the supervisor's boss is part of management, it would have been acceptable for him to know Tom's personal problem. However, since his knowing would not have aided in the solution of the production problem, the supervisor did not share that information with him.

Tom, the worker, either had a production problem that he did not know how to solve or was in no frame of mind to solve. The parts he was processing were arriving with burrs on them and that prevented him from running his machine properly. In an ideal world, Tom would have notified someone (a supervisor or a quality person) who would have taken care of the problem. Tom, however, had a personal problem that interfered with his work and though the supervisor is not supposed to solve Tom's problem, he should have been aware of it because it was interfering with production. When Tom's supervisor gets to Step 3, "Take Action," he might think to refer Tom to the

Human Relations Department if employee counseling is available. To improve production, the supervisor must first be aware of Tom's problem and then work through this problem with Tom to get at the organization's objective of solving the production problem.

However, the supervisor became aware of the reasons for Tom's actions only after he began collecting facts, and he did that by speaking directly to Tom. Furthermore, the supervisor did not have an in-depth conversation with Tom out on the shop floor because Tom was in the middle of production and was angry. After speaking with Tom, the supervisor wrote down the following list of facts about the situation:

- Was a good worker
- Quality and quantity down
- Broke safety rules
- Careless
- Warned before
- Talked back
- Lost his girlfriend
- Felt nobody cared
- Burrs on parts

By talking with Tom, the supervisor found that Tom had lost his girlfriend, which made Tom despondent, resulting in him feeling that no one cared about him and causing him to lose focus and interest in his work. The supervisor is not expected to function as a counselor, but by knowing this information, he or she can make a better decision of what to do next. Merely talking with Tom, showing some interest in him personally, the supervisor discovered that the real cause of the problem was an incidence of burrs on the parts. Notice that the supervisor showed interest in Tom's problem, but did not volunteer to help. In fact, he asked for Tom's help to improve the production. This case points out that most production problems involve facts about machines and facts about people, and it is important to define both sets of facts in order to correctly and quickly solve the problem.

Six Concepts for Collecting Information

In Session II the trainer continues with the problem review and finishes it by listing the actions that the supervisor took. Because ascertaining opinions and feelings is an important part of collecting facts, the trainer then discusses in more detail how to go about doing this. Specifically, the trainer explains six concepts:

1. *Don't argue.* Since you never settle anything by an argument, the supervisor should avoid arguing. Instead, step back and let the person talk, listen in turn, and continue to gather as much pertinent information as possible.
2. *Encourage the person to talk about what is important to him/her.* To uncover the true source of the production problem, the supervisor must find out what the employee thinks is important. Though the supervisor may believe it is not relevant, if it is important to the employee, then it may be the cause of the production problem.
3. *Don't interrupt.* This will help the other five concepts. Interruptions cause people to lose their train of thought, making them think that what they are saying is not important, or worse, causing the supervisor to miss important information that they were leading up to.
4. *Don't jump to conclusions.* Making a decision before the supervisor has all the facts will reduce the choices of possible actions to solve the production problem.
5. *Don't do all the talking yourself.* Often in situations in which supervisors are trying to uncover a problem, they have a tendency to "make a speech" or "preach" about the issues rather than finding ways to have the employee do most of the talking.
6. *Listen.* Actively listen by using appropriate responses that encourage the employee to continue talking, and ask for clarification only when required, without putting the employee on the defensive. Motions such as maintaining eye contact, nodding affirmatively, leaning forward to show interest, and asking questions to verify your understanding of the discussion are some of the actions involved in active listening. Note that it is important to show sincerity so the person believes you are interested in the situation.

Concepts three through six emphasize rudiments of active listening. The supervisor wants to be sincere in listening to the employee so that the worker will tell the supervisor what he or she believes is the real problem. The active listener "bites his tongue," and listens carefully, asking questions that will help the employee tell his or her story. More can be learned about this in Stephen R. Covey's book 7 Habits of Highly Effective People under the topic empathetic listening.

The last item the trainer covers in Session II is to review two problems that the participants were required to bring in. They handled them with the standard procedure the same way the trainer handled the sample problem (see Exhibit 10-8).[16] This procedure (columns 1 and 3 only) is included at the end of Sessions

Exhibit 10-8. Standard Procedure for Reviewing Problems

Standard Procedure

Used for Reviewing Problems
(Results Are From Shipbuilding Problem)

Trainer's Actions	Results	Trainer's Notes
1. Ask supervisor to tell problem	Trainer tells problem from manual	Trainer asks supervisor: Does problem involve you and someone who comes under your direction? Have you taken action? Tell up to final action.
2. How problems come up	Ran into, but supervisor had warnings with previous lack of cooperation	Where appropriate stress: You sensed or anticipated a change.
3. Get objective	Get the job done without upsetting the department	Get from supervisor: Something to shoot at. May be changed. What do you want to have happen here? Does this problem affect the group? What net result do you want after you have taken action? Get agreement from the group.
4. Get facts	Old-timer Foot hurt Inside for full pay Foot healed Asked transfer outside Shop busy Uncooperative inside Refused to get tools Department watching Supervisor sore	Supervisor first, as he recalls them. Review subheads with supervisor to check for any missed facts—use card. Get additional facts from group—use card.
5. Weigh & decide	Possible actions from group: Layoff Transfer Fire	Fit facts—look for gaps and contradictions with group. Possible actions: What facts used?—from contributor. Check practices and policies with supervisor. Check objective first with group, then last with supervisor. Check probable effect on individual, group, and production, with supervisor.

Exhibit 10-8. (*Continued*)

<table>
<tr><td colspan="3" align="center">**Standard Procedure**

Used for Reviewing Problems
(Results Are From Shipbuilding Problem)</td></tr>
<tr><th>Trainer's Actions</th><th>Results</th><th>Trainer's Notes</th></tr>
<tr>
<td>6. Balance of case</td>
<td>Additional facts:
Long OK service outside
Liked outside work
Not advised why inside—pay
ACTION: fired old-timer</td>
<td>Facts used (from supervisor)
{do not reveal action for
volunteers' problems}</td>
</tr>
<tr>
<td>7. Check Step 3</td>
<td></td>
<td>Review subheads with
  supervisor
Why? – How? – Timing?</td>
</tr>
<tr>
<td>8. Check Step 4</td>
<td></td>
<td>Review subheads with
  supervisor
When?—How Often?—What?</td>
</tr>
<tr>
<td>9. Check objective</td>
<td>Did not accomplish objective</td>
<td>Supervisor</td>
</tr>
<tr>
<td>10. Foundations
    (if applicable)</td>
<td>Did not:
Let worker know how he
  was doing
Tell worker in advance about
  changes
Make the best use of worker's
  ability</td>
<td>Supervisor</td>
</tr>
</table>

II–V to give the trainer a uniform method of leading the participants through their demonstration problems. The first column states what the trainer should do and the third column gives the trainer some questions he might ask the supervisor in order to elicit a good response. I included responses to the "Shipyard Problem" in the middle column. This column includes some of the material that the trainer would write on the board during training.

Job Relations Session III

The structure of Session III is the same as that of Session II:

- Review of the JR 4-Step Method.
- Present Sample problem.
- Do Participants' problems.

In reviewing the JR 4-Step Method, the trainer makes an analogy to how a doctor deals with a patient. The steps are the same, but we use different terms:

- Step 1—Get the Facts   Examination
- Step 2—Weigh & Decide   Diagnosis
- Step 3—Take Action   Treatment
- Step 4—Check Results   Follow up (exam)

The trainer uses the doctor analogy for several reasons. First, it demonstrates that other professionals have used the same method for many years. Second, a doctor uses this method no matter what the situation is or how much time is available. It is important to use all four steps. In an office setting with a non-threatening disease, the pace of the method would be deliberate. An emergency ward would use the same method only if it would occur more quickly. The method may seem cumbersome to the novice, but frequent use will make it almost second nature. Finally, the order of the steps is important. Would a doctor prescribe a treatment before doing a diagnosis? Would a doctor make a diagnosis before collecting facts in an examination? If the participants have not yet accepted the value of the method, this analogy usually makes a favorable impression on them. Once a participant is familiar with the 4-Step Method, he or she will be capable of going through the four steps quickly as well as being assured of a reasonable solution to any type of problem. For larger and more complex problems, participants will usually have to be more formal and write down the facts, alternate solutions, and so forth. However, participants can handle many smaller problems on a more informal basis. Before long, the use of the JR 4-Step Method will become routine.

Lessons from the "Shipyard Problem"

The emphasis in Session III is on Step 2, Weigh and Decide. The trainer introduces the story "The Shipyard Problem," and once again the situation ends badly (see Exhibit 10-9).[17]

In addition to not having all the facts for this problem, the supervisor did not properly evaluate the facts he did have. The facts that the supervisor knew about initially were:

- Employee had long-term service with company.
- Had hurt his foot.
- Given a job inside so would make full pay instead of workman's comp.
- Foot had healed.
- Had asked for a transfer back to old job.

Exhibit 10-9. Shipyard Problem

Job Relations

The "Shipyard Problem"
To Emphasize "Weigh & Decide"

The electrical shop supervisor told a man to get some tools. The man said he couldn't—he'd left his checks at home. So the supervisor reminded him he could get them by signing for them—the man refused, said he didn't like to work in the shop anyway, and he wanted to go back to outside work. The supervisor was pretty sore about the man's refusal to get the tools.

This man was an old-timer. He had always been on outside work, but he had hurt his foot, so as soon as he was able to fill a job in the shop, he was transferred into the shop at the same rate so he could get full pay instead of part-time pay under workman's compensation. His foot had been healed for some time, and he had asked when he was going back to his outside job. But the shop was busy, so the supervisor kept the man. He had been uncooperative ever since he came into the shop; now he flatly refused to do some work. People in the department were watching to see how it would turn out.

The supervisor decided it was time to take action.

The supervisor fired the old-timer. The old-timer protested to the union and his case was taken up. The union proceeded to get additional facts—facts which could have been obtained by the supervisor.

The old-timer had almost 20 years of satisfactory service out in the yard. He liked to work outside, although it meant being out in all kinds of weather. He did not like shop work. He did not know that he had been brought into the shop to increase his earnings over what he would have received from compensation. The yard supervisor was not even questioned about the man's long service outside.

Eventually the workman was reinstated in the yard on his old job with back pay.

Note that this problem has been updated to an office problem. In the new story, Mike has been successful at outside sales for many years; but was forced to an inside office job since he hurt his right foot. Now that his foot has healed and he can drive, he really wants to get back on the road again. However, since the office is very busy, he has been assigned to a 6-month project with another person. The other person has complained to the supervisor that Mike has done nothing on the project so far, and he failed to hand in a report that was due. In this version, the office supervisor reported the incident to his manager and then he fired Mike. After being fired, Mike went to his old boss who talked with the office supervisor's manager and gave him the additional facts.

It should now be easy to see how case studies can be updated for relevance without changing the content or impact of the case itself.

- Shop was busy.
- Was uncooperative at inside job.
- Refused supervisor's request to get tools.
- The department was watching.
- The supervisor was angry.

In "weighing and deciding" the information, the first question the supervisor might ask would reflect an inconsistency: "How has this uncooperative employee lasted so long in this company?" It does not make sense that someone who has been so uncooperative would have a long service with the company. Since no other facts are listed, we must assume that the supervisor knows nothing else about this situation. Another inconsistency has to do with the fact that the company was being flexible in providing the employee with an indoor job while his foot was healing. Without this inside job, the worker would have been on worker's compensation and would not have been earning full pay. In addition, the worker was now doing an indoor job, which is usually coveted because one does not have to deal with the weather. A normal reaction would have been one of gratitude, but this employee seems to be hostile. Since these facts do not "fit together," the supervisor should go back to Step 1 and collect more facts. He would do that, for example, by speaking with both the worker and the worker's last supervisor. With new facts, he would again "weigh & decide." A supervisor must continue this reiterative process until satisfied that he or she has "the whole story" and that it makes sense.

The key in being able to make sense of the facts is to treat each person as a unique individual rather then relying on classifying people into "types," or stereotyping them, which can easily lead to wrong conclusions. A better approach is to make a *positive hypothesis* about a situation and then try to defend or destroy it. For example, the supervisor sees someone who appears to be lazy and makes the positive hypothesis that people like to be productive and generally are not lazy. Since the person's actions are contrary to this hypothesis, the supervisor must find some facts to resolve the inconsistency. People may act like they are lazy but it may be because they dislike the work, are bored, or are not properly trained. Seeing an inconsistency should alert the supervisor to collect more information. Once the supervisor has sufficient facts, in this case, for laziness, he or she is in a good position to provide the correct solution.

This Shipyard case study also gives the trainer the opportunity to emphasize two of the Foundation Points. "Tell People in Advance About Changes That Are Going to Affect Them" pertains to the situation in which the worker did not know he was given a job so he could remain on full pay. Had the supervisor used this Foundation Point, the worker might have been more cooperative and other facts and information about his feelings might have been revealed. If the worker had known how long the temporary assignment would be and the supervisor knew the worker wanted to go back to his old job soon, the supervisor could have averted the problem. Had the supervisor used another Foundation Point, "Make the Best Use of Each Person's Ability," he might also have prevented the problem.

Job Relations Session IV

In this Session, the trainer uses a case study to emphasize the third and fourth steps, "Take Action and Check Results," as well as the third Foundation Point "Tell People About Changes That Will Affect Them."

Lessons From the "Woman Supervisor Problem"

The story in Exhibit 10-10[18-19] brings out three major points, prevention of a problem, working with people who are natural leaders, and dealing with large impending changes.

1. *Prevention of a problem.* This is the only case study that deals with the prevention of a problem. The events the supervisor reacts to have yet to impact production, so he takes actions to avoid this. For a supervisor this is the ideal position to be in because anticipating problems is better than having to correct them. The supervisor must have the ability to be aware of what is happening around him or her in order to anticipate effectively. In some situations, it takes courage to do what is necessary to prepare for change because the supervisor must expend effort for what some people may see as having no apparent purpose. People may even disagree and attempt to prevent the supervisor from taking any action. This is why it is still very important for the supervisor to quantify as many facts as possible in order to make as strong a case as is possible. In this story, all the necessary facts are available to the supervisor to create a reasonable solution.

2. *Working with natural leaders.* This scenario also points out that a supervisor can get help by working with people who are natural leaders. This takes an awareness of who has influence with whom in the organization, something the official organizational chart does not indicate.

3. *Handling impending change.* This scenario also shows how one supervisor dealt with a large, impending change. The trainer emphasizes that this problem concerns how to prepare the organization for change, not how to handle specific circumstances.

Exhibit 10-10. Woman Supervisor Problem

Job Relations

The "Woman Supervisor Problem"
Emphasizing Dealing With Change and Preventing Problems

The plant superintendent called Jim White, the General Foreman, into his office and told him that the management had decided to use women supervisors as well as men. The superintendent told Jim to fill supervisory vacancies with women on the basis of seniority and ability, as was the rule with men.

He also told him that both men and women supervisors were to have the same authority and the same opportunity for advancement. Jim considered this very carefully and reviewed the following facts:

One supervisory position had to be filled, and no qualified men were available. All men capable of supervisory responsibility had been upgraded or had been taken into the Armed Forces. Most of the new employees who had come to the plant in the last 18 months were women.

Jim selected the best qualified woman for the job. As she was to be the first woman supervisor in the plant, Jim anticipated trouble. This was a major change. Some men supervisors might resent it. Also some men and women employees might not like having a woman in authority. More women supervisors would be appointed later.

Jim thought the situation over pretty carefully. Then he talked individually with his supervisors and also he talked individually to those of the operators who were looked on as natural leaders. He gave them the facts and asked for their help.

There was quite a commotion—some people said they wouldn't stand for it. Jim gave them a chance to express their concerns. Eventually the workers agreed to work with the new woman supervisor.

By the time the new supervisor took over her work, the outburst was over and the people cooperated in accepting her. Jim told her that she was going to be the first woman supervisor in the plant and that she might run into some difficulty and that she must not be easily offended. He asked her to do her best because it would not only affect her but also other women supervisors who would be appointed later.

During the first day on her new job, Jim talked with the supervisors and later in the day with the natural leaders he had talked with before. They informed him that apparently the new supervisor was accepted and everything was OK. Jim, to be sure that his preventive action was effective, kept in close touch with the situation for some time.

This was another case study that was updated for relevance. Actually, the original problem was the introduction of the first African-American supervisor into the plant. Although that example worked quite well in all the test sessions, TWI got so many questions on it that they decided to change the problem to the one shown above. The current problem starts:

(continued)

Exhibit 10-10. (*Continued*)

"The plant director called Mary Brown, the production manager, into his office and told her that management had decided to change the organization of the plant to put more emphasis on small teams. The manager told Mary to begin asking team leaders to perform certain duties . . . which until that time were done by department supervisors."

In addition to the work that the other supervisor did, Mary also made sure that the team leaders received training in the use of the reports and evaluations for which they would now be responsible.

NOTE: It's helpful to know all three versions (gender, race, and teams) because by doing so, it becomes clearer that the problem is not one of race, gender, or job duties, but rather a problem of dealing with *change*.

After analyzing the "woman supervisor problem," the trainer then discusses the third Foundation Point, "Tell People About Changes That Will Affect Them." Changes often bring the fear and pain of the unfamiliar and the uncertain. People resist changes they believe will be detrimental to them. Conversely, people will be more likely to accept a change if they understand that it will be beneficial to them. A supervisor should anticipate this resistance and turn it into acceptance to avoid interruptions to production. TWI was never intended to be a "magic elixir" that will solve all problems. When it comes to organizational changes, the organization must determine if the employees are having difficulty dealing with rapid changes, and if so, provide the appropriate information through books, discussions, and courses so employees know what is expected of them.

Job Relations Session V

The last session completes reviews of any of the participants' problems that have yet to be covered, sums up the six concepts of the JR program of showing you *what* to do and *how* to do it. The trainer also solidifies the participants' acceptance of the JR 4-Step Method. The participants review the JR 4-Step Method and the foundation points. Then the trainer works to solidify acceptance of all aspects of the Job Relations program through a three-part conclusion, presented through three activities to the participants:

1. *The value of the JR 4-Step Method.* The first activity is to ask the participants what they think about the JR 4-Step Method and to create a list of how they and their departments will gain if they use it. Examples are:

- Better standing with those you supervise.
- Better standing with your boss.
- Less criticism.
- More confidence in ability to handle people.

When the participants can generate this list, the trainer can then say that the participants see the value of the JR program. Now the participants should return to their workplaces and achieve the listed results.

2. *The broad applicability of JR methods.* The second activity is a discussion of how the participants can use the six concepts of the JR program to manage relationships with a broad spectrum of people. The JR program, of course, has been focusing on a supervisor dealing with a direct report. However, in order for a supervisor to be successful, he or she must have the ability to interact and build good relations with many different people within and outside the organization, not just direct reports.

3. *The need for using the JR method.* The last activity attempts to demonstrate the breadth of influence that these supervisors have. To emphasize how broad their influence is in the organization, each participant is asked how many people his or her actions directly affect. As TWI points out, we ". . . are all working for the same thing: the prosperity of ourselves, the company and our community, we have a responsibility to create and maintain good relationships with everyone with whom we interact."[20] Having brought the participants to this frame of mind, the trainer has succeeded in his or her training objectives and the program ends.

Using the Job Relations Method After Training

A user must practice any skill to be proficient, and of course, to gain positive results. Depending on the organization, some supervisors may not have an immediate need to use the JR training, though typically personnel issues will eventually arise for them to apply the method. However, it is recommended that the supervisors who took the JR training meet periodically to discuss situations they have encountered and then apply the 4-Step Method. The purpose of these meetings is solely to review the application of JR methods to the problem at hand. As in the training sessions, the supervisor with the problem is the only one who can take action on it. However, it is very useful to check with one's peers to make sure that they are using the JR 4-Step Method properly. If there are no personnel problems, then these (monthly) meetings will serve as a review for all aspects of the JR method. By meeting regularly, the supervisors will become more proficient in applying their training.

---

1. A Foundation for Good Relations as noted on the Job Relations reminder card (training card).
2. *TWI Report*, p. 206.
3. *TWI Report*, pp. 207–208.
4. This is discussed in the following pp. and in the article in the Appendix B titled A Way To Look At The Supervisory Job, which appeared in the original JR Manual.
5. *TWI Report*, p. 207.
6. Job Relations Manual, p. 2.
7. Adapted from Job Relations Manual, pp. 5–9.
8. JR Manual, p. 31.
9. JR Manual, p. 46.
10. JR Manual, pp. 33–35.
11. Deitz, *Learn by Doing*, p. 22.
12. JR Manual, p. 99.
13. As mentioned during the discussion of the development of JR, the method had five steps at one time. TWI determined that by combining "weigh and decide" it would make the material more comprehensive, so the developers reduced the number of steps to four. I believe that having each of the programs have a 4-Step Method may have also played some part in that decision. On the JR training card, DETERMINE OBJECTIVE is written in capital letters at the top but is not actually considered a step. Thus, when first discussing the four steps, determining an objective is not discussed until Step 2 when the trainer and participants must consider how a possible action affects the objective. This appears somewhat confusing to me and I believe determining an objective should be emphasized more. The trainer uses a standard procedure to follow (Exhibit 10-6) in reviewing problems. TWI instructs the trainer to use it for all problems except for the first one when the 4-Step Method is first discussed.
14. Job Relations Manual, Reference 4, pp. 115-116.
15. JR Manual, p. 48.
16. Standard Procedure JR Manual, p. 66.
17. Original case study: TWI JR Manual pp. 69 & 71. Revised case study: TDO JR Manual, pp. 76, 77, 79.
18. Original version TWI: JR Manual pp. 78 & 80 Revised version TDO JR Manual pp. 88, 89, 91.
19. Before the 1940's there were few women in industrial settings. Because of the emergency during World War II, women entered the workforce in greater num-

bers and it was inevitable that the most appropriate people would be chosen as supervisors regardless of gender. Promoting a woman to a supervisory position was emotional for many people and it occurred more frequently as time went on. Today we do not see this as an unusual action and thus this problem was updated to one that would seem more reasonable to today's society. See Exhibit 10-10 for additional details.

20. JR Manual TDO, p. 107.

CHAPTER 11

Delivering Job Methods

"JMT taught supervisors to make incremental improvements continually to processes and operations, how to generate such improvements, and the importance of putting their improvement suggestions in writing."[1]

As discussed in Chapter 7, the purpose of Job Methods is to provide: "A practical plan to help you produce GREATER QUANTITIES of QUALITY PRODUCTS in LESS TIME by making the best use of the Manpower, Machines, and Materials now available." (This statement has been updated to change "Manpower" to "People" and "Machines" to "Equipment.") Let's break down the wording in this statement.

"A practical plan" means a method that anyone can use easily on a daily basis. Traditionally, organizations have assigned engineers, specifically, industrial engineers, the task of improving methods. Yet to a certain extent, everyone in the organization should be improving job methods. "To help you," means not telling you the answer, but enabling you to discover the best solution. You supply the thought and the process will guide you. "Produce" means that the method is designed to facilitate production of products, not help you decide which products to produce. It will not help an artist decide what picture to paint or an engineer what design to use for a sleeker car. *Job Methods focuses on improving work processes and not on creating designs.* "Greater quantities" means increasing production of the products that you already make. This actually goes together with "in less time" because if you don't want to increase production, perhaps you want to produce the same quantity in less time. In either case, the quantity made per unit of time should increase. "Quality" means that at a minimum, you will not increase production at the expense of reducing the level of quality at which you currently produce; and at best, it means you will be increasing the level of quality because the method will help you scrutinize and improve the process. "Making the best use" means optimizing the process by eliminating wasteful activities and changing, combining, and resequencing others. Anything that does not contribute to the desired outcome will be eliminated. "Manpower, machines, and materials" means that you will consider all resources, the people doing the work, and the equipment and materials they use to do it. "Now available" means that you are not going to be hiring more people, or buying more equipment or materials in making your improvements. You can consider such changes, but the focus will be on increasing productivity by eliminating waste and manipulating *existing* resources.

The two main concepts of the Job Methods program that should always be kept in mind, that are actually more important than the specific improved method that may result from applying the method, are 1) teaching employees to critically understand and improve their work, and 2) developing know-how to sell improvement ideas to others, including upper management.

The first concept "was designed to develop in supervisors a constructively critical attitude toward their work."[2] The Final Report refers to this as a "by-product"—"the development of thinking among supervisors, the identification of supervisors who were thinking . . ."[3] But as discussed in Chapter 7, there is much more to this statement, especially in the context of Lean Thinking, which leverages off training employees to improve continuously. One purpose of Job Methods is to teach *people to develop a habit of constructively questioning what they do*. "Constructively" means simply to find and understand the reason for their actions, which in turn can improve the organization's productivity and morale. Here's why. When organizations teach their employees to understand the reasons behind the way they do work, the employees often identify and eliminate many non-value-adding activities, saving the organization time and money. In addition to helping employees find a "better" way of doing the work, the Job Methods program can help an organization create and sustain an environment of continuous improvement where employees *continually* come up with a better way to do the work. If applied optimally, the Job Methods program's systematic approach can empower employees to implement one good idea after another, continually improving processes as needed.

The second concept addresses the failure to use employee ideas to improve productivity. The main reason organizations fail to tap into employee ideas is that they do not provide employees a vehicle or the training for presenting or "selling" ideas to upper management.

> "One definite aim of the program from its very beginning was to prevent people from presenting incomplete ideas. An idea may sound good, but when it is presented to the boss, he often finds it to be flawed in some way. Following the 4-Step Method means that the supervisor himself looks for flaws in his idea and eliminates them

before presenting his idea to management. Anyone who has had ideas refused or criticized as being incomplete or impossible realizes that this experience often keeps the supervisor from making a later, better suggestion."[4]

This idea was further reinforced by C.R. Dooley in an introductory letter in the Job Methods manual in which he states: "Your [the trainer's] function is to show them [the participants] how to fully develop their ideas for practical use and present them successfully to management."[5]

Like the other "J" programs, it will be easiest to understand the delivery of Job Methods by going through the five sessions of the program. Refer to Exhibit 11-1 for Course Contents. Most of this chapter will cover Session I.

JM Session I

The trainer uses more props than in the other "J" programs because he or she must demonstrate an actual job. The trainer has a checklist and a layout and should arrive at the site 30 minutes before the session starts to have sufficient time to prepare the room. As with the other two "J" programs, the first session starts out with an introduction by a company executive to show intent and support, the introduction of the trainer, and then introduction of the participants. "Putting the participants at ease" and "creating an informal atmosphere" are necessary activities at the beginning of every program.

Once the trainer is past the introductions, his or her job is to get participants interested in learning the JM program. The trainer discusses the "Five Needs of a Supervisor," followed by improving job methods. This leads into why everyone is at the training session and to the following points.

1. The Job Methods program will help you to produce greater quantities of quality products in less time by making the best use of manpower, machines, and materials currently available.
2. JM will not make people work harder or faster.
3. Responsibility for production is assigned to us, the supervisors.
4. We must increase production in spite of shortages of manpower, machines, and materials.
5. Reasons why we need increased production.

In this section of the training, the trainer lays out the intent of the JM program to show that it is about making changes that will help the participants do his or her job better. It is here that the trainer wants the participants to start buying into and accepting the program. In the 1940s, there was one last incentive, rallying the participants around the war effort.

Exhibit 11-1. JM Course Contents

Course Contents of Job Methods

SESSION I—2 hours
    Introduction
    The Supervisor's Five Needs
    Job improvements and the three types of work
    Sample job demonstration—present method
    Sample job demonstration—proposed method
    Introduction of the 4-Step Method using the Sample Job
    Assign improvement demonstrations
    Resistance and resentment

SESSION II—2 hours
    Review the 4-Step Method
    Volunteer's job demonstration—Stress Step 1
    Introduction of the Proposal Sheet
    Assign improvement demonstrations

SESSION III—2 hours
    Review sessions 1 & 2
    Demonstration of jobs (three volunteers)—Stress Step 2
    Presentation of Proposal Sheets from Session II
    Assign improvement demonstrations

SESSION IV—2 hours
    Review previous sessions
    Demonstration of jobs (three volunteers)—Stress Step 3
    Presentations of Proposal Sheets from Session 3

SESSION V—2 hours
    Review previous sessions
    Demonstration of jobs of remaining volunteers—Stress Step 4
    Presentation of remaining Proposal Sheets
    Review of Job Instruction Program
    Summary

- "This is the **critical year** of the **war**."
- "**Today, thousands** are **risking** their **lives—tomorrow,** thousands **more will face** the same **risk**."
- "**Your** complete **cooperation and suppor**t of this program **will help** to **meet** the **crisis**."

Though today organizations are not confronting a conventional war effort, the threat of global terrorism presents new challenges. Also in the last few decades, increased global competition and outsourcing make it hard for an organization to sustain a competitive advantage purely through product innovation. Today's trainer should contact the company before the session starts to understand the nature of its competition and its particular challenges. The trainer will appear more credible to the participants if he or she describes the organization's business challenges appropriately. If a company has 70% of the market, the discussion would center on staying ahead of the competition rather than meeting the competition. Today's key words might be "cost reduction," "meeting customer needs," and "beating the competition."

Toward the end of the first 20 minutes of Session I, the trainer discusses how supervisors fit into JM training and that having supervisors improve a company's job methods is not a new idea. Traditionally, methods improvement (or process improvements) has always been a regular part of every supervisor's job (in Lean Thinking this might be the team leader's role) and the supervisor has been the best source of ideas for improvements, because he or she has greater contact with the workers and the actual work flow than the managers above them. In fact, today, you can directly attribute much of the content of JM improvement to the contribution of supervisors. The important point the trainer must make is that the purpose behind the TWI Job Methods program is to provide tools and approaches that will empower and make it easier for supervisors to continue improving processes, removing non-value activities, etc., in their efforts to improve job methods. Again, the trainer's goal here is to convince participants to accept the need for the JM program fully before moving on.

Actual Demonstration Job

The best way to explain Job Methods is to demonstrate how you use it on an actual job. The trainer tells the participants that JM is easy to learn and apply and now they will see for themselves. Since it is not possible to select a demonstration job that occurs in every plant, the trainer asks the participants to view the demonstration from the perspective of their own jobs. The trainer then asks the participants what type of work they do, and then lists the only three possible categories of work:

1. Material Handling
2. Machine Work
3. Hand Work

This is a very creative way to get the participants to view the demonstration job in terms of their own work environment. The purpose of doing this is to counter the possible argument that "the demonstration is not like my job." The trainer wants the participants to see that this method can be used for their type of work and thus wants the participants to see the similarities between the demonstration and their work. Everyone's job is classified into one or more of these three groups because any job would require moving something, operating a machine, or doing something manually. If the supervisor is doing one of these three activities, then he or she is using a method or process that can be improved. The only exception would be brainstorming or thinking a problem through; an example would be the solving of a mathematics problem. JM does not apply to the thinking process because this type of activity involves no clear method. If, however, you use a series of steps to solve a mathematical problem, then JM could apply. The group discussions do not usually touch on "abstract" issues, but the TWI developers must have received feedback regarding this because they included the following in the reference material:

> "(Note—Thinking, Inspection, and other "nonproductive" operations are parts of all three types of work.)"[6]

The trainer's objective is to get the participants to look at the demonstration job in terms of the three types of work as opposed to what is actually being done, which is the assembling of a radio shield.[7] (We will be discussing the radio shields shortly.) In this way, whether the demonstration job is actually that of assembling a radio shield or operating a machine tool, the participants will immediately be able to identify any job by its category. They will be able to look at the job from its "type" perspective: a job that requires material handing, operating a machine, or manual work. The Reference Material states in a note to the trainer:

> "Emphasize that these three types of work are included in the demonstration job and that these three types of work are comparable to their jobs. IT IS VERY NECESSARY TO MAKE THIS COMPARISON CLEAR. In this way you will overcome the objection that the Plan does not apply to their jobs because "their work is different." It reduces any job of any kind to the common denominator of ONE or MORE of the three general types of work."[8]

The TWI developers knew it was very important that the participants understand this concept, otherwise, they might not be as attentive and would merely go through the motions and not accept, learn, or use the JM program.

If the participants happen to be office workers, the flow of paper would be equivalent to the flow of material. Moving files or papers from an 'out-basket' to an in-basket, or practicing file management with emails and electronic folders, is office "material handling." "Machine work" is replaced by "equipment work," and this can include copiers, fax machines, printers, computers, and so forth.

Now the trainer is ready to describe the demonstration job, which consists of joining two flat sheets of metal together with rivets. For the purposes of this demonstration, the trainer uses a colored cardboard instead of brass and copper sheets, and a stapler instead of a riveter. The sheets are 5″ × 8″ × 1/64″, and as a result, the actual sheets would be quite fragile. Scratches and dents are not allowed in the final product. The job consists of laying the brass sheet over the copper sheet, aligning them within .005″ and then joining them with four rivets, one in each corner. Once that has been done, the word "TOP" is to be stamped in the lower right corner of the brass sheet. The finished sheets are put into a tote box and taken to the shipping department where they are packed and shipped. On the way to shipping, the tote box is weighed and the weight is recorded on a slip of paper and put into the tote.

Four people do this work using four workbenches located in the area. A material handler supplies them with the brass and copper sheets. The operators assemble the shields and put them into a tote. Once a tote is full, they carry it to the scale, weigh the tote, and return to their workbench to repeat the cycle. A material handler takes the totes to shipping. The scale is about 50 feet from the workbenches and shipping is about 150 feet from the workbenches. The raw material containers are centrally located for the four operators and are about 6 feet away from each workbench. There are scrap bins located near each workbench. Before the session started, the trainer laid out the props for the demonstration. While the trainer briefly describes the demonstration, he or she quickly walks around the room pointing out the various props.

Once the trainer completes the tour and description of the props and job, the trainer stops at the workbench and says, "I am now going to start the job" to distinguish between all the instruction just delivered and the actual job. The demonstration job follows the 12 steps below.

1. Get, inspect, and lay out 12 copper sheets on the workbench.
2. Get, inspect, and lay out 12 brass sheets on the workbench.
3. Stack sets of sheets to the right of the riveter.
4. Rivet each set (do at least 3).
5. Stamp each shield. Pile shields on table.
6. Place 12 shields into tote box.
7. Carry 75-lb. tote box 50 feet to scale.
8. Weigh and make out ticket.
9. Handler takes tote box 100 feet to Packaging Dept.

10. Packer unloads tote box, puts 200 shields into packing case.
11. Packer closes, stencils, and weighs case.
12. Empty tote boxes returned by handler.

Because the copper and brass sheets are six feet from the workbench, the assembler does the first three activities while standing (we will assume the assembler is a male). This requires also that the assembler walk back and forth from the workbench to the supply of sheets. The trainer explains during the actual demonstration job that the assembler lays down only 12 sheets, but he must pick up 20 or so. It is difficult to pick up exactly 12 because the sheets are so thin and the assembler knows that he will damage some that must be discarded. Also, since the assembler picks up more sheets than he needs, he must return the extras to the stock bins. The sheets are laid out on the workbench in three rows of four so to make twelve piles. As the assembler is laying them down, he is inspecting them for damage. Periodically, the assembler will pretend to see a damaged sheet so that he can demonstrate the act of discarding it.

Once the assembler has 12 stacks of two sheets, he stacks them at 90° angles into one pile next to the riveter (stapler). The assembler then sits down, picks up the first set of sheets, and begins assembly. Four holes in each sheet are used for the rivets. The assembler must align these holes and the edges of the sheets within .005 of an inch, which is about the thickness of a piece of paper. The trainer explains that such close alignment requires experience and technique. Even an experienced assembler, however, can get tired eyes and a stiff neck by the end of the day. Once the assembler aligns the sheets, he puts it into the riveter (stapler) and rivets one corner. He shifts the shield and rivets the other corner. He then removes the shield from the riveter, rotates it, and rivets the last two corners as he did the first two. He removes it from the riveter and rotates it again so that it is in the correct position for stamping. He then lays the shield on the workbench, inks the "TOP" stamp, and stamps the shield on the brass side in the lower right corner. He then sets this shield aside, picks up the next two sheets, and repeats the process.

Once the assembler has completed all twelve sets, he puts them into the tote box and then gets more sheets and repeats the process. Once the tote box is full, he carries it to the scale, which is about 50 feet away.[9] The tote box is weighed at the scale, and a slip of paper with the recorded weight is placed into the tote box. The tote box is left there for the material handler, and the assembler returns to his station to repeat the process. When four or five tote boxes are completed at the scale, the material handler uses a two-wheel cart to take them to the packing area.

At the packing area, the packer unloads the shields from the tote, inspects them for damage, counts 200 shields, and packs them into a shipping container (we will assume the packer is female). She then seals the container, weighs the container, and adds the proper markings for shipment. The material handler returns the tote boxes to the assembly area. To emphasize the waste in the operation, the trainer distributes a "Present Method Layout" at this point to describe the material flow throughout the job (referred to today as a spaghetti diagram). At this time also, there is a brief discussion of the three types of work involved—material handling, machine work, and handwork—which helps the participants further see how they can apply the JM concepts to their own jobs.

Participants' Reactions to the Demonstration Job

A typical reaction of many participants to the above job method is that they would never do anything as wasteful or foolish as this. Actually, when the participants start analyzing their own jobs, they quickly see that some of what they do is at least as wasteful as the job demonstration example. However, because some improvements are so obvious, the trainer does not illicit comments at this point. Instead, when the trainer has completed the demonstration of the *Present method*, he then demonstrates the *Proposed Method*, to contrast results. The trainer quantifies the results in terms of productivity increase, machine utilization, scrap reduction, and better utilization of personnel. Usually the dramatic differences in results seize the attention of the participants, making them even more receptive to wanting to know how these results came about. The trainer saves this part for the end of Session I, when the trainer explains the JM 4-Step Method. The changes made to create the Proposed Method include:

1. The raw material was moved onto the work bench so it was closer to the worker.
2. Two riveters per assembler were used.
3. A magazine was created to dispense single sheets easily.
4. A fixture was used to align the sheets automatically.
5. Less experienced people were used and they did not have to be able to lift 75 lbs.
6. Scrap bins were placed under the workbench and slots were cut into it for easy disposal of scrap sheets.
7. Shipping containers were placed by the workbench for direct packing.

The trainer then distributes a layout of the Proposed Method to show the difference in travel distance between the two methods. A summary of the improvements is:

- Each assembler produces three times more shields per day than before.
- Each machine rivets 50 percent more shields per day than before.
- Scrap is reduced from 15 percent to <2 percent.

People generally accept the dramatic results, such as increased production by a factor of three for each assembler. There are usually some concerns also, so these are answered before other questions are asked.

For example, the material handler put the raw material sheets directly onto the workbench. It is explained that she agreed that it was no additional work for her. The addition of a riveter was not an added cost, because the second riveter was taken from one of the other four stations. Because production increased by a factor of three, two people now could use all four riveters and increase production by 50 percent.[10] It is noted that these changes also allowed people with less experience to do the job. The trainer then emphasized that the experienced people who were performing the job are upgraded to positions that make better use of their skills and experience. It is important to discuss this point to some extent, because the idea of losing one's job to method improvements is always a concern. One should not make too much of it and the trainer should be sensitive to the culture of the workplace. (Refer to Exhibit 7-1 for FAQs about Job Methods.)

Weighing the tote before it gets to shipping and stamping "TOP" on the shield are two steps that have been eliminated. Since they are somewhat subtle, many participants do not even notice that these steps are not followed in the Proposed Method. If no one asks why these steps were eliminated, the trainer points this out, underscoring how common it is to waste time in this way. First, you don't need the weighing because the shields were sold by count and the shipping operator weighed the final package for shipping purposes. This is an example of a step that people do but that no one can explain why it was ever started. Secondly, the word "TOP" was used for orientation purposes in assembly, but that need was eliminated when a notch was included in the shields. When the engineering change notice for the notch was processed, the stamping operation was never removed from the method sheet. Many people can relate to this.

The trainer makes two final points. First, none of the productivity gains were made by having anyone work faster or harder. Making a person work faster usually results in mistakes. "Production is increased *by eliminating unnecessary parts* of the job—*and making* the *necessary parts of the job easier and safer to do.*"[11] Second, you can apply the principles used in this demonstration to improve any type of job. In fact, these principles have been used on hundreds of jobs to create similar improvements.

So far, it has taken about 50 minutes of the first 2-hour Session to get to this point, and the trainer has not even discussed the JM 4-Step Method yet. This is because it is so important for the trainer to be sure the participants accept the results, to have accomplished the first objective of getting the participants interested in learning. It is now time to move to the second objective—helping the participants learn the JM method.

Introducing the JM 4-Step Method

Learning the JM program begins with the participants receiving the JM 4-Step Method training card (see Exhibit 11-2, which is the same as 7-1).[12] The trainer explains that everything that was used to improve the demonstrated job is on this card, and that if you follow exactly the four steps, and the auxiliary information on the card, you have all the information you need to help make any job method improvements. The trainer distributes the laminated reminder cards (training cards) one by one to emphasize their importance. The trainer explains that the training cards contain only 274 words describing the method, and that although they can easily be memorized, encourages the participants to carry it in one's pocket for reference at all times. Even after one memorizes the method, displaying the card is a visual sign that you are using, and always thinking about, the Method. Now the trainer goes through each step.

Step 1—Break Down the Job

Of course breaking down the job is the starting point for all job improvements. The value in going through this step is that you list all the details that are actually necessary to get the job done. When people are doing a job, they naturally forget about the details of each step. Writing down all the details makes people aware of the things forgotten and those things they never realized were part of the job. In developing this detailed list, it is critical to detail the "how' or "what" of a job. For example, "get the report" or "get the wrench" is not a detail because it does not tell you *how* we got the report or the wrench or *what* you had to do to get them. Once a person details how they got the report—out of their in-basket, from email, across the hall, waiting in line, etc.—they start to think about *what it is they are actually doing*.

The Job Methods manual defines a detail as "every single thing that is done, every inspection, every delay."[13] It is every single movement required to accomplish the job. Listing all the details of the job gives a complete and accurate picture of what is actually done, not just what you think you are doing. The details *give all the facts to help determine if there is actually a need for improvement*. For an emphasis of this point, refer to Exhibit 4-2 "Follow the Manual."

Exhibit 11-2. The JM 4-Step Method Training Card

How to Improve Job Methods

A practical plan to help you produce GREATER QUANTITIES of QUALITY PRODUCTS in LESS TIME by making the best use of Manpower, Machines, and Materials, now available.

STEP I—BREAK DOWN the job.

1. List all the details of the job exactly as done by the Present Method.
2. Be sure details include all:
   • Material Handling
   • Machine Work
   • Hand work

STEP II—QUESTION every detail.

1. Use these types of questions:
   WHY is it necessary?
   WHAT is the purpose?
   WHERE should it be done?
   WHEN should it be done?
   WHO is best qualified to do it?
   HOW is the "best way" to do it?
2. Also question the:
   Materials, Machines, Equipment, Tools, Product Design, Layout, Workplace, Safety, Housekeeping

STEP III—DEVELOP the new method

1. ELIMINATE unnecessary details
2. COMBINE details when practical
3. REARRANGE for better sequence
4. SIMPLIFY all necessary details—
   • Make the work easier and safer
   • Preposition materials, tools and equipment at the best places in the proper work area
   • Use gravity feed hoppers and drop delivery chutes
   • Let both hands do useful work
   • Use jogs and fixtures instead of hands for holding work
5. Work out your ideas with others
6. Write up your proposed new method.

STEP IV—APPLY the new method

1 Sell your proposal to the boss.
2. Sell the new method to the operators.
3. Get final approval of all concerned on Safety, Quality, Quantity, Cost.
4. Put the new method to work. Use it until a better way is developed.
5. Give credit where credit is due.

JOB METHODS TRAINING PROGRAM
Training Within Industry Service
Bureau of Training
War Manpower Commission

The trainer now shows the participants that it is not difficult or time-consuming to break down a job into its details. The trainer then asks the group to describe what he did first when he raised his hand to start the demonstration. Sometimes the answer will be, "You picked up some copper sheets." Of course, this detail is not fine enough to describe what the trainer did. The first three details are as follows:

1. "Walk to box of copper sheets."
2. "Pick up 15–20 copper sheets."
3. "Walk to the bench."

The trainer stops after the group has given the first 5 details and then distributes the complete list of 30 job details for the demonstration. It usually takes about 2 minutes or less for the group to create the first 5 details. Therefore, it should take another 10 minutes to list the other 25 details. The point of the exercise is to show that in less than 15 minutes, you can easily find many facts that will help you improve a method.

Once this point is made, the trainer is ready to move on to Step 2, but before covering this step, take a look at the complete job breakdown for this job in Exhibit 11-3[14] (original form) and Exhibit 11-4[15] (contemporary form).

Note that the original breakdown sheet has three columns while the contemporary has 14 columns. Distance was broken out because it often is a significant factor. The questions are included (why and what are combined) to keep track of the thought process. The results (eliminate, combine, rearrange, simplify) are included to further focus the thought process. This modification does not change the Method at all, but in fact makes it easier to use, while providing added information.

Step 2—Question Every Detail

The trainer makes two points initially. First, people learn only by asking questions. "The *success* of any *improvement depends on our* ability to develop a *questioning attitude*"[16] Children question everything; but as we grow older, we either assume we know the answer or are embarrassed to ask. The six fundamental questions are WHY, WHAT, WHERE, WHEN, WHO, and HOW. Answering these types of questions will give the information needed to make improvements.

The second point made is that you must ask the questions in this order. If we ask "How?" first, for example, we might spend a lot of time determining a better way to do something. If we then ask "Why?" and find out that the detail is not necessary and can be eliminated, we have wasted a lot of time. The trainer briefly goes over the six questions, but emphasizes the importance of the first question, "Why?" As mentioned, one main objective of JM is to develop a questioning attitude in people so that they can better bring out and formulate ideas for discussion. TWI found that once workers were using the JM method, it was possible to go far beyond superficial ideas and "evolve ideas which never could have appeared on the basis of suggestions."[17] They discovered that when asking the question "Why?" one should limit the question to the active verb. For example, the first detail in the demonstration job is,

Exhibit 11-3. Present Breakdown Sheet—Original Form

Job Methods Breakdown Sheet

Operation: Inspect, Assemble, Rivet, Stamp, and Pack   Product: Radio Shields   Department: Riveting and Packing

Your Name: Bill Brown   Operator's Name: Jim Jones   Date: June 14, 1944

List of All Details for { Present / Proposed } Method — Every single thing that is done: Every Inspection—Every Detail	Notes — Reminders—Tolerances—Distance—Time Used—Etc.	Ideas — Write them down— Don't trust your memory
1. Walk to box of copper sheets	Placed 6 feet from bench by handler	No, if sheets nearer bench
2. Pick up 15 to 20 copper sheets		Close to riveter; better way
3. Walk to bench		Same as #1
4a. Inspect 12 sheets	Scratches and dents; scarp into bins	Just before assembly; better way
4b. Lay out 12 sheets		No, if sheets nearer bench
5. Walk to box and replace extra sheets		Same as #1
6. Walk to box of brass sheets	Placed 3 feet from copper box by handler	Same as #1
7. Pick up 15 to 20 brass sheets		Same as #2
8. Walk to bench		Same as #1
9a. Inspect 12 brass sheets		Same as #4a
9b. Lay out 12 brass sheets	One on top of each copper sheet	Same as #4b
10. Walk to box and replace extra sheets		Same as #1
11. Walk to bench		Same as #1
12. Stack 12 sets near riveter		No, if no layout
13. Pick up one set with right hand		Better Way
14. Line up sheets and position in riveter	Line-up tolerance is .005"	Better Way
15. Rivet top left corner		Better Way
16. Slide sheets to the left and rivet top right corner		Better Way
17. Turn sheets and position them in riveter		Better Way
18. Rivet the bottom right corner		Better Way
19. Slide sheets to left and rivet bottom left corner		Better Way
20. Turn sheets around as you lay them on the bench		Better Way
21. Stamp "TOP" and tack them on workbench		Find out
For details 13 to 21 repeat the process 11 times		
22. Put 12 sets of shields into the tote box	For details 22 to 30, counting and packing	
23. Carry the full box to the scale and weight it	could be done anytime and anywhere after	
24. Fill out a measuring skip and place it into the box	riveting	
25. Take the tote box to the packing area		
26. Unload the shields from the box		
27. Put 200 sets of shields into the packing box		
28. Cover and seal the box and write address slip on it		
29. Fill out a delivery slip		
30. Store box until it is delivered		

"Walk to the supply box containing copper sheets." If we ask, "Why do we walk to the supply box?" the obvious answer is "To pick up copper sheets." However, if we limit our question to the verb, the question becomes, "Why do we walk?" which opens up additional possibilities of how to get the sheets and where they should be. The next question would then be "Why do we pick up sheets?" Which leads us to think of some other way of attaining the sheets. This method of breaking down questions into components and questioning the components is a foundation of *root cause analysis*, which is a method of resolving issues to prevent their reoccurrence. The question "Why?" provides you with information that you can use to eliminate unnecessary details. Eliminating unnecessary details (wastes) is the most effective way of improving productivity and that is the reason "Why?" is perhaps the most important question to ask. An integral aspect of Lean manufacturing's continuous improvement and process is the use of Toyota's five-why analysis.[18] When confronted by a problem, you repeatedly ask "Why?" until you get beyond the source of the problem to uncover the deeper root cause. Then you provide countermeasures to correct the problem. Toyota has had great success developing this type of questioning attitude in its employees.

Exhibit 11-4. Contemporary Job Breakdown Chart—Page 1

Job Breakdown Chart

Product: Microwave Shields   Made By: Anne Adams   Date: 3/18/01

Operations: Inspecting, Assembling, Riveting, and Packing   Department: Riveting and Packing

Page 1 of 2

PRESENT/~~PROPOSED~~ METHOD DETAILS	Distance	REMARKS — TIME/TOLERANCE REJECTS/SAFETY	WHY	WHERE	WHEN	WHO	HOW	IDEAS — Write them down, don't try to remember.	Eliminate	Combine	Rearrange	Simplify
1 Walk to supply box containing copper sheets	6 ft.	Already been carried by the material handler	✓					No, if sheet is nearer workbench			✓	
2 Pick up 15 to 20 copper sheets		Closer to riveter, better way	✓	✓							✓	✓
3 Walk to workbench	6 ft.		✓					Same as #1			✓	
4a Inspect 12 copper sheets		Rejects with dents and scratches go into scrap bin				✓	✓	Just before assembly, better way			✓	✓
4b Lay out 12 copper sheets			✓					Same as #1			✓	
5 Walk to the supply box and replace extra sheets	6 ft.		✓					Same as #1			✓	
6 Walk to supply box containing brass sheets	3 ft.		✓					Same as #1			✓	
7 Pick up 15–20 brass sheets			✓			✓		Same as #2			✓	✓
8 Walk to the bench .	6 ft.		✓					Same as #1			✓	
9a Inspect 12 brass sheets		Rejects with dents and scratches go into scrap bin; place on top of copper sheets				✓	✓	Same as 4a			✓	✓
9b Lay out 12 brass sheets			✓					Same as 4b			✓	
10 Walk to the supply box and replace extra sheets	6 ft.		✓					Same as #1			✓	
11 Walk to the bench	6 ft.		✓					Same as #1			✓	
12 Stack 12 sets near riveter								No, if no layout				✓
13 Pick up a set of sheets with the right hand							✓	Riveting – better way				✓
14 Line up sheets and place them into riveter		Line up tolerance is .005"									✓	✓

Exhibit 11-4. Contemporary Job Breakdown Chart—Page 2

		Job Breakdown Chart											
Product: Microwave Shields				Made By: Anne Adams					Date: 3/18/01				
Operations: Inspecting, Assembling, Riveting, and Packing			Department: Riveting and Packing						Page 2 of 2				

PRESENT/~~PROPOSED~~ METHOD DETAILS	Distance	REMARKS / TIME/TOLERANCE REJECTS/SAFETY	WHY	WHERE	WHEN	WHO	HOW	IDEAS Write them down, don't try to remember.	Eliminate	Combine	Rearrange	Simplify
15 Rivet the top left corner			✓					Riveting – Better way				✓
16 Slide sheets to left and rivet the top right corner			✓			✓		Riveting – Better way				✓
17 Turn sheets and position them in the riveter				✓				Riveting – Better way				✓
18 Rivet the bottom right corner			✓	✓				Riveting – Better way				✓
19 Slide sheets to the left and rivet bottom left corner				✓				Riveting – Better way				✓
20 Turn sheets around as you lay them on the bench				✓				Riveting – Better way				✓
21 Stamp "TOP" and stack them on workbench		Stamp on the bottom right corner			✓			Find out				
For items 13–21, repeat the process 11 times												
22 Put 12 sets of shields into the carrying box				✓				Anytime, anywhere, anyone, after riveting			✓	
23 Carry the full box to the scale and weigh it.	50 ft.	50 ft. from bench to scale	✓			✓		Not necessary to weigh				
24 Fill out a measuring slip and place it into the box		Total weight 75 lbs.				✓	✓	Not necessary to weigh				
25 Take the carrying box to the packing area	100 ft.	Carried by the material handler		✓				Anytime, anywhere, anyone after riveting			✓	
26 Unload the shields from the box		Unloaded by the packer			✓			Anytime, anywhere, anyone, after riveting		✓		
27 Put 200 sets of shields into the packing box		Inspection & packing box handled by packer			✓			Anytime, anywhere, anyone, after riveting	✓			
28 Enclose the box and write out address slip on it		Empty boxes are returned by material handler			✓			Anytime, anywhere, anyone, after riveting				
29 Fill out a delivery slip					✓			Anytime, anywhere, anyone, after riveting				
30 Store it until it is delivered					✓			Anytime, anywhere, anyone, after riveting				

Sometimes, however, it may be difficult to get an adequate answer to the question "Why?" Typical answers are: "That's the way we always do it" or "It's policy." You ask "Why?" in order to get "sound and reasonable answers."[19] The JM trainer will often ask a follow-up question. "*What* is its purpose?" The intent is to find out if the detail we are talking about adds quality to the product or has some other useful purpose. For example, what is the purpose of the policy? Note that the tandem use of these questions will always set the objective of the detail. If you cannot determine a useful purpose for the detail, then you should be able to eliminate it.

The trainer states a caution here, resulting from what TWI discovered through many of its trial sessions. Once people start thinking about what they do, they come up with ideas of how to make improvements. A usual reaction is to try out some of those ideas. As discussed in Chapter 7, the developers called them "flash" ideas because they would flash through a person's thoughts. Since these may be good ideas, you shouldn't ignore or lose them, but this is not the appropriate time to consider them. This is why the breakdown sheet includes a column for participants to captures ideas for later use. The next four questions, WHERE, WHEN, WHO, and HOW, are self-explanatory, but asking each one of them assures the person that he has thoroughly reviewed the structure and details for the entire job.

Using the Breakdown Sheet

The trainer then demonstrates how the supervisor would have used the breakdown sheet in analyzing the radio shield job (see Exhibits 11-3 and 11-4). Before this demonstration, the trainer distributes blank breakdown sheets and instructs the participants to fill them out as he goes through the procedure. Starting with Detail 1 (and focusing on the verb), one asks, "Why do we walk to pick up the sheets?" The answer is that we walk because they are away from the workbench. If the sheets were closer to the workbench, walking would be unnecessary. In the notes column, one would write, "Bins 6 feet from bench" and in the ideas column, one would write, "No, if sheets nearer bench." Because we now believe that walking to pick up the sheets may be unnecessary, we do not need to investigate further and we can go to the second detail. The contemporary breakdown sheets require that we put a check mark (✔) in the "Why?" column before moving to Detail 2. This will alert us to the fact that this step may be eliminated in Step 3.

The second detail is "Pick up 15–20 copper sheets." Since they are necessary for the assembly, it is necessary that they be picked up. By questioning this detail, one might start thinking about why I have to pick up the sheets (with my hands). Perhaps there is a better way to get these fragile sheets into production. Also, why do I pick up 15–20 sheets? I do that because I must lay down a pattern of 12. That is Step 4, so I can question it when I get there; but now my mind is anticipating questions in Step 4. Going sequentially through the questions results in the following:

- *What is the purpose*? Necessary to assemble the shields.
- *Where*? Closest to the riveter is best.
- *When*? Any time before assembly.
- *Who*? The riveting operator.
- *How*? Based on the above, there should be a better way.

The trainer can write appropriate notes on the breakdown sheet (Exhibits 11-3 and 11-4). The trainer continues with this technique for all 30 details, starting out slowly and increasing the speed so that it does not become too monotonous. For example, you do details 13 to 20 all the same. The trainer's emphasis is that one thoroughly questions every detail and writes down ideas but does not act on them at this time.

Note that the training card states that you must question everything. In fact, nothing is "sacred." This does not mean TWI is advocating anarchy, but merely that you need to understand why you do what you do. If a detail is, "Place two copies in the VP's in-basket," we might question why we place them in the in-basket at all, or why we need to place *two* copies in the in-basket when we could send an email instead. The answer, "Because the VP said so" is not sufficient and thus we would ask the purpose of doing so. It is not necessary to probe into the VP's operational habits and an answer of, "One copy is filed and one copy is sent on" may be sufficient. The possibility of using email could then be explored.

But this leads us to what TWI understood so thoroughly—*you should train everyone in the organization in the JM program*. If the VP knew the JM program, and someone asked why she needed two copies, that question would prompt her to analyze from a JM-perspective why she required two copies in that manner. Perhaps the copy does not have to be filed or perhaps the copy "sent on" is thrown out. During a contemporary training session, one engineer's demonstration job was the procedure of asking for a vacation day. Although it was a simple procedure, it was annoying to him. The procedure was that he would write up a request and then have his manager and his manager's manager sign it. When he asked his manager why he had to sign the request, the answer was to make sure there was sufficient engineering coverage on the days he would be gone. When he asked why his manager's manager signed the request, the answer was that it was the procedure. What was the purpose? There was no purpose. The senior manager placed the responsibility for vacation days with his direct report. The second signature was thus eliminated because it was not necessary. The senior manager did not object because he knew that by adding his signature, he was neither adding value to the process nor facilitating efficiency. In this case, the senior manager was actually in the training and he quickly accepted this process change. If he had no knowledge of the JM program, he may not have been so quick to accept the change.

Step 3—Develop the Method

Now that the participants fully understand the details, they are ready for Step 3. The techniques in improving a method are to 1) *eliminate* unnecessary details, 2) *combine* details whenever possible and practical, 3) *rearrange* details for better sequence, and 4) *simplify* details so they are easier and safer to do. The trainer points out to the participants that these four techniques of Step 3 are directly related to the six questions of Step 2 (see Exhibit 11-5).[20]

Exhibit 11-5. Relationship of Step II to Step III

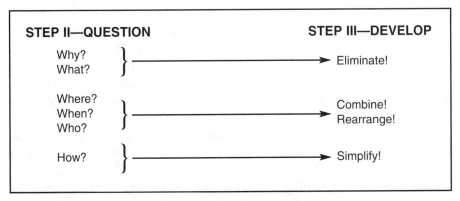

Again, note the importance of the order. First, you would want to eliminate anything that is unnecessary. The answers to the first two questions, "Why?" and "What?" give you information that allows you to do that. The trainer now explains how the supervisor uses the breakdown sheet to develop the new procedure. He looks at details that he believes he could eliminate, which were the ones that involved walking: Details #1, #3, #5, #6, #8, #10, and #11. He thought he could eliminate these details if the sheets were delivered closer to the workbench. He found that there was space on the workbench and the material handler said that the sheets could be as easily delivered to the workbench as anywhere else. So he eliminated those details from his method and consequently, he put a ✔ in the "eliminate" columns of those details.

In the contemporary breakdown sheet, there are columns for the six questions listed as five columns since "What?" is considered to be with "Why?" for the four techniques in Step 3. When going through the questions of Step 2, it is convenient to check the question that does not have a satisfactory answer. For example, when the participants ask why they walked to the supply box and discover that it is unnecessary, they put a check mark under the 'Why' column for that detail. When the participants get to Step 3, they confirm that they can eliminate the detail and put a check mark in the 'Eliminate' column of that detail. In this way, when you write the proposed method, you can easily recognize details that you have eliminated.

Eliminating unnecessary details is one of the greatest contributors to improving processes. Organizations can get instant returns by having its employees use the JM method as soon as they learn it. They can make even greater improvements once the employees learn how to question what they do and how they do it on a daily basis.

In another contemporary JM training session, one supervisor volunteered to demonstrate his job method first (on the second day). Because this supervisor did the first demonstration, he did not have the benefit of learning from watching his peers. He was the "guinea pig" so to speak. The job entailed checking the viscosity of a slurry used in production. The thickness of the slurry was important to its application and thus it had to be checked every 4 hours. The slurry tanks were in an automatic production line that included a conveyor and thus the first detail was to turn off the conveyor because of safety reasons. The inspection initially took about 30 minutes, so about an hour of production was lost for every 8-hour shift. Although this had bothered the supervisor for some time, he did not know how to address the situation until he took the JM program. By listing and then *questioning* all the details, he managed to reduce the inspection time from 30 minutes to about 18 minutes. The travel time (walking around) was reduced from 397 feet to about 54 feet.

Although a 40 percent reduction in time was an admirable result, the supervisor was still bothered by something. He kept thinking about the process during the week of training and by Thursday, he had his answer. It had to do with the first detail. "Turn off the conveyor." The answer to "Why?" was because of safety, but now, having learned the importance of questioning more thoroughly, he asked, "Is there *another way* to perform the inspection in a safe manner?" "Does the conveyor have to be turned off?" The answer hinged on whether he could keep the conveyor running *if* the inspector didn't have to enter the hazard area around the conveyor. After checking with the safety department, the supervisor realized that he did not have to turn off the conveyor because the inspector could access the slurry tanks outside of the hazardous area. Production, therefore, did not have to be stopped at all and an hour of production was gained during each shift, which was a considerable savings because the company ran two, and sometimes three, shifts a day. Besides eliminating the need to stop the production line, this process change reduced the inspection time by 40 percent. This resulted in 100 percent savings over time, which meant that the production line did not have to be stopped for inspecting the slurry. All of this occurred because the supervisor improved his skill in questioning.

Although elimination can give us 100 percent reduction of a detail, combining details will give us a smaller reduction. In the demonstration job, Details #22, #26, and #27 were combined. In the existing method, the shields were put into a tote box, taken out of the tote box, and then put into a packing box. The supervisor combined the details so that the shields were handled only once by having the riveter pack the shields directly into the packing container. If you cannot combine details, you may be able to rearrange them to make them easier to do. The questions, "Where?", "When?", and "Who?" lead one to think about how to combine or rearrange details.

"Because he had changed the location of the supply boxes, he had to rearrange the details of picking up the copper and brass sheets. (Nos. 2 and 7)"[21]

Finally, the question of "How?" leads you to uncover ways to simplify a process. Simplifying processes is what many people first think about when asked to improve a method, yet it is the last item one should deal with. It takes the most time, often incurs the greatest expense and may result in the smallest amount of time saved.

The five improvement techniques cited below are classic industrial engineering techniques that have been used for over 100 years and cover 90 percent of what a person needs to know about methods improvement.

1. Put materials and tools within convenient reach.
2. Use gravity whenever possible to bring parts to you or take them away from you.
3. Use both hands (and feet) when possible.
4. Use jigs (moveable devices) to hold parts or tools.
5. Use fixtures (fixed devices) to hold parts or tools.

Because the JM program is not intended to replace industrial engineers who have a great deal of specific knowledge, the developers intentionally made the process of questioning broad by using the six generic questions. For example, you could consider ergonomics as part of "put materials and tools within convenient reach." As the trainer discusses these five principles, he also explains how the supervisor used them in the job demonstration problem.

There are two other activities under Step 3. Since the supervisor is encouraged to "question everything" in Step 2, he or she has an opportunity to speak with a variety of people. These are the same people that the supervisor can return to when it is time to develop the new method. Therefore, the trainer reminds the participants to "Work out your idea with others." JM underscores that improvement ideas can come from many different places and that one should be seeking them out everywhere at any time. A valuable by-product of this "teamwork" is improved communication among most people across the organization. The training further emphasizes that the supervisor did not create the entire change alone in the job demonstration, but received much help from one of the four operators.

The last activity in Step 3, and an extremely important part of JM, is to write up a proposal for the improvement idea once a supervisor formulates it, because a written proposal is the first step to implementation. This is key because many improvement ideas are never implemented because people fail to convince the necessary parties of their value. The written proposal includes a form which is easy to use, and when used properly, will be accepted by any reasonable person. The only cause for rejection would be due to lack of information. Because this is such an important part of the JM program, the trainer will spend more time on this in the second session.

Step 4: Apply the New Method

Step 4 consists of four activities. The first activity is to sell your improvement idea, or new method, to both your manager and the people who will be using it. You may or may not require your managers' approval, but at a minimum, you should let the manager know what you are doing. Hopefully, the operators were involved in developing the new method, but if they, or anyone else who needs to know, wasn't, the supervisor should inform them before implementing the changes. This activity is more about "selling" than "informing." This is why supervisors need to show their proposal sheet to everyone who has an interest in the operation. Because the process change in question will make people's work easier, the "sell" should not be too difficult.

The second activity is to get approvals from required areas. The supervisor talks to these people twice, once to question the details, and once to work out his or her ideas. Now it's time for the supervisor to return and tell them what the final decision is. Keeping people informed in this way makes it easier to gain approvals and better participation when needed. Areas from which you may need to obtain approvals could include safety, quality, design, production control, accounting, sales, marketing, human resources, and plant engineering.

The third activity is to implement the change as quickly as possible. Many good ideas fall to the wayside simply because people do not immediately use them. Ultimately, they are forgotten. If necessary, it is better to pare down the size of a great idea, or break it into phases, so you can implement it quickly rather than delay implementation because you want to perfect the idea or implement all at once. It is easier for participants to accept this approach once they understand the concept of continuous improvement.

"Remember there will always be a better way. Keep searching for further improvements."[22]

In Lean Thinking, the way to create long-lasting improvement and strive for perfection is for a company to implement continuous improvements of all kinds over the long-term. You can always improve methods, though it may not always be practical to seek or make the improvement. Yet the potential improvement is always there. Also, a supervisor should not be overly "attached" to his or her new "great" idea, because in an environment of continual improvement, someone may come up with a better idea at any time. Sometimes you must be satisfied that, although your idea is not being used directly, it served as a catalyst to inspire someone else to improve the process even more. If the supervisor has been very thorough and creative, the time between process improvements will be greater.

The success of a supervisor can be traced back to Step 1, speaking to as many people as possible during the investigation period; and emphasizing the importance of activity 4, "giving credit." "Giving credit" means to show sincere appreciation for help. Studies by psychologists, such as Abraham Maslow, show that after satisfying basic survival needs, humans have a strong need for recognition.[23] Failing to give recognition or credit will slow or stop the flow of ideas. And conversely,

"The **more credit** we give the **more ideas** we get."[24]

At this point, the trainer has completed the discussion of the JM 4-Step Method (Exhibit 11-2) and is now ready to end Session I. The trainer makes a final effort to sell the program to the participants by engaging them in a discussion about whether or not they believe the JM program will help them. The trainer repeats such points as:

- The JM plan [method] will make it easier for you to make improvements that will make your job easier.
- One improvement each week would make any Supervisor's job easier, reduce "bottlenecks," and cut down the number of "trouble" jobs.
- One improvement today is worth ten times as much now as it would be next year.
- We can't afford to be 'TOO BUSY' to find time to continually search for improvements.
- The plan is applicable to all types of jobs in all types of industries.[25]

End of Session I and Preparation for Session II

Once the trainer believes that most of the participants have sufficient confidence to proceed, he solicits volunteers for a job demonstration in the second session. Before the end of the week, every participant must select a job from the workplace that he or she is familiar with and can improve.[26] The participants must also select a small portable job that can be set up in the room. The

trainer needs to make it clear what is expected of them. Because each participant will have only about 20 minutes to describe both the present and proposed process for the demonstration, it must be understood that the actual job
itself must take just a few minutes to complete. More important than the
demonstration itself, the trainer explains that the participants need to discuss
how he or she used the JM 4-Step Method to improve the job.[27] The main purpose of the demonstration is to have the participants learn the 4-Step Method
and show that they know it.

As I've mentioned before, some people are so sold on the Method that
they immediately want to apply it on a lengthy or involved process.

"Many try, in Session II, to rearrange the plant and perform small mira-
cles. Drive for the small jobs to start. The larger ones may follow later."[28]

So it is important that the trainer make it clear that though you can apply
JM to any process, selecting and improving a process is not the purpose of the
training. Studying, discussing, and learning the Method is.

The trainer can also supply additional reasons for selecting a short job.
The intent of the practice session is to both train the participants in the Method
and to impress upon them the importance of using the Method continually
with everything they do—even simple, small processes. Yes, product selection, design, and launch are three major activities that can dramatically change
things, but it usually requires a complex time-consuming process. However,
making smaller process improvements on a daily basis usually does not
require as wide an approval, which means you can implement them more
quickly and, over time, these many small improvements will add up to reflect
major benefits. Also, if you use the JM 4-Step Method for small changes, you
will use it more often; and the more something is used, the better a person gets
at using it. After a while, it can become second nature, which is when continual improvement will start becoming part of the culture.

Anyone involved with production knows that Japanese suggestion systems are legendary and most of those systems are based on the TWI Job Methods program which was introduced to Japanese industry in 1949 (see quote in
Chapter 3, page 2–3), Having 100 or 200 suggestions per person per year is
not uncommon in companies with these suggestion systems. Having two to
four suggestions per person per week may not be significant in itself. Implementing 50,000 suggestions in an organization of 500 people is significant,
however.

To prepare the participants so they can put together their job demonstration and improvement analysis, the trainer spends the last few minutes of Session I on 1) resistance to new ideas and 2) resentment and criticism. The trainer

explains that initially many people are resistant to a new idea because of past practice, custom, precedent, tradition, or habit. Examples such as the telephone, balloon tires, tubeless tires, and even the computer are discussed to show that people will resist most anything that is new. Since the participants (supervisors or team leaders) will be spearheading improvements that must be made, they need to learn to ignore the "nay sayers" within the organization. If workers or managers end up interpreting the supervisor's actions (or comments) as personal criticism of what they do or how they do it, then the supervisor must explain the purpose behind his or her actions or comments. The fact is, no process is perfect and the supervisor is merely examining the process to determine if there is anything to improve the job or to make it easier to do. There may be things that no one has considered in the past, and surely, there will be something to consider in the future. But others may not see it this way. The point is, it is the supervisor's role to continually observe and ask questions to improve processes, regardless of criticisms, but he or she also needs to have the skill to explain and "sell" the improvement.

Session II, III, IV, and V

The objectives of Sessions II, III, IV, and V are:

1. To make sure that each member understands each and every part of the 4-Step Method.
2. To convince every member that the principles of Job Methods Improvement apply to ANY job that has material handling, machine work, or hand work, whether repetitive or not.[29]

Because the JM 4-Step Method is basic, these objectives might sound too easy. This can be deceptive because when people think something is easy they assume they already understand it. For example, many people confuse a job "detail" with a job "step." A "detail" is the smallest element of a process while a "step" is a guidepost to steer you through a process. Also, as previously explained, knowing how to question thoroughly is a learned skill. Finally, some people think of an improvement before the questioning leads them to it and they apply the JM program after the fact.

In order to achieve the first objective of learning to question, the trainer uses the volunteer's job demonstration as additional training for the group. The Trainer's Guide specifically says:

"Remember if they fail, you have failed."
Keep always before you that your obligation is to *sell* the plan, so that at the conclusion of the ten hours each will agree that the JOB METH-

ODS PROGRAM is a PRODUTION TOOL that may be used daily on ANY job."[30]

To accomplish this, the trainer focuses on teaching one step of the JM 4-Step Method per session when the volunteers are conducting their demonstrations. So each session proceeds as follows:

- Session II stresses Step 1, breakdown the job.
- Session III stresses Step 2, question every detail.
- Session IV stresses Step 3, develop the new method.
- Session V stresses Step 4, apply the new method.

Each session begins with a review of the four steps, although the trainer simplifies this review throughout the week. When reviewing a job, the trainer uses additional time to emphasize one of the four steps with the volunteer. Group discussion is encouraged to get everyone to respond verbally to questions about the steps. By the end of the week, everyone should be completely familiar with the JM 4-Step Method and respond confidently to any of the trainer's questions.

Session II is critical because much learning will occur here. Also, ". . . the best for which you may hope, is that the group has absorbed 50% of what you put over in Session I, and you had to do a bang-up job if you approached this figure."[31] The trainer makes sure that the participants have an increased understanding of the JM program and further sell it in Session II; otherwise, the remainder of the week could be lost. Remember, at this point, the only job demonstration the participants have seen is the Radio Shield job and they may still have a lot of skepticism. It is not until they see how they can improve a job in their own organization, using the JM Method, that they become more inclined to accept it. The ideal situation is to have the first volunteer do a less than perfect job demonstration. As it happens, this is usually the case because the participants are still unfamiliar with applying the four steps and they probably still do not have a clear idea of what a "detail" actually is. This allows the trainer to properly break down a job into its details and demonstrate how this helps one to gather the information needed to expose areas for improvement. The Job Methods anecdote in Exhibit 4-2 gives a good example of how a trainer can use an imperfect demonstration to "sell" the participants on the use of the Method.

The procedure for demonstrating a job is standardized and posted in the room so that the participants can refer to it. It is also discussed with the volunteers at the end of Session I so they can prepare for their demonstration. Then the entire group discusses it at the beginning of Session II (see Exhibit 11-6).[32] The participants will follow this procedure for all the demonstrations.

Exhibit 11-6. Procedure for Demonstrating a Job

Demonstration Procedure

1. **Description—**
   Describe briefly the job you have tackled and explain samples and sketches you will use.
2. **Present Method Demonstration—**
   Demonstrate the present method step by step. Use your Job Breakdown Sheet.
3. **Present Method Details—**
   Read the details of the Job Breakdown Sheet.
4. **Ideas Obtained From Questions—**
   Explain what information and leads you obtained from the answers to questions in STEP 2.
5. **Development of New Method—**
   Explain how this information helped you to eliminate, combine, rearrange, and simplify details while developing the new method in STEP 3.
6. **Proposed New Method—**
   Demonstrate the Proposed Method.
7. **New Method Application—**
   Explain how you used, or will use, the items under STEP 4 to help you apply the new method.
8. **Summary of Improvement Results—**
   Sum up the improvements on your job: safety, cost, time, etc.

There are two requirements that the trainer must enforce for the demonstrations.

1. The job improvement must be new, not one that is already in place.[33] This helps assure that the participant will evoke a new improvement from a job using the plan and will not adjust the plan to an existing improvement.
2. You must complete the Present and the Proposed Breakdown Sheets. This also gives some assurance that the participant worked through the method and did not come up with an improvement by using another plan or method.

The trainer should confirm that these two criteria have been met before the start of each session in order to assure that the sessions run smoothly for both the trainer and the participants and preempt any awkward moments, such as the trainer not allowing a participant to give a job demonstration because he or she was ill-prepared.[34]

Because the participants review the job breakdown sheet on the second day, there usually is time for only one demonstration in Session II. As a result, the participants must cover the remaining nine demonstrations in 3 days. These are the main reasons why the class size should be limited to ten and why participants must select small job improvement projects. Since time is a factor, the volunteers should perform the Demonstration Procedure through Step 6, skipping Steps 7 and 8, without any group discussion. Participants can ask a question if something is unclear, but in the interest of time, the discussion should occur at the end of the demonstration.

Since Session II emphasizes Step 1, *Breakdown the Job*, the first thing the trainer does once the volunteer completes the demonstration is to explain the proposed new method. This is when participants can ask for clarification or what further improvements could be made. The intent of this session is to have the group develop any improvement ideas that the volunteer may not have uncovered or demonstrated. After this discussion, the trainer will ask the volunteer to perform the demonstration again, telling the volunteer when to start and stop his actions. The volunteer must actually go through the motions of what he has to do. The trainer says "Start" and watches the volunteer do the first detail and then the trainer says "Stop." The trainer then asks the group, "What did he do?" This is the first detail the trainer writes on the blackboard. In addition to writing down the detail, the trainer writes down any remarks or ideas. Once the group has captured 10 to 20 details—this is usually sufficient to proceed with the Method—they are written on the blackboard and the trainer proceeds to Step 2, even though the job may not be complete. It is important to make sure everyone understands the concept of creating the job details, so the trainer may have to spend extra time here.

Step 2, *Question Every Detail* the volunteer is asked, "Why is this detail necessary?" and "Can we eliminate this detail?" "What is the purpose?" is asked if necessary. The intent is to have the volunteer go through the six questions (Why, What, Where, When, Who, How) correctly. If he has already done this, then there is little discussion and the exercise proceeds quickly. Sometimes the volunteer has not sufficiently thought through the questions and discovers something new.

Step 3, *Develop the New Method*, is done quickly with group involvement by the trainer asking which details can be eliminated, combined, rearranged, or simplified. Because this is the volunteer's job, everything that is written down is first confirmed with the volunteer. The trainer goes through Steps 1 through 3 using a board, overhead projector,[35] or a specially prepared preprinted form with the print large enough for the participant to see from a distance. In any case, the trainer goes through the entire plan correctly so that the participants can see how to do it.

Whether the volunteer has done the analysis perfectly or left something to be desired, the group will always see how you can use Job Methods to improve a job in their organization. Again, the trainer's main objective is for the participants to learn the Method, so the trainer should take as much time as is required to ensure the participants are following and learning the JM 4-Step Method, rather than the technical aspect of developing and improving a job. "It is far better to have a clear understanding and realization of the value of each step, than to have a startling improvement that confuses thinking of the group."[36] See Exhibit 11-7 for the final job breakdown sheet and proposed method details for microwave shields.[37] (Note: Exhibits 11-4 and 11-5 are the original and contemporary JBS for the way the job is currently being done—*present* Method (or procedure). Exhibit 11-7 is the contemporary JBS for the way the job could be done—*proposed* Method (or procedure). The main difference between the two is that the present method has 30 steps, while the proposed method has 14.

Step 4, *Apply the New Method*, is covered briefly because the trainer hasn't yet discussed the concept of a proposal sheet. At this point, the trainer asks the volunteer about plans for implementation. The four items (sell, approve, use, credit) are discussed briefly and the trainer writes a summary of the benefits on the board. The trainer distributes blank proposal sheets and discusses their purpose. The people who appreciate these proposal sheets the most are those who are asked to review the job improvement, either for approval or for suggestions. Many people do not know how to properly capture and present ideas that they can share with others, and the proposal sheet is a good learning tool for this purpose.

The proposal sheet is a simple form that lays out the critical information in a way that is easily understandable. It actually serves three purposes. The first is that the originator can check to see if his idea is worthwhile before he presents it to someone else. It gives him a way to look at it from another perspective and acts as a check to make sure that all pertinent information is included. As mentioned previously, if the person has used the JM 4-Step Method and has filled out the proposal sheet completely, the decision to accept or reject the proposal will be obvious to both the person originating the proposal and the person approving it. Second, when presenting the idea, the sheet makes the proposal very clear by eliminating any unnecessary information that the originator might include in a verbal presentation. Ideas clearly presented are easier to evaluate and more likely to be accepted. Finally, because the proposal is written, it can be distributed and documented. In a contemporary JM session, when a manager reviewed a proposal sheet he was given for approval, his comment was, "The next time somebody says to me, 'Why don't we . . . .' I'll ask him for a proposal sheet."

At this point the trainer is instructed to tell the participants:

Exhibit 11-7. Final Job Breakdown Chart for Microwave Shields

Job Breakdown Chart

Product: Microwave Shields Made By: Anne Adams (Bob Burns) Date: 3/18/01

Operations: Inspecting, Assembling, Riveting, and Packing Department: Riveting and Packing

#	PRESENT/PROPOSED METHOD DETAILS	Distance	REMARKS TIME/TOLERANCE REJECTS/SAFETY	WHY	WHERE	WHEN	WHO	HOW	IDEAS Write them down, don't try to remember.	Eliminate	Combine	Rearrange	Simplify
1	Pile copper sheets onto the right jig		Materials are placed on the bench by the handler.										
2	Pile bras sheets onto the left jig												
3	Pick up copper sheet with right hand, brass sheet with the other												
4	Inspect both sheets		Rejects w/dents and scratches go into the scrap bins through slots.										
5	Position both sheets in the riveter		The guides in the fixture will automatically align the edges and holes. The brass sheet goes on top.										
6	Rivet bottom two corners												
7	Turn sheets around and position in riveter												
8	Rivet upper two corners												
9	Place the shields in front of the fixture												
	For Details 3–9, repeat the same process 19 times.												
10	Place 20 finished sets of shields into packing box (1 full box contains 200 sets.)												
11	Take the full box to the packing area	100 ft.											
12	Pack and address the box												
13	Fill out a delivery slip												
14	Store it until it is delivered												

1. List the improved uses of manpower, machines, and materials at the **beginning** of the proposal.
2. Include all other improvements in quality, safety, and housekeeping.
3. Tell exactly how you will make the improvement and what will be accomplished.
4. Fill in the heading completely.
5. List those who should be given credit.
6. Refer to the reverse side of the sheet for a review of the use of the 4-Step Method.

As you can see from Exhibits 11-8a and 11-8b,[38] the original double-sided proposal sheet merely listed an area for describing the details of the improvement. Exhibit 11-9,[39] the revised, contemporary proposal sheet has a specific area for results. This improvement makes it easier for both the writer and the reader. Also, some companies may want to augment this section with metrics that are unique or specifically important to their own organizations. The important point is to have such a comprehensive sheet so that you can quickly record and disseminate the ideas.

If the trainer accomplished the objectives in Session II, than the remainder of the week should go smoothly because the participants will be enthusiastic about developing and presenting their ideas. The trainer conducts the remaining three days for Sessions III through V just like Session II, with some small exceptions. As mentioned earlier, Session III emphasizes Step 2, Session IV emphasizes Step 3, and Session V emphasizes Step 4. There are multiple demonstrations but the trainer will choose only one to review closely, and selects an appropriate demonstration for a volunteer to go through the JM 4-Step Method. In addition, volunteers who have already demonstrated their jobs will read their proposals to the group. Though these sessions can be intense because of the amount of work in a two-hour period, the participants do have the advantage of returning refreshed each day.

Using the Job Methods Plan

Job Methods is different from the other two "J" programs where once the participants complete the training, they cannot use it until a situation arises at their companies. TWI made it very clear that is was important to make sure that once the training was completed, the organization would make an effort to have the trainees use the new skills. Although you can use the JM program immediately, it may require management's interaction to approve any changes. The purpose of using Job Methods, of course, should be for results; an organization can develop a program that sets goals for periodic improvements. A TWI

Exhibit 11-8a. Original Double-Sided Proposal Sheet (front side)

JOB METHODS
PROPOSAL

To R.V.Swift, Supt.   Date   June 14, 1944

From: Bill Brown, Riveting Dept.   Department   Riveting

Product or Part Radio Shields

Operation Inspect, Assemble, Rivet, & Pack

The following is my proposal for improving the method for doing this work.*

We can produce 2,400 shields per day per operator instead of 800—have
riveting machine drive 4,800 rivets instead of 200—decrease material scrap
from 15%to less than 2% and use 2 inexperienced operators instead of 4
experienced men by making the following changes:
1. Have brass and copper sheet boxes delivered to a specified place on
riveting benches by the material handler.
2. Put 2 riveting machines on each bench and use a riveting fixture to line up
and hold the sets of sheets so 2 rivets can be driven at the same time.
3. Use two jigs made from scrap material to hold sheets alongside of fixtures
so sheets can be picked up with both hands.
4. Eliminate the "TOP" stamp because it is not necessary on the present
style shield.
5. Have shipping cases delivered to riveting benches and let the operators
pack shields in cases by count.
6. Cut slots in bench so scrap can be dropped into scrap bins.
See Job Breakdown Sheets and sketch attached.

Credit is due: Jim Jones for helping with this improvement.

Note—Tell exactly HOW you believe this improvement can be accomplished.
Use another sheet for additional information or sketches if needed.
Attach Present and Proposed Breakdown sheets.

(over)

(page 1 of 2)

Exhibit 11-8b. Original Double-Sided Proposal Sheet (reverse side)

(PROPOSAL—REVERSE SIDE)

Before turning in your PROPOSAL, be SURE you have rechecked the New Method with the Job Methods 4-STEP PLAN.

STEP 1—BREAK DOWN the job.
1. List ALL the details of the job EXACTLY as done by the Present method
2. Be sure details include all:
   Materials Handling
   Machine Work
   Hand Work

STEP II—QUESTION every detail. Use these types of questions:
1. WHY is it necessary?
2. WHAT is its purpose?
3. WHERE should it be done?

4. WHEN should it be done?
5. WHO is the best qualified to do it?
6. HOW is "the best way" to do it?

Also, QUESTION the:

MATERIALS
Can better, less expensive, or less scarce materials be substituted?
Can the scrap from this job be used for another product?
Have the defects and scrap been reduced to a minimum?
Are the material specifications entirely clear and definite?
MACHINES
Is each operating at maximum capacity?
Is each in good operating condition?
Are they serviced regularly?
Is the machine best for this operation?
Should a special set-up man or the operator make all the set-ups?
Can use be made of the machine's or operator's "idle" time?
EQUIPMENT AND TOOLS
Are suitable equipment and tools available?
Have they been supplied to operators?
How about gauges, jogs, and fixtures?
Have equipment, tools, been properly prepositioned to permit effective work?
PRODUCT DESIGN
Could quality be improved by a change in design or specification?
Would a slight change in design save much time or materials?
Are tolerance and finish necessary?

LAYOUT
Is there a minimum of backtracking?
Are the number of handlings and the distances traveled at a minimum?
Is all available space being used?
Are aisles wide enough?
WORKPLACE
Is everything in the proper work area?
Can gravity feed hoppers or drop delivery chutes be used?
Are both hands doing useful work?
Has all hand-holding been eliminated?
SAFETY
Is the method the safest as well as the easiest?
Does the operator understand all safety rules and precautions?
Has proper safety equipment been provided?
Remember, accidents cause WASTE of manpower, machines, and materials!
HOUSEKEEPING
Are working and storage areas clean and orderly?
Is "junk" taking up space that could be used for additional operators, machines, benches, and operations?
Do away with anything that is unnecessary.
Be sure necessary things are in proper places.
See that good Shop Housekeeping reduces delays, waste, and accidents

STEP III—DEVELOP the new method.
1. ELIMINATE unnecessary details.
2. COMBINE details when practical.

3. REARRANGE for better sequence.
4. SIMPLIFY all necessary details.

STEP IV—APPLY the new method.
1. SELL your PROPOSAL to your Boss and Operators.
2. Get final approval of all concerned on SAFETY, QUALITY, QUANTITY, COST.
3. Put the new method to work. Use it until a better way has been developed.
4. Give CREDIT where credit is due.

Page 2 of 2

Exhibit 11-9. Contemporary Proposal Sheet

Improvement Proposal Sheet

Submitted to: Sam Johnson, Manager

Made by: Anne Adams, Supervisor   Dept.: Riveting and Packing

Product/Part: Microwave Shields   Date: May 20, 2001

Operations: Inspecting, Assembly, Riveting, and Packing

The following are proposed improvements on the above operations.

1. Summary

We worked on improving the assembly and packing process for the microwave shields. Our analysis shows that there is too much walking and handling of the product that leads to wasted effort and material. By rearranging the layout of the work and devising jigs to automate the assembly, we were able to make dramatic improvements.

2. Results

	Before Improvement	After Improvement
Production (one worker per day)	800 sets	2,400 sets
Machine use (one machine per day)	800 sets	1,200 sets
Reject rate	5%	Below 0.5%
Number of operators	4 skilled	2 nonskilled
Other—scrap	15%	Less than 2%

1. Operators will no longer have to walk to the supply box if the material handler brings the sheets to the designated area on the workbench.
2. Placing two riveters inside a fixture and guides on it to align the sheets will enable two holes to be riveted simultaneously.
3. Having two jigs with sheets on top and placing them near the fixture will enable workers to use both hands to pick up the sheets.
4. Stamping "TOP" operation will be eliminated since it is not necessary.
5. Empty packing boxes next to the bench will enable the operator to install the completed shields directly into the boxes (by number, not by weight).
6. Having two slots on the bench will enable operators to drop defective sheets easily into the scrap bins. (Refer to the attached breakdown and layout sheets.)

This proposal was made with the assistance and cooperation of Bob Burns.

3. Content

Note: Explain exactly how this improvement was made. If necessary, attach present and proposed breakdown sheets, diagrams, and any other related items.

suggestion system sets a goal of one improvement per week per person and rec-ommends that someone act as a tabulator of all completed proposals so the results can be summarized in a periodic report. This effort should not take a sig-nificant amount of time, and, when the published data is distributed around the organization, it is very useful. It not only gives people ideas of what they can do, but shows how many improvements have been made. Such data is required by ISO2000 and easily fits into that methodology. At one contemporary JM training session, so many ideas were generated as the result of the demonstra-tion jobs that a list was created during the middle of the week, which became the genesis of a continual improvement program. Although the participants had some experience with Lean Manufacturing techniques, the JM training and the list created from it were key to helping them change their culture so they could truly embrace and sustain Lean Thinking.

---

1. Robinson, Alan G., and Schroeder, Dean M., *Training, Continuous Improve-ment, and Human Relations: The U.S. TWI Programs and the Japanese Man-agement Style*, California Management Review, The Regents of the University of California, CMR, Volume 335, Number 2, Winter 1993, p. 41.
2. Final Report, p. 37.
3. Final Report, p. 39.
4. Final Report, p. 229.
5. JM Manual Introduction letter from C.R. Dooley.
6. Job Methods Manual, Reference p. 72. Note also that "inspection" was termed "unproductive" in 1944; and now, according to Lean Principles it is a form of waste. Also, "thinking" was deemed nonproductive because, by definition, it did not produce a physical product.
7. This has been updated to be the assembly of a microwave shield.
8. Job Methods Manual, Reference p. 72.
9. Note that the actual tote is supposed to weigh about 75 pounds. This, of course, occurred in the days before the OSHA weight limit. The trainer is encouraged to act a little here to demonstrate both the large weight of the tote and the dis-tance through which it must be carried.
10. Four people making 100 shields per unit of time = 400 sheets per unit of time. With a productivity increase of (3), each person would now make 300 shields per unit of time. Therefore, two people could make 600 shields per unit of time, which is a 50% increase over what four people would previously do.
11. Job Methods Manual, p. 12.
12. Dietz, Walter, *Learn by Doing*, Walter Dietz, NJ, 1970, p 18.
13. Job Methods Manual, p. 14.
14. Job Methods Manual, Reference Section p. JM-2.
15. TDO-TWI Job Methods Participant's Manual, pp. 16–17.

16. Job Methods Manual, p. 16.
17. Final Report, p. 234.
18. The number "5" is arbitrary and the question should be repeated as much as is necessary to make the root cause apparent.
19. JM Manual, p. 17.
20. Job Methods Manual, p. 27.
21. Job Methods Manual, p. 26.
22. Job Methods Manual, p. 33.
23. Abraham Maslow is known for establishing the theory of a hierarchy of five needs, showing that humans are motivated by unsatisfied needs, and that lower needs need to be satisfied before moving on to satisfying higher needs. These five are: Physiological needs, Safety needs, Love and belongingness, Esteem, and Self-actualization.
24. Job Methods Manual, p. 33.
25. Job Methods Manual, pp. 33–34.
26. There is no specific order for the participants. Some people feel more comfortable with presenting than others, so the trainer asks for volunteers to present during the next session. At the end of session 1, the trainer asks for volunteers for session 2, and at the end of session 2, he asks for volunteers for session 3, and so forth. If there is enough time, two people will present in session 1, but usually, there's only time for one since a lot of time is spent on the JBS. That means (with a group of 10), there must be three demonstrations in each of sessions 3, 4, and 5.
27. Thus it's very important for the volunteer (person putting on the demo) to show how he used the 4-Step Method to make the improvements. If this isn't made clear, people would just show the two ways of doing something and people watching wouldn't know whether or not he used the 4-Step Method.
28. Job Methods Manual Trainer's Guide, p. 15.
29. Job Method Manual Trainer's Guide, p. 11.
30. Job Method Manual Trainer's Guide, p. 11.
31. Job Method Manual Trainer's Guide, p. 12.
32. Original JM Manual p. 41, Contemporary JM Manual, p. 57.
33. Some people will take an existing improvement and use it for a demo. This is not acceptable because they are not doing what is really important, which is to show the 4-Step Method.
34. For example, if the volunteer hasn't used the 4-Step Method, it will soon become obvious and he will look foolish. The trainer will lead the participant through the method and the difference in outcome will be obvious. This happened to me once in JI. We had 12 people in the group and so had to be really efficient with the time. One day I didn't review a volunteer's (woman's) JBS before the session. When I called her to demo and asked for the JBS, she said that she wanted to use her own instruction method. At the end, the person receiving the instruction said she was confused and couldn't do the job. That

was an awkward moment for the volunteer, but that exercise did sell the class on using the method. In my train the trainer class, we were told to not let anyone present who wasn't prepared, which would be awkward. Now, I would try to read the person and either not let the volunteer present (which would make the volunteer feel awkward) or let the volunteer present and not do well (making the volunteer feel awkward).

35. A digital projector can be used for delivering the training, especially in Session 1, but a board or overhead projector is required when the demo is being reviewed because the material comes from the volunteer which most likely can't be prepared ahead of time. I encourage the use of a white board.

36. Job Methods Manual Trainer's Guide, p. 15.

37. TDO-TWI Job Methods Participants Guide, p. 21.

38. Job Methods Manual Reference Section JM-8 and JM-9.

39. Job Methods Participant's Guide, p. 25.

CHAPTER 12

Delivering Program Development

"[Training] content must come from evidence [of need]..."[1]

As discussed in Chapter 8, volunteering to be the "arsenal of democracy" meant that the United States had to increase significantly its industrial output, and the largest obstacle was training thousands of people to do jobs, many of which they never knew existed. Because TWI's agenda was to respond to industry's requests and then satisfy its needs on a national basis, it created the three "J" programs to answer the demands of quickly getting people 1) to learn their jobs, 2) to work through personnel problems better, and 3) to improve how they did their work. These three programs addressed a majority of the challenges and problems to provide a trained workforce for industry. Because these challenges and problems were common among industries, TWI created programs applicable across all industries. You can use the same JI program techniques to train someone to be a secretary or an engine lathe mechanic. Likewise, you can use the same JM program to train that secretary to analyze and improve his or her work methods, just like the engine lathe mechanic.

TWI realized that though the three "J" programs increased productivity significantly, they did not address all production problems. Though most companies face similar challenges and problems, companies have cultures that are as individual and unique as the people they employ. For example, the extent to which supervisors are involved with costing varies greatly from one company to the next. (A costing problem is the first sample problem Product Development [PD] deals with in Session I.) A costing problem might cause a difficulty in one company, whereas it might have no effect in another. What TWI needed was to develop a program that addressed everything that the "J" programs did not.

Companies Learn How to Create and Direct Their Own Training

The concept of "Five Needs of a Supervisor" (Exhibit 4-4) explains that the three "J" programs deal with three skill needs: 1) Skill in Improving Methods, 2) Skill in Leading People, and 3) Skill in Instructing, which people can learn through uniform courses. Companies must handle the other two needs:

4) Knowledge of the Work, and 5) Knowledge of Responsibilities, by creating individual training courses tailored to their specific job situations. TWI created the PD program to train "training directors," that is, *people responsible for creating and directing training within an organization.* Program Development did not contain the word "job" in the title because it is not related directly to a job.

Because TWI's task was to assist companies in solving production problems, it limited participation at the *PD Institutes* to those people directly responsible "for spotting and analyzing problems, planning and recommending training action, taking appropriate steps for getting the training into operation, and checking results."[2] One's title did not matter. Many of the PD Institutes consisted of representatives from several companies because most small to midsize companies have only one person in such a position. With larger companies, however, it was expedient to have a PD Institute dedicated to a single company. Initially,

> "Several of these in-plant Institutes were run on a mistaken basis. In some cases, members were line executives who were not going to have any staff responsibility for planning to meet production problems through training. Their interest was solely in PD. Step 1; that is, in the statement of the problem, the gathering of evidence that a problem existed, and the consideration of various actions. In other cases, the members attending these in-plant Institutes were going to use the second step of PD or, in some cases, only a part of that step. In other words, they were instructors, not training directors."[3]

In order to understand why it was unacceptable to have people without training director responsibilities at a PD Institute, one must understand that at the time, TWI was operating on a limited budget and staff. At its peak, it had about 400 paid workers to cover the entire country. Many in TWI (including the Director and Assistant Director) did not receive a salary. Therefore, sending a TWI staff member to conduct a PD Institute when the outcome might not be any training would be a waste of their resources. In addition, a PD Institute took place over a period of at least two weeks. Three days of training were followed by a five-day period in which the participants would create their training plans. The participants would present their plans to the reconvened group on the last two days. In the five days between the training and the presentations, the *Institute conductor* would visit each participant and make sure that he or she understood what to do and how to do it, which meant the conductor had to devote a full two weeks to one PD Institute. If an organization's training plans did not result from the three days of training, this would be a waste of TWI resources, which it tried to avoid.

Accordingly, when an organization requested an in-plant Institute, TWI would require that one participant attend a different PD Institute ahead of time to train so he or she could take the place of the Institute conductor by coaching the other participants in his absence during the 5-day period between the training and the presentations. TWI did this because of the shortage of TWI personnel. A shortage of training personnel is not, of course, an issue for today's organizations. The PD program is very simple and is available to everyone. Reread the quote on page 266 and think about what would happen if everyone in an organization were skilled in Step 1 of the PD 4-Step Method:

- State a problem.
- Gather evidence & develop a plan.
- Put the plan into action.
- Check results.

Using the PD 4-Step Method, people think through the problem and arrive at an appropriate solution, whether or not that solution includes a training program, which makes the tools and skills taught in the PD program as versatile and applicable today as they were in the 1940s.[4]

PD Institute Format Outline for Delivering the Sessions

Because of the amount of material to present, the particular content, and the type of participants involved, TWI created the PD program as a two-week-long Institute. The PD program is similar to the "train the trainer" Institutes conducted in the "J" programs; however, the PD program takes 2 weeks to complete, with morning and afternoon sessions adding up to approximately 35 hours and ten sessions. The program also contains drill (work project), requiring that participants return to their workplaces and practice what they are learning (see Exhibit 12-1).[5]

As with all TWI programs, the emphasis is on *learning the 4-Step Method and not on solving a problem.* Thus, there is a requirement for drill on the PD 4-Step Method or some part of it. The contents of the PD Institute include introductory information to emphasize that companies can solve production problems through training designed by the training director. The participants use a PD 4-Step Method for analyzing problems, determining proper training solutions, and then following up on results. Although this is the core material, the PD program also includes the following topics:

- Methods and Aids.
- Getting a Plan Into Action.
- How to Get Continuing Results From Plant Training Programs.

Exhibit 12-1. PD Institute Format for Delivering Sessions

Program Development Institute Outline

Day One

Morning

    Plan of the Institute

    Definition of Terms—Production, etc.   2 hours

    Training Ties to Management   55 min.

    Problems Solved Through Training

    The 4-Step Method

    Sample Problem—Cost Records—Using the 4-Step Method

Afternoon

    Introduction and drill on Worksheet 1 for Step 1, Worksheet 2

        for 3 hours Step 2, and Steps 3 & 4   30 min.

    Assignment of Problem

Day Two

Morning

    Review 4-Step Method   3 hours

    Three participants present their homework problems

Afternoon

    Induction of employees (using the 4-Step plan)   3 hours

    Three participants present their homework problems   45 min.

Day Three

Morning

    Three participants present their homework problems   2 hours

    Information on training services through War Manpower Comm.   55 min.

Afternoon

    Plant Meetings

    Last participant presents his assigned problem   1 hour

    Discussion of assignment of training plan   55 min.

Day Four

Morning

    Discussion of problems/programs/plans   3 hours

    Three participants present their training plans

Afternoon

    How to Select Supervisors   3 hours

    Two participants present their training plans   40 min.

Day Five

Morning

    Two participants present their training plans   3 hours

    Discussion of Checking Results

    One participant presents his training plans

Afternoon

    Two participants present their training plans   not more

    Discussion of Relationship of Plans to Programs   than

    One participant presents his training plans   2 hours

    Summary   55 min.

- Induction.
- War Manpower Commission Training Services.
- Plant Meetings.
- Selecting Supervisors.

Program Development—Sessions I and II

The "J" programs state that the participants view themselves as supervisors even if they do not have that title, because the program is designed for supervisors. The only criterion for attendance for the "J" program is that the person "directs the work of others." PD emphasizes a similar theme. A person's title is not relevant as long as he or she has "*responsibility* for organizing and coordinating training to meet production problems . . . [they] are *not trainers* . . . [but they] . . . *plan training*, see that it gets done, and check results."[6] The objective of the PD program is for participants to learn how to solve production problems through training.

The Institute conductor has the participants discuss the PD training definitions at the outset. This is an important part of the training because it clearly defines seven training concepts to help keep participants focused throughout the training. In Chapter 8, we discussed these and they are: 1) What is production? 2) What is a production problem? 3) What is training? 4) What is a training plan? 5) What is a training program? 6) What is a training director? and 7) What is management? (See Exhibit 8-4, for definitions.)

TWI defines production as the end result of an organization. If that organization were the company, it would be the product sold to the customer. If the organization is a department within that company, then it would be whatever product or service is given to accompanying departments. Production is easy to visualize in a manufacturing plant, but people sometimes have difficultly understanding the concept with a service provider. Participants must have a clear understanding that accounting, for example, includes production items, such as budgets, cost sheets, profit and loss statements, and so forth.[7]

The TWI manual emphasizes that every participant should have a clear understanding of what the product is in his or her organization. Every organization, including a dentist's practice, an attorney's practice, a hospital, and a courtroom has a product, and creating that product is called production and whatever interferes with production is a production problem. Training is *one* way to solve a production problem. The PD 4-Step Method may reveal several possible activities that a company should perform to solve the problem.

Because PD's purpose is to use training to solve the production problem, the *training plan* is defined as *an organized way of solving a specific part of a production problem.* To address the entire production problem may require several training plans. A *training program*, then, is defined as a <u>combination of training plans coordinated to meet the training needs caused by a specific production problem.</u> The word "specific" is important because the participants may uncover several production problems while solving one specific problem. However, TWI stresses that participants should address only one production problem at a time.

Exhibit 12-2. PD 4-Step Method Training Card

WAR MANPOWER COMMISSION
Bureau of Training
TRAINING WITHIN
INDUSTRY SERVICE

PROGRAM DEVELOPMENT
How to Meet a Production
Problem Through Training

1. SPOT A PRODUCTION
   PROBLEM
   Get supervisors and workers to tell
   about current problems.
   Uncover problems by reviewing
   records—performance, cost,
   turnover, rejects, accidents.
   Anticipate problems resulting from
   changes—organization, production
   or policies.
   Analyze this evidence.
   Identify training needed.
   Tackle One Specific Need at a Time.

2. DEVELOP A SPECIFIC PLAN
   Who will be the trainer?
   What content? Who can help
   determine?
   How can it be done best?
   Who should do the training?
   Where should it be done—how long
   will it take?
   Where should it be done?
   Watch for relation of this plan to
   other current training plans and
   programs.

3. GET PLAN INTO ACTION
   Stress to management evidence of
   need—use facts and figures.
   Present expected results.
   Discuss plan—content and methods
   Submit timetable for plan.
   Train those who will do the training.
   Secure understanding and
   acceptance by those affected.
   Fix responsibility for continuing use.
   Be Sure Management Participates.

4. CHECK RESULTS
   How can results be checked?
   Against what evidence?
   What results will be looked for? Is
   management being informed?—
   How?
   Is the plan being followed?
   How is it being kept in use?
   Are any changes necessary?
   Is the plan helping production?

Responsibility for Training Results
   The LINE organization has the
   responsibility for making
   continuing use of the knowledge
   and skills acquired through
   training as a regular part of the
   operating job.
   The STAFF provides plans and
   technical "know-how" and does
   some things FOR but usually
   works THROUGH the line
   organization.

Source: Dietz, *Learn by Doing*, p. 26.

The participants also have discussions about how the PD training fits into the overall organization. The Institute conductor draws a blank organizational chart showing the line organization. Next to it, the Institute conductor draws the staff positions, one of which is for the supervisor of training. The line organization does the actual production, while the staff organization supports the line. There are production problems that are common among all organizations and these are discussed to promote the idea that though all companies have similar problems, no two problems are exactly alike. Each plant must solve its own particular production problems.

PD 4-Step Method Introduced

The Institute conductor then discusses the PD 4-Step Method along with a caution point listed on the PD training card (see Exhibit 12-2, which is the same as Exhibit 8-1).

To complete the morning activities on the first day, the Institute conductor and participants apply the PD 4-Step Method to a cost records problem case study (see Exhibit 12-3).[8]

To summarize, the scenario is that the training director went to a weekly staff meeting. The plant manager was angry because he knew 50 men had worked the last Sunday and should have received double-time pay. Yet, cost

Exhibit 12-3. The Cost Records Problem

Program Development
The Cost Records Problem
(As read by the Institute Conductor being the training director)

Last Monday I went to the works manager's weekly meeting. The cost accountant and I were there as well as the six superintendents. The works manager was all worked up about the cost records, and got pretty tough with the chief accountant. He asked, "How does it happen that those 50 men at double time the Sunday after the breakdown in Department 2 didn't affect costs? That got me started on going over a lot of our cost records and you can't make me think our estimates are so good that every job hits the estimate—never over, never under."

He went on to say, "Costs don't seem to mean a thing around this place. Do you think I'm going to wait for a government auditor to find out what's wrong? And what kind of fix are we going to be in to go after business when the war's over? I want to know what's wrong, and I want it fixed up."

[Discussion]

(Continued)

Exhibit 12-3. (*Continued*)

The cost accountant said this wasn't anything new—he'd questioned the superintendents' weekly reports before, and he didn't want the same old story—that they just made them up from the foreman's Daily Operating Reports.

The superintendents said they never realized how their weekly reports tied in with the company's operations and profits. They said they had never made much of this point with the foremen.

The upshot was that the superintendents said they would get their foremen together so the cost accountant could discuss this cost record problem with them. I too went to that meeting. Both the chief accountant and I learned some things there. A foreman has an estimated cost on each job in his department. If he's going to run over more than 5%, he has to get advance approval. It isn't hard to get, but it does take a lot of paperwork.

If he saves time on one job, he can take care of running over on another. In that way, he can avoid asking for a change in the estimates. The cost accountant was horrified that they juggled costs like that.

Here's how it boiled down. A foreman may have 20 to 50 workers. Now, each worker has a time card and even the accountant agrees it is a very detailed and complicated card.

The time cards are a sore subject. Most of the time clocks are in out-of-the-way positions and the average is one clock for 200 people.

Well, nobody bothers filling in the job numbers on time cards. The foremen would just as soon not have them filled in—they mark them up after they see what labor costs they should charge, according to the estimate! The foremen spoke up and said they had never understood how important their Daily Operating Reports were.

Don't think they said this without saying plenty about new time cards, moving the time clocks, and making it easier to revise estimates. The superintendents and the cost accountant answered quite a few questions. The cost information does have to be recorded. The plant cannot charge more than 5% over the estimate without getting the army in on it.

As to the time clocks—we can't get any more, but we may be able to find better locations. Maybe the time card can be changed—but not overnight. I looked at some of the time cards and I know I'm really going to have to dig into this time card angle, too. But the cost records have to be corrected *right away*.

---

records did not show an increase in project cost. The Institute conductor stops the case study here and engages the group in a discussion so that they can agree on what the problem is.[9] Once everyone agrees that the problem is defined as "inaccurate cost records," the conductor completes describing the case study and then distributes the PD cards. The participants then address the cost records problem while reviewing the four steps on the PD card.

Step 1—"Spot a Production Problem"

In this cost records case, the plant manager saw the problem first, but this problem could have originated from any of several sources. One of the items under Step 1 notes that the organization's supervisors and workers should bring up for discussion any problems they see. Problems can be uncovered by reviewing various records (performance, cost, turnover, rejects, accidents, etc.). You can also anticipate them by looking at changes that are taking place. Note that even if someone gives the problem directly to the training director, he or she probably won't get enough information to plan training at this point. The training director must therefore do additional investigation to make sure all the facts are collected.

Furthermore, it is very important for the training director to make the distinction between a "production problem" and a "training problem," because if something is slow, wasteful, or expensive, it may be (but doesn't have to be) a production problem. For example, if the time cards in the sample problem were used *only* to record attendance and total daily hours, they would not reflect job cost numbers. Thus using them incorrectly would not constitute a production problem related to cost records. Perhaps training in the correct use of time cards is warranted, but even if they were used correctly, that would not help solve the cost records problem.

The next part of Step 1 is to *analyze the evidence.* Note that the intention is to break down all the information into "facts" and "causes." TWI used the term "evidence" because people were getting confused between cause and effect.

"The purpose was not to train people in how to distinguish between cause and effect, but just to make sure that, before a training plan is made, the designer has a true knowledge of just what is going on in the plant in order that he can remedy specific situations which produce the problem . . .

"Following very brief use of this approach it was decided that it could be made more clear by using "evidence" in place of "facts," using "underlying conditions and causes" in place of "causes," and considering for each item of evidence the action that was needed whether it was training action or some other kind."[10]

The Institute conductor now reviews the Cost Records case and asks the group to state all the facts (evidence) as they know them, which is then listed on Worksheet 1 under the "Evidence" column (see Exhibit 12-4).[11] (Note that this is a case study and not all the evidence may be available.)

The point is to learn the method. The PD manual emphasizes that:

Exhibit 12-4. Cost Record Problem—Sheet 1

(For use with Step 1 of P.D. Method – Use card)

What is the Production Problem?   <u>Inaccurate Cost Records</u>

EVIDENCE	TRAINING ACTION NEEDED		OTHER ACTION NEEDED
	Training for Whom?	Training in What?	
50 men Dept. 2 double time didn't affect cost records	Foreman of Dept.2		
Every cost report agrees with estimate			
Supt. makes weekly report from DOR's			
Supts. didn't understand relation of costs to operations	Superintendents	Importance of cost records	
Cost accountant had complained before			
Advance approval to run more than 5% over estimate			
Estimate change procedure complicated	Foreman	How to change estimate	Simplify procedure?
Cost reports juggled to match estimates	Foreman	Importance of cost records	
Foreman makes DOR's from estimate, not from time card	Foreman	How to make out DOR	
Foreman has 20 to 50 workers			
Time clock location bad			Move clock?
Time cards not filled in by workers	Workers	Imp. of time cards	
Time cards complicated	Workers	How to fill time card	Simplify card?
Foreman doesn't require filling in time cards	Foreman	Imp. of cost records	
Foreman fills time cards to match estimates	Foreman	Imp. of cost records	
Foreman didn't understand relation of DOR's to operations	Foreman	Importance of DOR	

"TACKLE ONE SPECIFIC NEED AT A TIME"

"It is only when we get at underlying causes, reasons, and related conditions that we really see what can be done about the problem."[12]

This approach is similar to using the "5Why" tool in Lean thinking to find the root cause of a problem and then to find a countermeasure. Once the group records all of the available evidence, the participants determine whether or not any training action is needed. Again, the word "needed" is emphasized because there is much training that can be done: "We are not interested in training that could be undertaken on a general basis—just on that which must be done."[13]

The group fills in the two columns "Training for Whom?" and "Training in What?," which then determines the content of any training programs that will be designed and who will receive that training. Here the participants take note about training that would overcome present or anticipated deficiencies, or improve performance. At this time also, the group determines if any other action is needed. In this case, the "estimate change procedure" is complicated and time consuming. Although the foremen should be trained in how to use the procedure, additional action might be to simplify the procedure. Another item, "Time clock location bad," does not require any training, but additional action would be to move the time clocks to a better location. Another piece of evidence not listed was that approximately 200 people had to use one time clock. This was not included on the original TWI worksheet because additional time clocks were not available because of the "emergency" war situation. However, today it might be prudent to include it for reference if your organization is going to keep the worksheets on file. The rule of thumb is that if a worker is doing something incorrectly because the worker does not know the right way, then training is in order. If the worker is doing the job correctly, but the result is wrong, then other action is needed. Naturally, this may take some persistent questioning to discover what the actual situation is because things are not always clear-cut.

Note that this analysis results in five individual training plans:

1. Superintendents—Importance of cost records
2. Foremen—
   a. How to change a job estimate.
   b. The importance and accuracy of cost records.
   c. Daily Operating Report—Their importance and how to complete them.
3. Workers—Time Cards—Their importance and how to complete them

Because the PD method cautions the training director to "Tackle one specific need at a time," he or she needs to consider training supervisors in the use of the Daily Operating Report (DOR). This is not a capricious choice. By immediately training the foremen in the correct use of the DOR, you will get the greatest return for improving the accuracy of the cost records. It is important to note that knowing more about the organization might lead them to make a different decision.

Step 2—"Develop a Specific Plan"

Exhibit 12-5[14] makes this step self-explanatory, but first the Institute conductor should mention a few items. First, the organization's training director does not create the content. This worksheet helps him determine what is necessary to cover in the training, but the training director should seek help from the subject matter experts. In the cost record case, this would be the chief accountant and the general superintendent. The next factor in this case is determining who should deliver the training. The Institute conductor points out that there are two main considerations. First, the foremen had to be convinced of the importance of the cost records and the easiest way to do this is to have it done by someone with significant authority. However, this is a decision that can only be made when the person knows the personnel involved. Hence, the General Superintendent was chosen to deliver this part of the training. In other situations, it may have been necessary to go higher up the organization chart—or it may not have been necessary to go as high. The second topic is determining who should fill out the forms. It would be a good idea for an organization to have as the instructor someone who really knows the forms well. The training director and the subject matter expert (the accountant) would work together to choose the best possible person. If the accountant is a very poor trainer, someone else might do the training and the accountant could be in the room to answer questions.[15]

The caution point at the end of the step is very important: "Watch for the Relation of this Plan to Other Current Training Plans and Programs." Remember the training director creates the training plan to solve a specific production problem. The organization may have many other production problems and plans in play, which means the training director must set a proper priority for the current training plan. The training director states at the bottom of the worksheet that, "This is the most important problem in [the] plant right now ... " Whoever is approving the training will verify that determination. The important point is that whoever is approving the training should consider the priority and make a decision based on facts, which is the evidence on worksheet 1.

Step 3—"Get Plan Into Action"

Steps 3 and Step 4, "Check Results," do not require the use of a formal worksheet. The TWI developers attempted to create worksheets for these steps, but

Exhibit 12-5. Cost Record Problem Sheet 2

(For use with Step 2 of P.D. Method—Use Card)

What is the Specific Plan? Daily Operating Report

Training for Whom? Foremen   Training for How Many? _____ 30

What Content?	How Can It be Done Best?	Who Will Train or Help?	When? How Long?	Where?
1. Importance of DOR Government audit Legal responsibility Prospective orders Post-war business	Personal appeal	General Supt.	1½ hr. each group; all 3 groups; 10 each next Monday	General supt's office
2. Analysis of DOR Use in making weekly report Errors and effect	Blow-up chart of weekly report, explanation, questions Sample sets of time cards, DORs, weekly report, job cost reports	Chief Accountant	2 hrs. each group all on Tuesday	Conference room
3. Filling in DOR Time card basis Charges to specific jobs Delay—charges to overhead Day work—how charged Job charges vs. estimates Material charges	Practice on sample material Analysis of own reports	Chief Accountant	2 hrs. each group; Wednesday 2 hrs. each group; Thursday	Conference room

What is the Relation of This Plan to Other Current Training Plans and Programs? This is the most important problem in Plant right now—this takes precedence over any other training program. This is only one part of the whole problem, but the only one we can get at immediately.

quickly realized that, although participants should take notes, the steps and their items act more importantly as a checklist for the training director. Therefore, the training director can just list the items and make sure he or she has properly covered each one.

Step 3 is not trivial because, like the Institute conductor in the TWI training, it is usually necessary for the training director to sell his or her training program to the organization. In the cost records scenario, 30 foremen are going to spend 6½ hours each (195 hours total) in training. The effect on production has to be justified somehow. Therefore, the first item under Step 3 is to stress to management the need for the training. The training director should use facts and figures, not qualitative arguments to sell management on training. After establishing the evidence, he or she should state the anticipated results and a training schedule. Again, being quantitative is just as important as it was in defining the problem, but the training director will never have all the facts, so it may be necessary to make some reasonable assumptions in presenting the plan. The training director may also want to prepare a backup plan in case the training proposal is rejected.

It will probably be necessary for the organization to train and cross-train personnel who will do the training. In the cost records scenario, the accountant may have to learn how to instruct, or the instructor may have to learn how to use the cost record. Initial versions of the PD 4-Step Method included several hours of the three "J" programs. Because other material in the PD syllabus was added, a review of these three programs was reduced, and then eliminated. The training director should be familiar enough with these programs, however, so that he or she would have some skills in instructing that could be passed on to the accountant.

Perhaps the most important item of Step 3 is to "Secure understanding and acceptance by those affected." This is vital for two reasons. If the foremen do not think the training is necessary, they may have a difficult time learning or remembering it. Also, after the training, they may not use what they learned, which means they will not solve the production problem. In the cost records scenario, the foremen do not like the cost records and regard them as a nuisance. From their perspective, the foremen may see that other problems should have a higher priority. For example, you could consider simplifying the procedure for the cost record change. They may say that the change procedure should be simplified first (noted under "other action to be taken") and then they should receive the training. If this is the case, it may be necessary to reveal to them the thought process of the training director to show why he or she came to that conclusion. Everyone must accept (not necessarily agree with) the decision in order for the plan to go ahead successfully. Accordingly, it is necessary to "fix responsibility for continuing use." To do this, management must participate. "Participation" takes more effort and awareness than mere "approval."

Step 4—"Check Results"

If the training director can give a meaningful answer to each of the questions listed under Step 4, he or she will have successfully checked the results. The training director should mention the method of verifying results when discussing the plan with management (Step 2). In the cost record case, the detail and precision will vary with the method. Previously, all cost records matched all estimates. Thus, one way of tracking training results would be to see if the cost records now had any variation from the estimates. If they did, the training was successful. Another way would be to follow the jobs, showing an obvious variation between the estimate and the cost record. The job that led the works manager to uncover the problem involved 50 men working double time for a day. Because we do not know the size of the organization, we do not know if the addition of 50 person-hours to a job is significant; but working on Sunday might be. If those costs were recorded properly in future transactions, then the organization would have a better sense that the training was effective. Naturally, one's confidence level in the training program rises if the organization performs random and periodic audits. All this activity has little meaning however, if the time cards are not filled out properly. Therefore, the type of audits will vary over time.

The last item under Step 4 is "Are any changes necessary?" Do some foremen need remedial training or coaching? Has another problem been created? Has this training triggered other training to have a higher priority? For example, is it now imperative to train the workers in the correct use of the time card?

Finally, the caution statement for Step 4 is: "Is the plan helping production?" To answer this question, one only has to refer to the worksheet for Step 1 and look at the list of evidence for the production problem. If statements like "50 men in dept. 2 working double time didn't affect cost records" are no longer applicable, then the training did what it was supposed to do. It corrected the problem hindering production and that statement is no longer valid. It is important to follow up on determining whether or not you have actually achieved the anticipated results so that particular problem does not occur again.

One of the items under Step 4 states: "How Is it Being Kept in Use?" If an organization has identified and verified a training need, and it has solved the problem, the organization should continue the training sessions so the problem will not return. Sometimes, however, the organization can incorporate specific training into other training so it does not have to stand by itself.

TWI recognized that you should discontinue training if it no longer serves a purpose. Therefore, organizations should review training plans periodically...

"Training can outlive its usefulness.

"If the need for training has ended, the training director should be the first one to recognize that fact.

"Occasionally, the need for the training ceases abruptly—the training director should be the one to see that a plan which is not needed is chopped off."[16]

Discussing the Program Development training definitions (seven concepts) and introducing the PD 4-Step Method consume the morning of the first day. The group spends the afternoon (Session II) working through two more case studies going from Steps 1 through 4. The Institute conductor directs the group to use the two worksheets for Steps 1 and 2. Step 1 is especially emphasized because if training directors find production problems quickly by merely talking with supervisors or workers, they might not use other measures or contact additional sources to gather and corroborate existing evidence. As the TWI Report noted:

"It is now stressed that the training director must go through the other ways of finding evidence—that is, reviewing records and anticipating effects of changes—before he is ready to make any plans for training to overcome the problem."[17]

The only way to view a problem realistically is after collecting information from all possible sources. Participants each write comments for Steps 3 and 4, then compare, and discuss their notes.

The last activity of day one is an overnight assignment. Using the 4-Step Method, the participants are to consider their own companies and design a hypothetical training plan to address an increase of production, affecting not more than 200 workers in a time frame of four weeks. The conductor gives them no further details and the participants must address actual conditions in their own plants. Then they make presentations to the group in days two and three.

Program Development—Sessions III–X

The next two days include going over the participants' plans for the hypothetical problem assigned. The Institute conductor leads each participant through each training plan starting with how he first became aware of the situation. The conductor asks for the definition of the problem and continues through the PD 4-Step Method with sufficient probing questions so that everyone in the group can learn from this example. The group also thoroughly reviews worksheets for Steps 1 and 2, and the notes for Steps 3 and 4. Typically, as with all TWI programs, you want to limit the group size to ten people, so that by the end of these 2 days, everyone in the group has gone through ten examples.

At the end of Session VI on the third day, the Institute conductor gives the participants an assignment to return to their own plant, identify a problem, and then create a training plan. The usual PD training schedule is for the first 3 days and six sessions to take place on Monday through Wednesday. The next 5 workdays are for each participant to design the training plan and reconvene on the following Thursday and Friday for Sessions VII–X. During the five-day break, the Institute conductor contacts each participant, either by telephone or in person, and spends an hour or two confirming that he or she understands what to do and how to do it. If the conductor has done well in the first 3 days (6 sessions of training), there will be no need for additional coaching.

After returning from the 5-day break and over the next 2 days (Sessions VII–X) each participant presents his or her training plan in the same way as he or she did with the examples on days two and three. This means that during Session VII–X each participant will experience ten more training plan method reviews. In addition, they have their own training plan that they will take back and implement. This then, is the end of the PD training. However, the Institute conductor hands out some supporting material throughout the training that we'll discuss next.

Additional Topics Covered in PD Training

Interspersed among the reviews and lectures, the Institute conductor presents additional supporting material. Though the participants might not have an immediate use for it, it is important for concluding successful training plans. Some of the material is in the form of a handout that may or may not be discussed; and some material is discussed without a handout. Table 12-1 shows the eleven bulletins and corresponding Appendixes in this book. Although TWI provided these bulletins to anyone who wanted them, they were specifically included in Program Development. The bulletins are self-explanatory and will not be discussed here.

Induction and War Manpower Commission

The concept of "Induction" and the presentation of the services of the War Manpower Commission (WMC) did not include any written material aside from what was in the training manual. The services of the WMC are of interest today only for historians, and the reader can obtain the information from

Table12-1. Additional Material Presented During Program Development

# Title	Description	Bulletin on CD
1. How Training Can Be Done— Methods, Aids	Bulletin + brief discussion	Bulletin 25
2. How to Get A Plant Training Plan Into Action	Bulletin + brief discussion	Bulletin 21
3. How to Get Continuing Results From Plant Training Programs	Bulletin + brief discussion	Bulletin 22
4. Introducing The New Employee To The Job	Bulletin only	Bulletin 18
5. Management and Skilled Supervision	Bulletin only	Bulletin 20
6. Improving Supervisors' Knowledge of the Work	Bulletin only	Bulletin 23
7. Keeping Supervisors Informed About Their Responsibilities	Bulletin only	Bulletin 24
8. How to Select Supervisors— A 6 Step Program	Bulletin + 1 hour presentation	Bulletin 17
9. Plant Meetings (in "How Training Can Be Done")	30 min. presentation (Bulletin included in #1 Methods, Aids)	Bulletin 25

the author or from your local library. Induction is the concept of getting a new employee acquainted with an organization, including a new department. "Induction is the introduction of a person to the very place where he is going to work."[18] Induction does not include, however, all the necessary paperwork done in the human resource department.

Induction deals only with employees and usually starts after an organization has hired a person. Each induction plan is different because each company is different. Induction does not require creating any information because all the information already exists; and because it exists, induction technically is not necessary. Sooner or later, an employee will discover the necessary department information on his or her own. "If you learn a rule by breaking it, you will remember it the next time. But is that the best way to learn?"[19] Typically, organizations just give the new person the standard human resource packet and employee indoctrination information, but this does not guarantee that the person will learn, remember, or use it. Induction training is the only way to ensure a new employee gets "up to speed" and productive as quickly as possible. It also improves an organization's employee retention rate.

On the afternoon of the second day (Session IV), the Institute conductor devotes an hour and a half to induction, presenting it as a solution to a production problem while at the same time reviewing the PD 4-Step Method with another example emphasizing Step 1 and 2, "Spot a Production Problem" and "Develop a Specific Plan."

The scenario is that the company is operating at 80 percent capacity, while orders are being entered at 100 percent capacity. The problem of this backlog is discussed at a plant superintendent's meeting, which the training director attends. The plant superintendent believes that the machinery is worn out because there is at least one line idle in each department he passed as he walked to the meeting. The chief engineer said that the machinery is not worn out, but the employees are annoyed because they have not received raises in a long time. Therefore, they are very careless. The personnel director says that the plant is on piecework and thus they can earn more money if they want, but she believes they do not know how to do the work properly. This may sound like a far-fetched scenario, but before you find the real cause to a problem, you discover that everyone has an opinion of the cause of that problem. All seem plausible and all probably represent situations that could be corrected. A proper analysis of the problem is necessary to lead to the solution that will correct the "real" problem in question.

At this point, the Institute conductor stops telling the story, gets the group to agree that the production problem is "Production is down to 80 percent," and then continues the story. Since the training director is the hero of the story, she is the one who pursues the problem. First, she went to one department and asked the foreman why it was idle. The foreman said that he did not have enough people at work that day to run the line. After talking with many other foremen, she got the same answer–not enough people. Having sensed a pattern, she decided to verify the reason by getting more information from various records. She collected data from personnel records and listed the evidence on Worksheet 1 as the first ten items (see Exhibit 12-6).[20]

Seeing this information led her to speak with more supervisors and especially with those workers whose actions resulted in the data. That is, she spoke with people who were frequently absent and those who were waiting to be discharged. She added the additional evidence to two headings: "Quits" and "Absenteeism." The Institute conductor notes here that the evidence falls under two categories: "facts and figures" and "underlying causes." The facts and figures were found from the records and they serve two purposes. First, they led to additional information; and second, they serve as benchmarks for checking results. Once you ask enough questions, you will discover the underlying causes (or root causes) which suggest the proper actions to take. *Therefore, facts and figures will give us benchmarks for checking results, while underlying causes lead to action.*[21]

Exhibit 12-6. Induction Problem Sheet 1

(For use with Step 1 of P.D. Method – Use card)

What is the Production Problem?   <u>Production down to 80%</u>

EVIDENCE	TRAINING ACTION NEEDED		OTHER ACTION NEEDED
1000 jobs in plant	Training for Whom?	Training in What?	
Never more than 950 filled			Investigation too long
Never more than 900 at work any one day	Every absentee	Importance of work	
Turnover 5% a month plantwide			
Turnover 20% a month, less than 3 month service			
Turnover 30% a month, 3rd. shift, under 3 mos.			
Absenteeism 5% a month plantwide	Every absentee	Importance of work	
Absenteeism 15% a month, under 3 months' service, approximately same all shifts	All new people and present short service	Importance of work	
Average 10 months to get up to guarantee on piece rate	All new people and present short service	Work they are to do	
90% of rejects from less than 6 months' service	All new people and present short service	Work they are to do	
Quits Provoked discharges			
Transportation, 3rd shift			See bus company
Didn't like jobs	All new people and present short service	Importance of work	
Didn't like supervisor	Supervisors	How to work with people	Better supervisory selection
Thought work dangerous	All new people and present short service	Safe practices	Check safety equipment
Didn't like pay	All new people and present short service	Work they are to do How to figure pay	
Absenteeism Didn't think work important	All new people and present short service	Importance of work	Hall displays of completed product, news pictures
Looking for a better job	All new people and present short service	Work they are to do Importance of work	Investigate provoked discharges
Tired	All new people and present short service	Work they are to do	Any better methods?

"TACKLE ONE SPECIFIC NEED AT A TIME"

In this scenario of "production is down to 80 percent," analyzing the evidence led the training director to prioritize her solutions. The top priority would be to get the new employees off to a good start and as quickly as possible after that, bring all employees with short service up to date. Finally, the organization should investigate the supervisors and employees with excessive absenteeism. Note that the training director will make the suggestion to management that this is to be the order of priorities for handling this problem and is subject to change because of circumstances or differences of opinion from the manager approving the training plans.

In this scenario, the analysis results in three or four training plans, one for each of these groups: new employees, short service employees, absentees, and supervisors. Since PD suggests creating and implementing one plan at a time, the training director chose to create one for the new employees on Worksheet 2 (see Exhibit 12-7).[22]

She has called the plan "Induction" and she has estimated there will be about 50 people per month who will need this training. The content has been determined by three ideas:

1. What new *people need* to know.
2. What new *people want* to know.
3. What the *plant wants* them to know.[23]

The training director cannot just hand this information to the people (employees) because she has no assurance they will understand and retain it. She must present it through training, using training techniques. The training director divides the training into four parts and presents it at four separate times. There are several reasons for this. First, you do not want to inundate people with too much information. Second, giving people information when they can easily relate it to something increases understanding and the likelihood they will ask questions. For example, discussing how a person is paid is more meaningful after some work has been done and payroll figures are available. Finally, the training director is conducting some of the training with one individual at a time, while some training is done in groups, with different people responsible for implementing different parts of the total plan. Note that item three under the "What Content" column in Exhibit 12-7, "How people learn jobs," is just a quick overview of what the company thinks is important: safety first, then quality, then quantity. The actual job training would be handled under another training plan using the Job Instruction 4-Step Method. Notice that in Exhibit 12-6 that some part of the training plan has addressed all 19 items of evidence. Finally, in addition to creating other training plans, there are other action items to be addressed,

Exhibit 12-7. Induction Problem Sheet 2

<table>
<tr><td colspan="6" align="center">(For use with Step 2 of P.D. Method—Use Card)</td></tr>
<tr><td colspan="6">What is the Specific Plan?   Induction</td></tr>
<tr><td colspan="6">Training for Whom?   All new employees   Training for How Many?   50 a month</td></tr>
<tr>
<th>What Content?</th>
<th>How Can It be
Done Best?</th>
<th>Who Will Train
or Help?</th>
<th>When?
How Long?</th>
<th>Where?</th>
</tr>
<tr>
<td>Company production—
  Mobile mounts for rocket guns
  One of the newest weapons
  Decreases infantry casualties</td>
<td>How completed product
Point out what employee will do</td>
<td></td>
<td>Individually as soon
as new employee is
brought to department</td>
<td>Supervisor's desk</td>
</tr>
<tr>
<td>Size of company orders—
  Not up to full production</td>
<td>Sketch on paper how daily lag
  piles up</td>
<td></td>
<td></td>
<td></td>
</tr>
<tr>
<td>How people learn jobs
  Safety—first
  Quality—second
  Quantity—third, but very
    important—Army and your pay</td>
<td>Description of job training</td>
<td></td>
<td>If necessary to keep
waiting, provide some
employee magazines</td>
<td></td>
</tr>
<tr>
<td>How pay is figured
  Guaranteed minimum
  Piece rate
  Deductions</td>
<td>Figure with him at his own rate;
  stress advantages of beating
  guarantee
Summarize deductions</td>
<td></td>
<td></td>
<td></td>
</tr>
<tr>
<td>Company policies
  Interests of employees
  "Good place to work"</td>
<td>Mention company standing
and attitude; tell him he will
like plant</td>
<td>Supervisor</td>
<td></td>
<td></td>
</tr>
<tr>
<td>Company rules
  Badges
  No smoking</td>
<td>Explain 2 rules, give rule book
  to take home and study; invite
  questions</td>
<td></td>
<td>30 minutes to 1 hour
depending on
employee</td>
<td></td>
</tr>
<tr>
<td>Company facilities
  Lockers—showers
  Lunch
  Package passes
  Driving clubs</td>
<td>Take him to locker
Arrange worker to take to lunch
Does he need a pack pass
  now?
Find out how he gets to work</td>
<td></td>
<td></td>
<td></td>
</tr>
<tr>
<td>Detail on pay
  Minimum
  Piece rate
  Pay period—lag
  Deductions
  Withholding tax
  Social Security
  War Bonds
  Union dues</td>
<td>Uses his daily time cards
Figure with him what his pay
  envelope will contain
Answer questions
Show him how he can increase
  his pay—on job every day,
  increased production</td>
<td></td>
<td></td>
<td></td>
</tr>
<tr>
<td>Detail on rules</td>
<td>Go through booklet—answer
  questions</td>
<td>Supervisor</td>
<td>Individually, end of
first week—15 min.</td>
<td>Supervisor's desk</td>
</tr>
<tr>
<td>Official company welcome</td>
<td>Speech and rocket news reel</td>
<td>Plant superintendent</td>
<td></td>
<td></td>
</tr>
<tr>
<td>Detail on facilities
  Recreation, sports
  Employee store
  Employee magazine</td>
<td>Explanation</td>
<td>Personnel Director</td>
<td>End of month, all new
employees,
approximately 50 in
group</td>
<td>Auditorium</td>
</tr>
<tr>
<td>Detail on vacations and pensions
  Eligibility dates
  Provisions</td>
<td>Explanation
Distribute printed plans</td>
<td>Personnel Director</td>
<td>1½ hours</td>
<td></td>
</tr>
<tr><td colspan="5">What is the relation of this Plan to Other Current Training Plans and Programs?.</td></tr>
<tr><td colspan="5">This can and should be undertaken for all new employees as soon as they come to work; we should catch up on all short service employees as soon as possible. Other plans can't start until people are trained to handle. Supervisors can do this now.</td></tr>
</table>

such as: "Something should be done about finding out about transportation for people on the third shift," and "Safety training will be included under job instruction training, but it would be prudent to confirm that all the safety equipment is in proper working order."

As mentioned, Steps 3 and 4, "Get Plan into Action" and "Check Results," are checklists for what has to be done. In this induction scenario, the results would be a dropin turnover and absenteeism. The figures obtained (5 percent turnover plantwide) are a benchmark that can be used to measure the results. The Institute conductor distributes the bulletin, *Introducing the New Employee to the Job* (Bulletin 18) with little discussion. It provides another induction plan that the participants can use as a model. Although this scenario and the others discussed in this chapter may seem trivial, they evolved from real-life problems. The important point is to learn how to apply the 4-Step Method and not worry about the problem. Because Program Development adapts the scientific method into a very useable form, training is not the only benefit. Anyone, or any team, can easily use it to solve any type of problem, large or small.

Using Program Development

Because all of the TWI programs use the "learn by doing" concept, they all require participants to bring work samples into the training sessions. Program Development is the only program that requires the participants to return to their organizations with an assignment to implement a (training) plan that they developed during the first 2 days and four PD training sessions. This assignment will tend to help participants maintain the momentum they gained during the initial training, and through iteration from the other participants, reinforce the learning of the PD 4-Step Method. This assumes, however, that management requires the "training director" to demonstrate the usefulness of training by having employees use the PD 4-Step Method once they have learned it. In the end, for program development to be successful, companies must learn how to create, direct, and implement the PD training program across the organization.

---

1. Standard Procedure for Handling a Problem and Plan According to Program Development 4-Step Method, Program Development Manual Reference Section, p. 92.
2. *TWI Report*, p. 259.
3. *TWI Report*, p. 259.
4. As stated in *Learn by Doing* by Walter Deitz, (Deitz, Summit NJ, 1970) the Training Within Industry Foundation added Job Economics Training (JET), Discussion Leading (DL) and Management Problem Solving (MPS) courses to the four core courses. Although Mr. Deitz does not fully describe the MPS course, he does include a reminder card in his book. Based on only the reminder card,

the author believes that the PD course would be more robust than MPS if general problem solving were stressed (as opposed to problem solving to create a training course).

5. Program Development Training Manual, p. 2.
6. PD Manual, p. 1.
7. Today, this concept of "production" is often referred to as a "value added activity."
8. PD Manual, pp. 8–10.
9. Note that this is a pivotal part of the process. If one does not define the problem or if it is defined incorrectly, extreme amounts of waste may be created and the solution will be no closer than it was before. This may seem like an obvious point, but going after the wrong objective is a very common mistake.
10. *TWI Report*, p. 253.
11. PD Manual, p. 13.
12. PD Manual, p. 22.
13. PD Manual, p. 22.
14. PD Manual, p. 15.
15. When selecting someone to deliver training, do you choose someone who knows the material well or someone who can deliver training well? Ideally, the person should do both, but that doesn't happen often. The answer to this question depends upon the situation. One must consider both how technical or involved the material is and also how well the available subject matter expert can train. In some cases it may be better to teach the material to a trainer, while at other times, it may be better to teach a SME how to train.
16. PD Manual, p. 36.
17. *TWI Report*, p. 256.
18. PD Manual, p. 46.
19. PD Manual, p. 47.
20. PD Manual, p. 13.
21. PD Manual, p. 52.
22. PD Manual, pp. 53 &54.
23. PD Manual, pp. 53 & 55.

CHAPTER 13

Continually Developing TWI— Where Do You Go From Here?

The last chapter of the Training Within Industry Report is titled "Development Work Ahead." It was included because the developers believed that any training program must continually evolve to meet new challenges. Some of the ideas for development might be considered minor, such as creating better problems for the Union Job Relations Manual, or putting the development of the JM method in between the present method and the proposed method.[1] One of the most substantive suggestions was the creation of a manual that would blend the Job Relations and the Union Job Relations manuals. The former does not include any mention of shop stewards while the latter does not mention supervisors in any way.

> "It would have been possible to develop one program which considered both stewards and supervisors. This development work did not get done by TWI—it is left for someone else to do."[2]

Subsequent users of TWI programs have followed through on some suggestions. As mentioned, the JM breakdown sheets now have 14 columns and cannot be confused with the JI breakdown sheets. Also, some of the reference material has been extracted and placed in the manual itself.

TWI thought that organizations should identify and address process bottlenecks so they would modify the most critical procedures first. They were proved right. TWI programs served industries quite adequately until the development of a Value Stream Mapping manual some fifty years later.[3] Readers who are familiar with Value Stream Mapping (VSM) can see the logical progression from TWI to VSM. Once people use the "J" programs, they learn how to identify process bottlenecks and problems. As a result, addressing those areas should come naturally for the operators versed in the TWI problem-solving methods. VSM is an improvement on the TWI methods because it immediately highlights those areas where you most need to remove non-value-adding activities. Having employees already trained in TWI, however, will make it easier to create and implement VSM improvements.

C.R. Dooley, Walter Deitz, and others from the TWI service formed the TWI Foundation in 1946 and continued with the development ideas they compiled in the TWI Report. The intent was the same as that of the original TWI service:

> "The technique which is best suited for a particular use can be made into a more trustworthy tool if it is developed, clarified, and made easy to apply by the joint action of several qualified persons from different companies facing the same problem. To provide the stimulus, direction and continuity for such cooperative research, through joint action, the Foundation arranged with interested member companies, for the means of testing, trying out, and integrating their results. Thus a better solution could be reached than any single company could uncover working alone. The individual company must, of course, determine the use it will make of any technique which is available."[4]

In addition to updating the manuals, replacing "Win the War" with "Meet Competition," the TWI Foundation also added some additional programs. *Job Economics Training* promoted better understanding of U.S. economic factors. *Discussion Leading* was a program to help supervisors discuss matters to achieve better understanding in groups. *Management Problem Solving* enabled senior managers to develop an ability to recognize a problem, decide what needs to be done, and develop a way to take action.[5] Though the TWI Foundation continued to spread its message across the United States, it also went overseas to countries such as New Zealand, Australia, New Guinea, Taiwan, and Indonesia. Walter Deitz's book *Learn by Doing* was published in 1970 and documents very active TWI programs throughout the United States and the rest of the world.

At about the same time the TWI Foundation was being formed, TWI, Inc. was created in Ohio by Lowell Mellen, who had been the TWI District Representative for Northern Ohio.[6] TWI, Inc. won an Army contract to implement TWI training in Japan. At that time, the Japanese had already obtained the TWI manuals and had trained ten people to be TWI conductors, or master trainers. These conductors in turn trained "approximately 500 JIT trainers and 70 JMT trainers."[7] These efforts must not have been enough to trigger the "multiplier effect," because it was determined additional help was needed. The Occupation Army in Japan solicited bids and awarded a contract to TWI, Inc. The contract provided for TWI, Inc. to train selected Japanese personnel in the TWI methods.

> "In the six months that it would be in Japan, TWI, Inc. would select and prepare follow-through trainers, quality control specialists, and

installation specialists, and it would produce a core of Institute conductors, that is, people who could train instructors. If all went according to plan, the same "multiplier effect" that had been so successful in the United States would be triggered, and the TWI programs would spread rapidly throughout Japanese industry and perpetuate themselves."[8]

As we now know, as I touched upon in Chapter 3, this is exactly what happened. Most, if not all, employees of Japanese companies experience some sort of TWI training today, which is considered the genesis of kaizen (continuous improvement). There are two main reasons why TWI has been so successful in Japan. First and most important, top management makes it integral to the operation plan, making it an essential part of an employee's workday. Second, the Japanese do not substantially modify the program unless a governing body first approves potential changes. In addition to training the Japanese, TWI, Inc. used simple and very effective programs, such as "follow-through" specialists, and "quality control" specialists, and "sold" the program to top management. As stated throughout this book, the correct use of the TWI programs will give a stimulus to your company in the areas of training, methods, and personnel relations, and will change your company's culture to focus on standardization, increased safety, and documentation.

Adapting the TWI Manuals for Today's Companies

The majority of this book is based on the original training manuals written in 1940–1945. Occasionally, reference has been made to contemporary manuals published by the Central New York Technology Development Organization (CNYTDO), a Manufacturing Extension Partnership (MEP) center in Syracuse, NY. There are two reasons for referring to the CNYTDO manuals. The manuals are updated so they are applicable to today's culture. And if you compare the CNYTDO manuals with the original TWI manuals, you will see clearly the types of changes you can safely make without destroying the integrity and effectiveness of the original TWI programs.

Before making changes, you must ask, "What are we trying to accomplish?" and "Do we have the ability to test or try-out the changes to see if they effectively achieve our objective without reducing the quality of the program?" The answer to the first question may seem obvious, but when some trainers first see the "J" programs, their initial reaction is to modify them. Here is a simple example. One usual modification suggestion is to use PowerPoint® slides. However, before transforming the program from one of conversation and board work to a presentation, one should ask how the slides improve the program. How will the participants benefit from the use of the slides? What problem is being solved by using the slides? Just because one has the capability of using slides does not mean that one should use slides. One rule of thumb when making changes is that you can add material, but you should not take any away. Adding material, however, lengthens the program. If the participants are aware of, and can deal with, the added length in the training program, then this option may be open to you without diminishing the original program.

One suggestion made to me concerned delivering Job Methods to "engineer-type" employees who were trained and being paid to improve methods. I was hesitant when I delivered Job Methods to my first group of engineers. At the conclusion of the training, however, I discovered that the training was beneficial to them for two reasons. First, the JM 4-Step Method was not new to them because engineers are trained in the scientific method, and with discipline, use it daily in everything they do. However, TWI JM did demonstrate to them how they could apply it to non-engineering tasks at work, like applying for a day of vacation. The program showed them an easy method to make such a suggestion. Second, their company already embraced TWI so that when an engineer completed a proposal sheet, the management recipient understood what it was all about.

After delivering JM to another group of "engineer types," someone suggested delivering the training in such a way that the participants would come up with the solution to the microwave shield problem by improving it themselves. The advantage would be that by doing this, the engineers would have more of an acceptance of the method. The comment is valid and could be tried, but the result might not be worth the effort. Real acceptance of the JM method comes when the participant applies it to his or her demonstration work that is shown to the group in Sessions II through V.

TWI Is Finely Tuned to Deliver Results

As discussed in earlier chapters, if an organization decides to make a change to a TWI program because of some uniqueness of the organization, the proposed change should receive extensive trials before being implemented permanently. However, a single organization does not have the advantage TWI did in using numerous companies to examine alternative approaches and consequences. The TWI Service could propose a change and then test it extensively throughout various industries to see that the change had the intended effect and no deleterious effects. As mentioned, Dooley and Deitz recognized that a conglomerate could develop a better program than could a single company. Patrick Graupp, associated with CNYTDO, assembled the contemporary manuals after twenty-plus years of experience delivering TWI "J" courses. He has maintained the quality and integrity of the programs, while updating them only for societal changes.

In contrast to this approach, in the mid-1960s, a large U.S. company had successfully used Job Instruction and decided to apply the method to its office staff. At the time, *programmed learning* was a popular new method of training and the company thought it could alter Job Instruction Training to fit in with programmed learning because JI was so simple. The advantage of programmed learning is that the participant can progress at his or her own rate, at his or her own time, without an instructor, keeping costs down. As mentioned in Chapter 4, however, there are certain characteristics of the "J" programs that are required for their success. In this case, the people who received the training no longer participated in the group demonstrations; and as a result, they no longer benefited from observing or participating in other demonstrations, or receiving feedback about their own demonstration. That is, the entire concept of "learning by doing" had been lost. The result was that employees using it might have been able to discuss Job Instruction, but there is no assurance that they could actually perform it. And, although the training described the concept of Key Points, it was applied incorrectly because the company had substantially changed the text in order to fit it to the "programmed learning" format. All of these changes along with the new training format made JI ineffective, and therefore the company stopped using it.

I have also spoken with other sources who are familiar with job instruction training that involves teaching someone how to tie a knot. When I questioned further, I learn that the training is delivered in one 8-hour session. Without giving participants time to go back to their work areas to create a JBS and assemble materials for a demonstration, I don't know how the training could be effective. In addition, receiving 8 hours of input continuously is analogous to watering a garden with a fire hose. People can absorb only so much information at one time.

If your organization is considering TWI programs, do not change the material without a detailed quality review. To stay as true as you can to the original program, you should:

- Take the suggested change.
- Determine what problem that change will correct.
- Make the change.
- Monitor the training's effectiveness.
- Determine if the training appeals to more employees.
- Determine if it is easier to deliver and is just as effective.

If the training is either less effective or does not solve the defined problem, then you should eliminate it and revert to the original material. Simply put, if you don't thoroughly investigate the consequences of any proposed changes, do not make them.

Creation of a Governing Body

When a program works well in one company, you should not blindly transfer it to another company without accounting for the differences between the two organizations. That is why the TWI Service so painfully vetted the "J" programs to make sure that they were universally applicable. Having done this, the TWI Service knew it had to have rigid control over how the "J" programs were applied. Quality control is important. As mentioned, this is one of the reasons for TWI's continuing success in Japan. Having the Ministry of Labor oversee TWI does not mean a company that delivers TWI and then changes it to better suit its organization is penalized for making changes. If adaptations work, then use them. However, an organization that wants to start offering TWI to its employees has a source from which it can obtain a "pure" form of the training that has been time tested to work in any organization. It can go to that source, have employees trained to be trainers and purchase the necessary manuals and materials. Without a source or governing body to house unadulterated materials, companies will repeatedly modify TWI to the point it will soon become ineffective. Practically speaking, without a governing body from which to obtain such materials, the materials also would be more difficult to obtain. In my opinion, the governing body should be a government organization because TWI is fundamental training that should be equally available to everyone. Several government organizations could assume this duty, but I also believe that a good fit would be for the Manufacturing Extension Partnership Centers (MEP). Its funding has been increased in the 2005 federal budget because it provides a valuable service to small and mid-size companies. Furthermore, it is already delivering Lean training as one of its functions. The point remains, however, that it is less important what national body assumes responsibility for TWI quality control than that some organization should.

TWI and Lean—Brings the Best out of Employees

Both the original and the contemporary manuals have been used successfully in hundreds of different companies. Its design and format are as basic as reading, writing, and arithmetic, and just as universal. TWI training emphasizes that:

1. People are less likely to waste resources that they are responsible for and value. Because TWI makes people aware of how they do their

jobs, they become more aware of the resources they use in those jobs. They become aware of their "ownership" of these resources and thus the value and responsibility of managing those resources. When TWI training is done throughout an organization, the value of resources is more commonly understood.

2. People are more willing to change when it means improvements because people seek change to increase their pleasure or decrease their pain. The changes created through TWI methods focus on achieving the participants' stated objectives, which directly and immediately improves the persons' situation.

Lean Thinking also emphasizes these positive tendencies in people. Why then is Lean Thinking not more successful and widespread? I believe one reason is that when people learn about Lean, they are not learning the whole story—the human concepts that underlie the tools of Lean. To understand this, people must start at the beginning of Lean, when TWI and Toyota came together. The fact is that Toyota started its production system using TWI as a foundation along with the vision of Taiichi Ohno. Today, Toyota is still using both TWI and Ohno's visions to get *people* to understand, implement, and sustain Lean behavior. If TWI training were obsolete, Toyota would not be using it. But the fact is, over fifty years later, it is an integral part of the Toyota Way, and without it, Toyota would not be the learning organization it is today. Looking at Toyota's success, one could say that the basic training concepts of TWI may be the missing link that will help an organization successfully apply and sustain a Lean transformation. My hope is that in now understanding TWI concepts, others have a renewed appreciation for Lean Thinking. More importantly, I encourage others to use the TWI programs so that their Lean initiatives will have a strong foundation.

---

1. Currently, the present procedure of making the shields is immediately followed by the proposed procedure. The 4-Step Method is then explained by using it to analyze the present procedure and create the proposed procedure. It was suggested that learning might improve if the analysis and development of the proposed procedure follows the present shield procedure. Ref. Final Report pp. 262–263.
2. Final Report, p. 262.
3. *Learning to See* by Mike Rother & John Shook, Lean Enterprise Institute, 1999.
4. *Learn by Doing*, p. 51.
5. *Learn by Doing*, p. 53.
6. Training, Continuous Improvement, etc., p. 46.
7. Ibid, p. 47.
8. Training, Continuous Improvement, etc., p. 47.

APPENDIX A

TWI Timeline

June 22, 1940—France falls to Germany (page 3)

June 24, 1940—William S. Knudsen named as Commissioner of Industrial Production; Sidney Hillman named as Commissioner of Employment (Per Federal Register) (page 5)

Aug. 1940—TWI started; C.R. Dooley and Walter Dietz go to Washington, DC (for 6 weeks) to start TWI Service (pages 5–6)

Aug. 28, 1940—TWI holds a lens grinding conference to address the problem of the shortage of skilled workers in this field (page 18)

Sept. 1940—TWI divided the country into 22 geographical districts according to main industrial use

Sept. 16, 1940—The Selective Service Act was passed by Congress, which allowed up to 900,000 men between the ages of 20 and 36 to be drafted for military service for one year.

Sept. 24, 1940—TWI issued its first bulletin declaring its purpose (page 5)

Nov. 1940—bulletin "Helping the Experienced Worker to Break in a Man on a New Job" included seven steps of instruction and the concept of "key points" (page 19)

Jan. 1941—National Academy of Sciences states the most useful service TWI might perform is help "in the human relations problems of handling men." (page 39); exploration of JR begins (page 41)

Jan-June 1941—several hundred surveys made in war plants (page 30)

Note: Page numbers refer to the *TWI Report*.

March 1941
- first nationwide radio broadcast; National Director spoke from New York as a start for the cross-country stops, which ended at the Lockheed plant in CA (page 55)
- Steel Workers' Organizing Committee (later the United Steelworkers of America) issued a booklet, *Industrial Training*, which reported on the TWI program. (page 57)

April 1941—first Detroit District TWI conference which served as a pattern for Program Development; assisted by GMI of Flint, MI (page 236)

May 10, 1941—J.C.Furnas' article "Battle for Skills" appears in the *Saturday Evening Post* (page 25)

June 19, 1941—A slogan, "If the worker hasn't learned, the teacher hasn't taught," was adopted. This put a new light on the foreman's responsibility for getting new, green, sometimes non-too-promising, people into production quickly. First outline written for the five sessions of JI. (page 193)

August 1941—District heads meet in Washington and agree to adopt a proposal for a 4–step, 10-hour Job Instruction course (pages 30–31 & 32)
- New Jersey TWI staff believes that success of JI program leads logically to creation of a Job Methods Program (page 223)

Oct. 1941—first JI Institute held in Washington (page 34)

Nov. 1941—JI program on a national basis (page 34)

Nov. 11 & 12, 1941—District heads agree to create supervisory programs in Human Relations and Production Supervision (page 35)

Dec. 1941—The first "quality control" session—The New Jersey District brings its trainers together to answer common questions and get uniformity of procedure. (page 197)

Dec 6, 1941—first draft of JR complete (page 41)

Dec. 7, 1941—Japan attacks Pearl Harbor

Dec. 8, 1941—US declares war on Japan

Jan. 1942—first JR trial group (page 41)

Jan 1942—Job Methods program was named; 4-step card was made (page 229)

Jan 1, 1942—first tabulation of JI trainees—15, 767 (page 35)

Jan 1942—first version of JR tried at Simplex Mfg Corp; nine versions to follow (p 205)

Feb. 17–22, 1942—first "Training Within Industry Conference for Training Coordinators" held @ GMI in Flint, MI (basis for Program Development Program)

March 1942—TWI issues its last bulletins: *Increasing War Production through Employment of Women and Safety on the Job for New Employees* (page 51)

May 1942—JM presented to district heads & approved; followed **"package"** **principle**—10 hours, 10 men, 4–step method, demonstration, individual practice (page 37; page 230)

Sept. 1942—A Master Institute was held @ TWI Headquarters in Washington (page 232)

Sept. 1942—JM begins national use (page 37)

Dec. 1942—JM featured at an A.M.A. conference in New York (page 37)
  • First JM manual (3rd edition) produced in Washington for national use (p 232)

1943—Stuart Chase writes three articles about TWI, which are published in Readers Digest (page 16)

Feb. 1943—TWI field organization has over 225 paid staff members (page 8)
  • **JR officially launched at an A.M.A. meeting in Chicago** after several months of preparation and more than a year of trial sessions (page 40)
  • Mr. Dooley writes in *Fortune* magazine, " ... This includes women, Negroes, handicapped, Chinamen, and Spaniards. The only differences between ... men and women in industry is in the toilet facilities." (page 52)

Spring 1943—union stewards are included in a number of JR sessions in Michigan, beginning the UJR sessions (page 79)

April 1943—Program Development adopted as the name of the program for designing training programs and plans to meet specific plant needs (page 45; page 242)

Aug. 1943—National War Labor Board ruled on giving cash awards for Job Methods suggestions (page 39)

Jan. 1944—TWI established another district in Hawaii

Jan. 19, 1944—stewards and other union members were made specifically eligible in so far as use of federal war training funds was concerned (page 80)

June 1944—Purdue University gives honorary Doctor of Engineering in Human Relations to Mr. Dooley and Mr. Deitz in recognition of their establishment and direction of Training Within Industry

Fall 1944—**Program Development Institute** made available nationally (page 249)

1945—a special Union Job Relations manual was prepared (page 41)

Early 1945—Union JR program available (page 81)

April 1945—UJR Program is recommended for all local and district machinist lodges in Iowa at the Iowa State Conference of Machinists

May 5, 1945—US Office of Education begins to close its war training programs, providing for their termination by June 30. (page 111) It issues a letter stopping the use of Federal funds for payment of TWI trainers.

May 7, 1945—Germany surrenders

May 31, 1945—U.S. Office of Education announces that all programs will be concluded by this date (page 72)

June 1945—5-day Program Development Institute Manual made available nationally (page 249)

Summer 1945—lens grinding training reduced from 4–6 months to one day (was 5 years before JI)

July 28, 1945 (Saturday)—TWI district offices notified that they were to cease operations on Sept. 30 (page 124) July 28th is 9 days before Hiroshima was bombed.

Aug. 6, 1945—Hiroshima bombed

Aug. 14, 1945—Nagasaki bombed; Japan agreed to surrender unconditionally

Sept. 2, 1945—Japan signed surrender terms aboard the battleship U.S.S. Missouri in Tokyo Bay; Truman later declares Sept 2 as V-J Day (Victory over Japan)

Sept. 28, 1945—TWI's last day (Friday)

Sept. 29, 1945—Arthur Gorman, financial writer for the *New York World Telegram*, writes an article entitled, "Training Within Industry Group is Disbanded, but Ideas Go ON." (page 74)

APPENDIX B

Job Relations Manual Reference 4

A WAY OF LOOKING AT THE SUPERVISORY JOB

"Getting out the work" seldom runs along smoothly without interruption. About the time a group is working together smoothly changes usually occur. Whether these changes are in the form of expanding schedules, improvements in methods, shifts in organization, or new employees, they always create problems. Supervisors need to know not only the operations and machines in their departments, but the people as well.

Expert knowledge of the job as an operator is not sufficient to make a good supervisor. In fact, such knowledge may make it difficult to notice the other supervisory problems. The supervisor needs to give attention to the particular characteristics of each individual for no two of them have exactly the same experience, abilities, and desires.

The supervisor will not always find it possible to apply these particular practices to his own situation, since they were used in different situations. But if he will look for the general ideas which the other fellows' practices illustrate, he will find that they can be applied to his problems too. These ideas have been derived from the experience of men in the shop.

It must be remembered that to the worker a job means more than just a pay check every week or doing mechanical operations over and over between in-and-out whistles. It means that he is part of an organization, wherein he has a particular place. It means that he is a human being who wonders what kind of people his fellow-workers are, what they are going to expect of him, how he should approach his supervisor, etc. Consequently, job training is more than just teaching a shop skill. It includes helping the worker to adjust himself to his surroundings, giving him an idea of the organization of which he is a part, and the particular place he is to fill in it.

This is the point of view from which we approach these five sessions.

The supervisor facing hour by hour the difficulties of getting out the product may easily overlook the difficulties of his workers. It is natural for him to think most of results and to spend little time on people. Yet there are conditions in each department which hinder the employees from coming up to full productiveness quickly and easily, and prevent the development of wholesome attitudes toward associates and the plant.

New supervisors can look back and remember a few things—what difficulties did you run into? Try to look at the department situation through the operators' eyes.

In getting out the product in the shop, the instructor or supervisor may fix his attention only upon materials. Look at the men—their minds, muscles, feelings, and attitudes. Observe them and talk with them. Notice what they do. Attempt to analyze their actions. Listen to their comments and encourage them to talk because the more clearly you know each operator as a person, the better you can supervise.

Hindrances to Understanding Men

Understanding people is not a simple process. The supervisor or instructor who says, "I can size up a man as soon as I put him to work," is usually fooling himself. It will be helpful to notice some of the habits that actually hinder us in understanding them.

The *"Die-Casting" Habit*—Too often, as we observe individuals, we try to sort them into types or, to put it another way, to force them into imaginary molds that we have set up in our minds, much as the die-caster squirts metal into different kinds of molds. They may be different shapes before they go in, but they're all alike when they come out!

We feel that we have completely cataloged Bill Jones when we say that he is a "good mixer," that we have defined Tom Smith when we put him down as a "tough customer." But we can't do that with people, if we really wish to understand them. We must study each one from all sides, not pour them into molds or cast them into types.

The *"Just Like" Habit*—"He reminds me for all the world of Bill Brown," we say, and thereafter we notice more easily the traits that are like Bill Brown and ignore those which are different. Once we have made up our minds he is "like Bill Brown," we close our minds to the possibility of his having other characteristics that we may need to know. We stop studying him, with the result that we never discover many of the interests and abilities that are part of him.

The *"Go, No-Go" Habit*—"I can tell whether a man will make a good operator in this job as soon as I see how he follows directions," said a supervisor. "If he listens carefully to my directions for doing the job and does it exactly as I tell him, he will make a good man. If he doesn't get the directions the first time, but tries to 'dope out' his own way of doing it, he seldom learns to do good work here." This supervisor, if he really does follow the way of thinking which he described, is classifying all employees into two classes: (1) Those who follow directions to the letter, and (2) those who try to figure out methods of their own. His gage of men is two-valued, "go" or "no-go." There are no "in-betweens." He is applying an inspection technique not an understanding one.

People are seldom "either-or." Studies of individuals show that approximately two-thirds of them have each of the commonly observed traits to a moderate degree, that is, they are close to the average in it, and that only a small percentage have markedly large or small degrees of any trait. Not "either–or" but "the degree to which" should be the guiding concept in studying people.

Similarly it is easy to fall into the habit of judging employees solely by how well they do that particular phase of the job in which the supervisor prides himself, overlooking their skill or lack of skill in other important parts of the work. For example, in one assembly and adjusting job the supervisor had worked out a better way of tensioning a small spring. He took pride in this. It was very easy for him to fall into the habit of judging operators almost entirely by the way they tensioned this spring and to pass over other parts of the operation. People's reactions cannot be measured fairly with any single gage. They are too complex.

The "Formula" Habit—Closely related to these "stereotype" ways of looking at people is the practice of dealing with each "type of person" in a certain set manner. It has been said that the way to "handle" the "oldtimer" is to "let him alone," that the best way to get along with the "chronic kicker" is to "lay down the law," that the way to teach the new worker is to "show him how" to do the job and "tell him what" the requirements are.

Of course, these methods work a good deal of the time with many of the people with whom supervisors and instructors have to deal. Otherwise they would not be so commonly accepted. But they become a hindrance when they are used as excuses for lumping people together in groups or types and avoiding the responsibility of trying to understand each person as an individual.

In short, people cannot be handled like piece parts or apparatus. Each is an individual, different from every other. "Stereotyping" them, classifying them, standardizing them, or reducing them to formulas—habits of thinking that work well with inanimate things—often prove to be actual hindrances in handling people.

The "Standardization" Habit—Supervisors and instructors may become accustomed to thinking in terms of standards that they look only for *common* responses of "the worker" and pay little attention to the *special* interests, abilities, and peculiarities of individual employees. Yet it is these special characteristics that yield fruitful contacts upon which to base effective supervision. It is the ways in which a person is different, and especially the ways in which he is superior to the "mine run" of people, which furnish the key to his special interests, for he tends to develop strong interests in the fields in which he possesses ability. The instructor has the problem of taking each of these unique and different personalities, finding out what he is like and to what he will respond, and fitting him into a job and into a working organization.

How to Understand the Individual Employee

How can the supervisor understand a person who comes into his organization well enough to fit him into the department? He can talk with him, question him, observe him, throw out conversational leads to draw him out, listen to him, and think and listen and think, seeking ever to look behind appearances and first impressions into the background of feelings, sentiments, and other reactions-to-experience which make up the man himself.

Keeping in mind that it is not a question of "either-or" but rather of "the degree to which," the supervisor can use the following questions in his study of each individual. In each question, however, the supervisor must think constantly, "To what extent does he do this? In what degree is this true or not true of him? How far is this aspect important to this individual? Why does he react the way he does?" Here are the questions:

1. Is he "doing a good job?"
2. Does he fail to understand instruction?
3. Does his attention wander from the job?
4. Is he interested in his job?
5. How does he respond to recognition?
6. Does he stand on his own feet?
7. Does he seem ill-adapted to the job?
8. Does he get along well with the other people in the department?

Each of these questions may now be considered a little further.

1. Is he doing a good job?—Does he miss a part of the instructions when he is given a start on the new job? Most likely he does. Is he therefore stupid or careless? Not at all. He is merely human. The human mind has a perfect mechanism for avoiding overload. It simply ignores. If parts of the situation are wholly unrelated to the individual's past experience or to his present interest, he "pays no attention to them." If the total situation demanding his attention—for example, the new job—is complicated, his eyes and ears first grasp only those aspects which interest him most. If his experience with these is satisfying, he soon explores further and is ready for more instruction. The supervisor or instructor can help, first, by noticing the points of the job he seized upon at the beginning, as cues to his interests, and relating the rest of the instruction to these interests; and second, by noticing what points of the job the worker missed and bringing these to his attention as soon as he is ready for them. Are you sure he knows just what you expect of him? Have you over-sold the job and is he let down?

2. Does he fail to understand instructions?—Does she misinterpret them? Does he fail to catch the point of the explanation? Does he seem "a bit thick?" The easy way out is to label such a person "dumb" and thus avoid all responsibility for making an efficient operator of him. This, however, neither saves the man nor gets the work done, and what is more, it is usually unnecessary. Most workers who have passed the employment office are high enough in mental capacity to learn readily the jobs to which they have been assigned. When they fail to understand, it is not from "dumbness" but from *narrowness of experience.* They are like the city boy who, on his first visit to a farm, tried to get a pail of water by calmly holding up the pump handle, waiting for the water to come. Why shouldn't he? He has seen hydrants with pull-up handles but he had never seen a pump in a well.

The worker who learns slowly because of narrow experience can usually be trained by patient, well-planned instruction and often makes a superior operator. Clues to his background and his interests may be gained by encouraging him to talk about the job, listening to him without interruptions, and giving attention as much to what he takes for granted as to what he actually says. Gaps in his background can be filled by giving him actual experience in the shop.

The worker who misinterprets instructions and thus makes mistakes is a similar problem. On account of the narrowness of his experience he fails to understand. Where others might have got meaning he draws a blank because he doesn't know the "code." Yet he fears to reveal his ignorance. What does he do? He bridges the gap by using his imagination and, whenever he guesses wrong, he makes mistakes. The remedy is to make connection with his meager experience by finding out as much about it as possible and to win his confidence to the point where he is willing to ask questions. It often helps to have him repeat instructions in his own words: "Now just to be sure I've made it clear, tell me what it is you are going to do."

Care in explaining shop terms will help greatly. One worker tells of his first day in the shop thus: "The boss gave me a big pan of little gadgets and said, 'Take these parts over to that bench and "mike" 'em. The "max." and "min." are six and ten.' Then off he went and I spent the next 3 hours trying to figure out what mike, min., and max. had to do with the job, and what I was supposed to do with the pan of gadgets."

Ignorance of shop terms and shop customs is by no means confined to "new" employees fresh from the employment office. Picture an experienced employee newly transferred from a different department, trying to adjust himself to a new location and learn a wholly new kind of job. During his years on the old job he has gone along paying little attention to other organizations, yet now on the new job he is ashamed to reveal his ignorance. He is grateful to the instructor who will take the trouble to discover the limits of his experience and give him the help he needs.

3. Does his attention wander from the job?—Does he seem to be oversensitive to noises, changes in light and ventilation, presence of other workers or passers-by? If so, he is merely responding naturally—acting "like a human being." Most individuals find it hard *not* to pay attention to all that is going on around them, especially to noises and people.

The new worker, in addition to mastering his skill, has to become accustomed to a "total situation" which is strange and fascinating. In fact, a part of any skill is an ability to ignore everything except the activity itself—to concentrate one's attention on it. Witness the ability of the champion athlete to forget his gallery and lose himself in the game.

Complete absorption in a task and disregard of surroundings amid the distracting noise and activity of a manufacturing plant is not a natural act. It is an achievement—that is, it can be learned. Fortunately, most workers are able to learn it for themselves in a relatively short time. Sometimes it is possible to help the worker who is unusually sensitive to distraction by placing him in a less exposed location where noises are more uniform or monotonous or by transferring him to work which requires a broader spread of attention or which includes dealing with a large number of people.

4. Is he interested in his job?—Does he fail to put forth the necessary effort to learn to do the job well? A boy will have an interest in a job if he feels that it is in harmony with his own purposes, that it is "getting him somewhere." If he can identify the job with himself, see its connection with his own life, with his cherished ambition, then he is "interested in the job" in the same way that a man who buys an interest in a business is "interested in" that business. When this happens, there is no trouble about effort.

But often the new worker cannot see any relation between his own plan for the future and the job to which he is assigned. The instructor can explain to the worker how upgrading takes place and what avenues of advancement are open to him if he is efficient in each job along the line. Some young workers are victims of the "white-collar" craze; their only idea of advancement is to get out of the shop and into the office, without any clear understanding of the possibilities of either. A supervisor or instructor can render a real service to such young people by giving them facts regarding the values of shop experience, no matter where later promotions or transfers may lead, and helping them to think over their plans and ambitions in light of these facts rather than on the basis of family or personal prejudice regarding "overalls" or the "white collar."

Occasionally the supervisor or instructor finds an individual who has "hitched his wagon to a star" far beyond the limits of his capacity, background, and education. He may have to help such a person to get his feet on the ground. On the other hand, some learners in the shop seem to have no definite ambition or plan of action for their lives at all. By talking with them and becoming better acquainted the instructor may be able to discover such an ambition and help the worker connect his job to it.

Under war conditions it is a powerful stimulus to show each man what he and the department do for the war effort.

One instructor, in training a man to turn out a bushing on a turret lather, said, "This part will be hardened and ground and put into a molding machine to guide the mold down into place accurately each time it is closed to mold a casting."

Many instructors make it a point to tell the operator how his product will be used: "This goes into an airplane to show the pilot so and so—." "This goes into an instrument panel to show so and so—."

In a highly specialized factory it is difficult to provide the interest which the old craftsman felt in the product of his hands because it was all his own, from raw material to finished master piece. The modern shop, where the worker can see the whole product fabricated before his eyes, provides an opportunity to revive this kind of interest. For the same reason, moving workers about from job to job until they have become familiar with all the operations on a particular product adds to their interest. Each job takes on meaning and significance as its relation to other operations and to the whole product is seen. The worker can "see what he is doing" and can see that it is worthwhile.

Likewise a worker has more interest in his machine if he understands how it works, the principles of its operation, what it can do, and just as important, what it cannot do; i.e., the limits of its operation. When the worker knows these things, instead of blindly following the directions of the machine setter or the equipment man, he takes an interest in the machine. Because he feels that he understands it, he comes to identify it with himself, just as he does the job in which he "has an interest." It becomes his machine and thus a new interest in the job is born.

A simple key to the worker's interest is some activity which he enjoys doing for its own sake. One supervisor makes a practice of talking with the new worker about his hobbies. He discovers what the worker likes to do and often is able to relate the job to these interests or to help him transfer to a job he enjoys.

Knowledge of his own progress stimulates the learner's interest. Supervision long ago discovered the value of operators' performance records as an incentive, especially when presented in graphic form. We like to beat our own record, to see ourselves grow in skill, and most of us like to engage in rivalry with others. Rivalry in output, however, is a form of stimulation which has to be handled wisely, especially during the training period. Progress in learning does not always register in daily output. While learning correctness of "form" and developing the ability to reach quality standards, output may not show a daily increase and the worker should not judge his progress by it. The instructor can prevent discouragement and loss of interest by directing his attention to this fact.

Then there is the matter of social approval. Any experienced supervisor knows the value of recognition as a stimulation of interest in the job. Praise is discussed further in a different connection below.

The effectiveness of all these ways of reaching the worker's interests and relating them to the job lies in the fact that a man reacts as a whole. We sometimes talk of training his muscles or his brain or his hands. We can't. His whole self is being trained by every experience he has. We teach the man, not his hand. When he has mastered a skill, the whole man has it, uses it, and is proud of it. The man himself has ambitions to which the job may or may not be related. The man himself enjoys doing it, or is indifferent to it. The man himself basks in the appreciation of his fellow workers when they recognize that he has done the job well. Anything which connects with his interests affects all parts of him. His eye brightens, his mind becomes more alert, his hand more sure. Recognition of success in one part of the job reacts to heighten his interest in the job as a whole, and he does the whole job better. Conversely, failure in any part of the job depresses the whole man, his work and his attitude toward the job—unless he and his supervisor regard the failure as a challenge, analyze it, and learn how to overcome it.

The largest factor with which a supervisor or instructor has to deal is his worker's "interests." This emphasizes again the need for the supervisor to become well acquainted with his workers as persons, to understand their backgrounds of experience, their hopes and purposes for the future, their bents and special abilities, all in order that he may help them to discover real and lasting connections between themselves and their jobs.

5. How does he respond to recognition?—Does praise stimulate him? How does he take criticism?

Experienced supervisors know that a little recognition adds zest to the job and stimulates a man's efforts. This is especially true of the learner, because he feels insecure and uncertain about himself anyhow. Building his confidence is part of the job.

Recognition of good work can be done in many ways. Posting records of progress has been discussed above. Advancement to a harder or more important job stimulates a learner just as it does an experienced worker. Whenever he is ready for a more difficult step in the learning of the job, the instructor can use this for stimulation by saying, "You've done well with that. You're ready for this harder job now."

The most tangible form of recognition is of course the weekly pay envelope. An increase in his rate is a visible goal. But so many factors over which the supervisor has no control enter into determination of wages that he finds other forms of recognition also necessary as instruction incentives. Using an advanced learner occasionally as an instructor is a form of recognition. It adds prestige and gives a bit of recognition to those who are competent.

Praise in the presence of the group is an effective form of recognition, so long as it is fair. It is usually stronger than praise in private but more difficult to give because the members of the group are always making comparisons. Both approval and correction are necessary, but criticism given before the group usually results in confusion or resentment.

The new worker learns more from praise than from censure. The reason is simple. He is blundering about, seeking the right way to do each part of the job. When he happens upon a right way, and the instructor approves it, he *knows* he has got that part of the job, and seeks to repeat it. At the same time he experiences a glow of satisfaction which spurs him on to master other parts of the job. But suppose he tries a wrong way and is "bawled out." What has he learned? Simply that that one way is wrong. He still does not know a right way and may try many other wrong ones before he finds a right one. Meanwhile he feels discouraged because of the disapproval. The alert supervisor will of course seize such a moment to demonstrate again the "right way" to do the operation, though that is beside the point here. It is often necessary to point out mistakes but, even at its best, censure or adverse criticism helps the learner too slowly on his way to skill. Instead it is better to catch him as often as possible doing the right thing, even by chance, and speed him on his way with a word of appreciation.

6. Does he stand on his own feet?—Does he lean on the supervisor too much, or go to the opposite extreme and act as if he knows it all?

Most new workers are a bit fearful and lacking in confidence, some more and some less. They show it in curious and contradictory ways, as the above questions suggest. A little fear when facing a new situation serves to awaken most persons to greater alertness and effort. They are able to rise to the occasion and soon overcome their fears. They "take things in their stride." Yet there are many individuals who lack emotional balance, who have not learned to take life as it comes, to face reality as adults. It is important, however, to remember the caution about "die-casting" people into molds, to notice "the degree to which" the individual lacks emotional balance. Differences in individuals range all the way from the person who adjusts himself to the job situation promptly, stands on his own feet and quietly tackles everything in a matter-of-fact way, to the person who leans on others and expects favors, who covers his fears with overboldness, or who seeks to "make a good impression" instead of concentrating his attention on learning the job.

While the supervisor or instructor cannot go along indefinitely trying to help a maladjusted person "grow up," he can often add to the timid man's confidence by pointing out his successes and, on the other hand, bring a bluffer back to reality by facing him with the demands of the job. He is interested at all times in each operator's reactions to the job and to his fellow-workers, because they are facts which affect his doing the job, his attitude toward it, and toward the whole organization.

7. Does he seem ill-adapted to the job?—In spite of the best efforts of line supervisors and personnel organizations, employees are sometimes placed on jobs they cannot do satisfactorily. Two cautions are in order here, however.

First: Do not assume an employee is a misfit in a job until he has been fully and correctly instructed on that job and has shown that he cannot do it successfully. Many men have been called misfits on jobs they never had a fair chance to learn. Often a slow learner makes an excellent operator. It is a misfortune for him if he has to begin the job under a supervisor or instructor without patience and willingness to instruct.

Second: Do not assume that when a worker is a misfit in one job he is useless. Any supervisor of long experience could tell stories of "misfits" who found other places where they made good. Few misfits are totally unfit.

Get acquainted with the employee, win his confidence, discover what he can do and likes to do, find out his difficulties on the job, and see that he either learns it or gets a fair trial at other jobs for which he is better adapted.

8. Does he get along well with other people in the department?—Sometimes men know how to do their jobs well, and yet they are not effective because they do not get along well with the people with whom they work.

Consider whether any differences in your relationships with the various people are part of the situation.

You may need to re-align the team in order to get a group to work together.

SUMMARY

Good supervision is not a skill which can be mastered overnight—human beings are complex. But it is a skill in which you improve on the job, and one which returns to you, your department, your plant and the war effort.

BIBLIOGRAPHY

The Fifth Discipline: The Art and Practice of the Learning Organization, Peter M. Senge, New York: Doubleday, 1990.

The Learning Alliance: Systems Thinking in Human Resource Development, Robert O. Brinkenhoff and Stephen J. Gill, Jossey-Bass, 1994.

Learn by Doing: The Story of Training Within Industry 1940–1970, Walter Dietz, published by Walter Dietz, 1970.

Lean Thinking: Banish Waste and Create Wealth in Your Corporation, James Womack, Daniel Jones, Simon & Schuster, 1996.

Learning to See, Mike Rother & John Shook, Lean Enterprise Institute, 1999.

The Machine That Changed the World: The Story of Lean Production, James P. Womack, Daniel T. Jones, and Daniel Roos, Harper Perennial, 1990.

Robinson, Alan G., and Schroeder, Dean M., *Training, Continuous Improvement, and Human Relations: The U.S. TWI Programs and the Japanese Management Style*, California Management Review, The Regents of the University of California, CMR, Volume 335, Number 2, Winter 1993.

The Roots of Lean Training Within Industry: The Origin of Kaizen, Jim Huntzinger, The Tribune, published by The Society of Manufacturing Excellence, Second Quarter 2002.

Strategy Maps: Converting Intangible Assets into Tangible Assets, Robert S. Kaplan and David P. Norton, Harvard Business School Publishing Corporation, 2004.

The Toyota Way: 14 Management Principles from the World's Greatest Manufacturer, Jeffrey Liker. The McGraw Hill Companies, 2004.

Training Within Industry Service, The Training Within Industry Report: 1940–1945 (Washington, D.C.: War Manpower Commission Bureau of Training, 1945).

Training, Continuous Improvement, and Human Relations: The U.S. TWI Programs and the Japanese Management Style, Alan G. Robinson & Dean M. Schroeder, California Management Review Reprint Series, CMR Volume 35, Number 2, Winter 1993, pp. 45–46 .

INDEX

ABOUT THE AUTHOR

Donald A. Dinero

Donald A. Dinero is a Lean consultant with MainStream Management, LLC. As such, he draws on over 30 years of industrial experience in engineering, manufacturing, and independent consulting.

Don's first Lean project was actually done in 1985, before the term Lean was coined. His success with that project and subsequent experiences has led him to the realization that a company's culture is at least as important as its employees' technical knowledge. To this end, he chose to complement his engineering and MBA degrees with a degree in human relations, with a concentration in Organization Development. Consequently, Don considers himself fortunate to be a member of the MainStream team, which emphasizes organizational development activities in its lean implementations.

During Don's first encounter with TWI, he immediately recognized it as a necessary link between mass production and Lean production that is often missed. After concentrated study, he now sees how TWI can also form the basis for developing a learning organization.

Don resides in Rochester NY with his wife Maureen and invites and welcomes your questions and comments. He can be reached through his web site, www.RoundPondConsulting.com.